D1297575

The Houston Astros' Golden Era

Bill Brown

with Phil Boudreaux

and Mike Acosta

2

Acknowledgements

Special thanks to Phil Boudreaux and Mike Acosta, who contributed valuable stories, memorabilia and information from their extensive files of Astros' historical data. Phil has spent much time over decades keeping records of significant events and has shared tidbits with many broadcasters and others. Mike is the Astros' team historian. He has been immersed in the history and lore of the team, as well as the organization of information about the team for future generations. Much appreciation to Tal Smith and John Frost for serving as consultants.

Tal Smith and George Gentry were vital to the outcome of this book with their proofreading, editing and suggestions about content.

This book is for the true baseball fans who kept their loyalty to the sport despite work stoppages, a pandemic and personal travails for some. It's been a marvelous diversion for those who have spent much of their lives absorbed with a sport that has a magnetic attraction.

Information from articles in *The Houston Chronicle, USA Today Sports Weekly, Dome Sweet Dome* by SABR, MLB.com, baseball-reference.com, AstrosDaily.com and FanGraphs.com is included in this book.

All net proceeds (25% of retail) go to the Houston Food Bank. All of the authors and consultants volunteered their services.

Luke 12:48

From everyone who has been given much, much will be demanded; and from the one who has been entrusted with much, much more will be asked.

TABLE OF CONTENTS

INTRODUCTION

As the Houston major league team arrived at its 60th season in 2021, baseball moved to a new inflection point. Its record-setting popularity was being tested by a world pandemic and the personal financial troubles it created for many sports fans and businesses. Priorities changed for many in a rapidly-evolving society.

Then there was the state of the game itself. Theo Epstein resigned as president of the Chicago Cubs in order to focus on making the sport more enjoyable for the fans. In January he was hired as a consultant to Major League Baseball to bring that focus to the way the game is played. In the current game, the home run is so prolific that countless observers long for a return to previous eras (such as the 1970s and 1980s) with fewer home runs and strikeouts but more doubles, triples, stolen bases, sacrifice bunts and great defensive plays.

With batting averages plummeting and punchouts at an epidemic rate, there are questions about outlawing shifts. Requiring two players between second and third and two between first and second would open up the middle for more hits into center field and more great infield defensive plays. The science that permeates the sport has robbed it of action. Yet, the 2021 playoffs brought a great and popular show to big screens everywhere. The star power of the players is extremely attractive. The game could be tweaked some, but the sport still has much to offer the sports fan, especially with the terrific young talent on display.

Chapter 1

UP TO DATE

When the founders of the Houston major league team shared their mutual goals, they may have exchanged dreams that their team could be the forerunner of something this good.

With division titles in each of the last four full (162-game) seasons, five ALCS teams and three World Series appearances in the last five years, the Houston Astros have climbed to a new plateau as one of the top teams in the sport. Their star players are among the most popular in the sport. Their brand has progressed from a ragtag group of expansion players in 1962 to a collection of elite athletes among the best baseball can offer.

In the last decade, the Astros have shed the image of a basement-dwelling group who endured 324 losses in three seasons from 2011 to 2013 to a dominant, flamboyant unit of champions who rolled to 311 triumphs in three years from 2017 to 2019. There were only three seasons between the basement and the penthouse.

Reality in 2021 for 2014 holdovers Jose Altuve and Jason Castro was prime-time excellence and big money, not the lack of attention and ridicule for being on a team stuck in the mud as they experienced before this era started.

This story of the Astros' ascent from a dream with a plan to an era that refuses to be closed out is chronicled backwards. The early history of the team can be found in the last half of the book. The present is where this story starts.

2021

AS the early months of the pandemic year of 2021 moved slowly forward, President Joe Biden was sworn in at the same time George Springer was signing his six-year, $150 million contract with Toronto. Springer was one of the best to play in a Houston uniform. In 2011 the Astros made Springer the 11th overall choice in the first round after his excellent career at the University of Connecticut. General Manager Ed Wade presided over that draft. It was Springer who graced the cover of *Sports Illustrated* in 2014. Writer Ben Reiter predicted that the Astros would win the 2017 World Series in that issue of *SI*. Springer again adorned the cover in 2017 when *SI* reported the story of the prediction coming true.

When the Astros were hitting the century club in losses in 2011, 2012 and 2013, Springer was being followed closely by Astro Nation as he progressed through the minor leagues. The organizational plan was to draft wisely and develop players in the minors, and Springer was a poster boy for that plan. When he was promoted to the major league club in April of 2014, the Astros waited until his service time in the big leagues would start after a couple of weeks of games, giving them seven years of Springer before he would be a free agent instead of six. This kind of manipulation of service time is common at a time when payrolls are at the $200 million level or above for the top teams. Although it was well within the rules of the collective bargaining agreement in the sport to manage the service time of star players, players could harbor resentment of the practice of depriving them of a shot at free agency one year sooner. Sometimes teams felt the player needed more minor league seasoning at the beginning of a campaign. Players seldom agreed when big money was around the corner.

The 2017 World Series Most Valuable Player departed the Astros as the franchise's all-time leader in postseason home runs (19) and doubles. His .892 OPS in 292 postseason plate appearances was close to his career regular season OPS (.852).

In the 2017 World Series alone, Springer pounded eight extra base hits, five of them home runs, in just 29 at-bats. Only Craig Biggio was a better leadoff hitter in Houston history.

Springer moved ahead of Derek Jeter as the all-time RBI leader among leadoff men in the postseason with 34. His 39 career leadoff home runs in the regular season through 2020 ranked him eighth on the all-time list.

George Springer brought a high level of energy to the clubhouse and the playing field. People who had seen him walk into the clubhouse and bring that energy to his teammates wondered how much of an effect his loss to the team would have in 2021. His importance to the team regarding the level of emotional support he provided his teammates was substantial. His determination to make every play in the outfield and run the bases with abandon brought some noticeable responses from the bench. His smile was infectious. His career batting average of .270 with 567 runs scored, 174 home runs (fifth on the Astros all-time list) and 458 RBIs were quantifiable; his leadership and emotional impact were not.

The Astros sustained other major free agent losses on their way to the upper tier of teams. Dallas Keuchel left as a free agent after 2018. Gerrit Cole closed the door on his Houston years after 2019 and entered the most lucrative level of free agency, reeling in a $324 million deal from the New York Yankees. Springer became the third big-name Astro to move on in three years.

Although Houston's payroll escalated to above $200 million pro rata in 2020, which put the Astros in line for paying a luxury tax, the Astros had not been known for lavishing many lucrative contracts on top free agents. Their operating plan was to build from within and acquire free agents who fit into their budget or trade for established players near the end of their controllable years. Their largest free agent expenditure under owner Jim Crane was the four-year, $52 million deal for outfielder Josh Reddick.

They took on $53 million for pitcher Zack Greinke over 2 ½ years when they made the trade with Arizona. They had extended Jose Altuve for $150 million, Alex Bregman for $100 million and Justin Verlander for $66 million (over two years) to keep those players. They lost free agents Charlie Morton, Will Harris and Robinson Chirinos in an escalating market.

Michael Brantley re-signed a two-year, $32 million contract to return to the Astros just after Springer left. Catcher Jason Castro returned on another two-year agreement, setting up a possible platoon arrangement with Martin Maldonado. Those two signings addressed priority spots for GM James Click.

Their 2021 roster gave them a chance to enter the postseason tournament again, but after 2021 they had many millions coming off the books. Verlander, Zack Greinke, Lance McCullers, Jr. and Carlos Correa were the four big lynchpins who could have become free agents. McCullers signed a five-year, $85 million extension. They had flexibility to extend Correa if they could keep enough excellent players on the team who could produce at reasonable payroll figures. Unlike Springer, Correa stated publicly that he wanted to be an Astro for life. "I love this organization. I love the Astros. I would love to be an Astro for life," said Correa in January of 2021. "I hope they're on the same side I am. If they're on the same side, I'd love to be an Astro for the rest of my life."

With Correa not yet 27, he was entering his potential prime years, unlike Springer at 31. Although there is no form chart for a player's prime years, the general pattern for most players places them in their prime before age 31. It's unusual for a player's prime to continue much past the age of 33, but there are many exceptions to that age. Players are more attuned to staying in top condition longer in life now, partly because of the financial rewards of a longer career. Teams are more likely to spend in the neighborhood of $25 million per year for a star player if he is younger than 31, though. At 2021 prices, especially after the year he had in 2021, Correa was considered a bargain at $30 million per year. His representatives turned down Houston's offer in spring training of 2021 for five years, $125 million. They rejected a larger offer after the season ended.

The previous market top of a $300 million payday or more for a ten-year contract was set by San Diego's Fernando Tatis, Jr. and the New York Mets' Francisco Lindor, both shortstops.

As Correa and Jose Altuve began their seventh season as major league teammates, the team around them was built to win its division. The experts were expecting the Astros to take another American League West title. They began that pursuit with Greinke their Opening Day starter in the final year of his $34 million contract (for 2021). Lance McCullers, Jr. was the other highly-regarded starter in the rotation. Jose Urquidy had shown great promise. To bolster that group, youngsters Cristian Javier and Luis Garcia returned from their successful rookie seasons in 2020. Veteran Jake Odorizzi joined the rotation as a late-signing free agent in spring training. The bullpen was anchored by closer Ryan Pressly and supplemented by setup men Ryne Stanek and Pedro Baez, both free agents. The other bullpen arms were relatively inexperienced. The starting lineup was packed with potent hitters. In April, the Astros were 14-12 despite some COVID-19 victims. Their schedule was tougher in the first half of the season.

In May, their starting rotation held up well and the offense outscored every other team in the American League. The Astros were ½ game behind first-place Oakland at the end of May. They had a great offensive month, but Jose Urquidy went down with a shoulder injury and there was concern about the innings Cristian Javier was piling up. The load was not sustainable for him at that pace projected over an entire season in the estimation of the medical analysts. Javier went to the bullpen to fortify the weakest area of the team. Framber Valdez joined the rotation at that time after his broken finger healed.

One doctor thought Valdez would miss the entire season because of his spring training injury. Without him, it would have been difficult to reach the playoffs. Odorizzi, with Tampa Bay connections to James Click, was signed as a contingency.

In June, the Astros broke out with an 11-game winning streak. But by July, the long absence of Bregman because of persistent leg injuries began to weigh on the lineup. Aledmys Diaz filled in capably at several positions, but Abraham Toro was traded in late July to Seattle for Kendall Graveman and Rafael Montero.

Graveman was sensational in the first half of 2021, but after an initial impact on the Houston bullpen he fell off into a less predictable performance. Phil Maton, who came from Cleveland in the Myles Straw trade, was able to bolster the middle-inning relief. Chas McCormick and Jake Meyers shared center field in Straw's absence and kept the lineup in a good place.

August brought a slump, with six losses in eight games shrinking the Astros' lead in their division from six games to a 2 ½-game edge over Oakland.

That's where the diary of the final weeks of the season begins on the next page.

August 19, 2021

CRUNCH TIME IN THE 2021 PENNANT RACE

Things were closing in on the Houston Astros. They had mastered every hurdle throughout the 2021 season until now. Injuries, a thin minor league organization, constant booing by crowds on the road and a stronger challenge from Oakland and Seattle than many expected had not deterred them from their goal of returning to the playoffs. But now, in the dog days of August, their lead over Oakland had dwindled from 6 to 2 ½ games. And one of the worst teams in the American League – the Kansas City Royals – had them down 3-0 and were threatening to sweep a four-game series from them.

A four-game losing streak was pinned on a slumping lineup. Some good pitching had been wasted, and what had been the best offensive team in the league until a few days earlier was sagging.

Some of the team's mainstays, including Jose Altuve and Yuli Gurriel, were struggling. Alex Bregman had been missing in the lineup for two months, and his leg injuries continued to deal him setbacks and shed doubt on when he might return and how much he might contribute. Kyle Tucker was on the injured list for health and safety protocol reasons. In June, he missed a group of games with illness and lost ten pounds.

The Royals sent inexperienced pitchers Brady Singer and Daniel Lynch to the mound, but the pair of 24-year-olds mowed down the Astros routinely and got terrific defensive support from their fielders.

The Royals won the third game, 3-2 when left fielder Andrew Benintendi fired a one-hop strike to catcher Salvador Perez for a tag for the final out on headfirst-sliding Chas McCormick, who was out by a couple of inches. Maybe. Kansas City shortstop Nicki Lopez played like Omar Vizquel during the series.

In the finale, McCormick drove in three runs and stopped the bleeding, 6-3 in 10 innings. The Seattle Mariners, who had stayed on their trail, were coming to Houston only 5 ½ games behind them.

The Mariners' clubhouse was inflamed with angry reactions from players the day Houston and Seattle agreed on a trade July 27. With the Mariners surprisingly in the wild card playoff race, their general manager, Jerry Dipoto, dealt free agent-to-be closer Kendall Graveman and Rafael Montero to the Astros for Joe Smith and Abraham Toro. The perception was that Dipoto was abandoning his team's chances to reach the playoffs for the first time since 2001. Dipoto agreed that appearances would lead to those opinions, but he cautioned that more trades were on the way and they would give clarity to the situation.

He followed by acquiring Tampa Bay closer Diego Castillo and starting pitcher Tyler Anderson. In the next three weeks, Toro caught fire and became the starting second baseman.

The starting pitching had held up very well for the Astros. Without Verlander and two seasons removed from Gerrit Cole's exit, the starting rotation of Greinke-McCullers-Valdez-Garcia-Odorizzi was keeping the club in a good position in August. Urquidy was rehabbing in the minors and doing well.

The offense was a different story. Weighed down by the absence of Bregman for two months, the hitters were showing signs of fatigue. Most of the position players had missed time during the season.

Michael Brantley, who was leading the American League in batting average through mid-August, was down for two weeks in late May and early June with sore legs.

Kyle Tucker lost ten pounds and missed ten days in June with illness. In mid-August he went out of the lineup again for another ten days.

Yuli Gurriel had two weeks of down time in August with a neck injury.

Supersub Aledmys Diaz missed seven weeks with a broken left hand.

When the bullpen faltered, Cristian Javier was moved out of the starting rotation to serve as a multiple-inning reliever in late May. His 3.14 earned run average in the starting rotation was solid, but Ryan Pressly was the only reliable late-inning reliever at that time. Jose Urquidy was in the rotation then, and Odorizzi had built up his arm after spring training miseries. Valdez's addition, though, was the biggest catalyst to the rotation. His first start was May 28 after a broken ring finger in spring training caused his season to open two months late. Garcia was like Javier in that: the Astros were pushing them beyond their career highs in innings.

THE FINAL WEEK OF AUGUST

As the Astros plowed through 13 straight games in the "dog days" of August, they handled a two-city road trip by halting a four-game losing streak and then added to their lead in the tight American League West. Their 7-6 record in the 13-game stretch allowed them to extend their lead to five games over second-place Oakland.

LUIS GARCIA

Luis Garcia dialed up one of his best efforts in a 4-0 shutout win over Kansas City August 24. The 24-year-old righthander continued to pitch with poise, stopping the aggressive Royals on four hits and a walk in 6 2/3 innings over his 90-pitch effort. The Royals stole two more bases, capitalizing on Garcia's slow delivery. But when Michael A. Taylor dashed from third to home, Garcia quickened his delivery and fired to catcher Jason Castro for the tag on Taylor to foil the steal of home. Garcia was one of the most important cogs in the 2021 Astros, with an 11-8 record and a 3.48 ERA through 28 starts and two relief appearances. He ranked among the American League rookie leaders in wins, ERA, innings and WHIP. He finished second in AL Rookie of the Year voting.

Garcia had a meteoric rise through the Houston organization, pitching just five major league games in 2020 but starting Game 5 of the 2020 ALCS as the opener against Tampa Bay. He built on that success by rising to the number 6 prospect in the organization in 2021.

Garcia signed for only $15,000 and developed his stuff in the Astros' minor league system. His steady presence in the starting rotation allowed the Astros to work around injuries to Odorizzi, Valdez and Urquidy and maintain their standing atop the division.

With no first or second-round draft choices for a two-year period because of punishment for the cheating scandal, the Astros were fortunate to have Valdez, Javier, Urquidy and Garcia in their organization while they bought time to develop the next wave of starting pitchers.

As it turned out, Bregman brought an impact to the lineup with two hits August 25th and he scored the winning run in the tenth, 6-5. The Astros finished a 4-2 homestand against Seattle and KC and went into a day off before the next road trip to Arlington, Seattle and San Diego.

With the New York Yankees reeling off a 13-game winning streak, they grabbed the top wild card spot. Boston remained slightly ahead of Oakland for the second spot.

As the final quarter of the season played out, the Astros proved again that they did not need to cheat by stealing signs in order to lead the majors in offense. They also responded to repeated loud booing in road venues by performing well and winning games. Their road record was 34-27 through August 26. The Houston players seemed to be able to channel their answer to the booing into a focused effort on the road.

After a fan in Kansas City yelled, "Cheater" while Carlos Correa stood at the plate, Correa clobbered a slider over the left field wall. As he typically did on home run trots, he cupped his right hand behind his ear when he crossed third base. Earlier in the season, he was asked about intense booing at Dodger Stadium. "I was like, 'This is awesome,'" said Correa. "I loved every bit of it."

Correa, Altuve, Bregman, Gurriel and McCullers were the only five remaining Astros from their 2017 World Series championship season. But fans booed other Astros as well.

"At the end of the day, it's an entertainment business," said Correa. "And we want to entertain people. When we go on the road, it's entertaining to make the fans go quiet." He was seen wearing a tank top with the message "H-Town vs. Everyone." "My last year with the Astros, hopefully we can win another championship," Correa told *The Athletic*. "I can leave this great organization with two of them." Manager Dusty Baker, in his 24th managerial season, had plenty of respect for his players after joining the team in 2020. "Our guys come out to play," Baker told Andy McCullough of *The Athletic*. "They come out to fight. And you know something? It's not always fun."

Dodger reliever Joe Kelly fired a pitch near the head of Bregman in a 2020 game. Then he made a face at Correa after striking him out. Kelly was suspended for his actions. Correa got his revenge by ripping a Kelly pitch for a home run in 2021.

Kendall Graveman pitched for Oakland in 2017, but when he joined Houston in a 2021 trade, opposing fans yelled at him and other newcomers. "I'd only been there for like a week, and people were yelling at me," Graveman told *The Athletic.*

A nine-game road trip for the Astros began in Arlington, where the downtrodden Texas Rangers had swept Houston in May, twice on walk-offs. But with a 44-84 record, the rebuilding Rangers were one of the worst teams in the majors. General Manager Jon Daniels and owner Ray Davis gazed upon thousands of empty seats in second-year Globe Life Field while watching their dismantled team head for its first 100-loss season since 1973. After a 2020 record of 20-40, the Rangers put themselves near the top of the list for draft choices. They were one of 12 major league teams with payrolls under $100 million. Four were below $60 million. The Los Angeles Dodgers were circling high above the field at $267 million in search of another world championship.

As the collective bargaining agreement between ownership and players moved closer to expiring, quiet negotiations were under way to change the landscape of the revenue-sharing situation.

The Major League Baseball Players Association was determined to prevent teams from tanking with low payrolls and pocketing revenue-sharing funds to regroup for their next run at relevancy. A salary floor of $100 million for each team had been suggested. The players sought more competitive bidding for their services in free agency, and their opinion was that too many teams were withdrawing from competing financially for players. Astros fans could remember when their team's payroll was lower than the Rangers' Josh Hamilton's annual salary.

The Chicago Cubs had built their championship team in 2016 by avoiding major free agent contracts and building through the farm system as well.

The Rangers, in the spirit of development, sent their 25th rookie player of 2021 to the mound to open the Houston series. He was a Houston product of Concordia Lutheran High School and Rice University, 25-year-old Glenn Otto.

Drafted by the Yankees and traded in the Joey Gallo deal, Otto dazzled the Astros in five shutout innings. His slider was unhittable. He left the game with a 4-0 lead. But the Astros came alive in a five-run seventh and captured the game, 5-4. It was one of the biggest comeback wins of the season for a team that was 5-36 at the time when trailing after six innings. The Astros were 76-52 August 27, and their lead grew to 6 ½ games over Oakland. The Athletics were on the losing end of the Yankees' 13th straight win – their best since 1961.

The Astros reached 25 games above .500 at 77-52 when they stopped the Rangers again, 5-2. Alvarez belted his 27th home run and Correa reached the "20 mark" for the fifth season.

For the first time since June 13, they had their starting lineup healthy and playing together August 28.

The next day backup catcher Jason Castro went on the injured list with a right knee problem. The Rangers blasted the Astros, 13-2. Losing pitcher Zack Greinke was awful. Still a long way from the playoffs, the Astros were forced to think about Greinke and his playoff readiness. He was on a pace to work more than 200 innings and was leading the league in innings pitched. At the end of August, both Valdez and McCullers appeared fresher than Greinke.

The next long trip began in Seattle, with the Astros getting key hits from Kyle Tucker and Jake Meyers in the eighth inning to overtake the Mariners, 4-3. Both RBI hits came off former Astro Joe Smith. Greinke and Taylor Jones hit the Injured List the next day after testing positive for COVID. Dusty Baker's plans for a six-man rotation changed without Greinke. Instead, Jose Urquidy would be coming off the IL to replace Greinke in the five-man rotation.

As August rolled to a close with a 4-0 loss to Seattle, former Mariner Kendall Graveman was victimized by an eighth-inning grand slam from Abraham Toro, who was traded for Graveman a month earlier.

Graveman said of pitching against his former teammates, "There's a familiarity that goes a little bit deeper than just looking at numbers and iPads and things like that. I've just got to execute. That's all it boils down to. I'll be better for this outing and I think I'll learn from it and continue to move forward." The Astros finished August with a 78-54 record, five games better than Oakland. They had some decisions to make about postseason roster eligibility before September 1 arrived. The backup catcher spot was the primary concern, with Jason Castro down with a knee injury.

Did you know that....

Jerry Goff tied the major league record with six passed balls in a game against the Expos in 1996. He is the father of NFL quarterback Jared Goff. His one game with the Astros in 1996 was the last game of his six-year major league career.

Scoreboard at Colt Stadium

SEPTEMBER

The September song started on a sad note for Astros fans. Seattle fans were joyous. Earlier in the day, Jerry Dipoto was promoted to president of baseball operations and given a multi-year contract extension. Manager Scott Servais also was given a multi-year extension. Hours later, the Mariners shut out the Astros for the second straight day, 1-0. They finished their home season series with a 5-4 edge over the Astros, and their deficit shrank to 6 ½ games in the AL West. Oakland beat Detroit the next day to move the Athletics to within 4 ½ games of the first-place Astros. Houston had not scored in 19 innings.

The player Dipoto pried from the Astros in the controversial July 27 trade, Abraham Toro, provided the only run on a sacrifice fly in the sixth inning. Starter Jake Odorrizzi was pitching as well as he had all season when Dusty Baker removed him in the sixth with one out and two men on base. Paul Sewald earned a 27-pitch save by stranding two runners in the eighth. Sewald had been the winning pitcher with a scoreless inning the night before.

Toro gained a footnote in history the previous night. He became the first player to belt a grand slam off the player who was traded for him (Graveman).

The final stop on the trip was in San Diego, where the Padres had lost valuable ground in their own pennant race. As Jake Arrieta took the mound with a 5-12 record and a 7.13 ERA, he was trying to reverse a long slide for the Padres' pitching staff. The Padres had lost 14 of their last 19. When Fernando Tatis, Jr. belted a tape-measure game-tying home run off Ryan Pressly May 29 in an 11-8 San Diego win after the Padres trailed by five, the Padres were rated a 98 per cent chance to reach the playoffs.

That was before Tatis' troublesome left shoulder popped out of place twice, robbing him of playing time and a chance to play shortstop. The Padres moved him to the outfield to protect the shoulder.

Tatis was in right field September 3 at Petco Park with the game tied 3-3, leaping for Kyle Tucker's two-run homer in the eighth inning that snapped a 3-3 tie and sent the Astros to an important 6-3 triumph.

Jose Urquidy started the game for Houston for the first time since June 29. His two trips to the injured list with right shoulder problems derailed the Mexican righthander, who hoped to establish in September that he was a playoff starter. He threw the ball well early but got no offensive support. Arrieta set down the first eight Astros until Urquidy, 0-for-6 with 5 strikeouts in his career as a hitter, stepped toward third base and slashed a line drive past a lunging Eric Hosmer into right field to become the first Houston baserunner. Urquidy said after the game that it was his first hit since childhood. He threw the ball well but was removed after 4 1/3 innings on a pitch count, leading 3-2. Carlos Correa snapped a 22-inning Houston scoreless stretch with a two-out, three-run homer off Arrieta. Tucker's go-ahead home run, his first in 21 days, gave Ryan Pressly a chance to nail down his 23rd save.

The White Sox were sinking in a sea of injuries. Starting pitchers Lucas Giolito and Lance Lynn were both on the injured list. Dallas Keuchel was mired in a slump. The White Sox had the luxury of buying time for the injured arms to recover in September since they were under no pressure to win their division. Their home record was terrific, and they preferred home field advantage over Houston. But their best players needed to be healthy above any other consideration.

Jose Siri joined the Astros September 3 from Sugar Land (.318/.369/.552) after a banner AAA season. Siri, 26, was not expecting the promotion when it came. He had been passed over for outfielders Chas McCormick and Jake Meyers. He had toiled for eight minor league seasons in four different organizations in a checkered past. But it seemed that Dusty Baker wanted him for one purpose: speed. He stole three bases in four tries with Houston.

Baker didn't need another outfielder, but he needed a pinch runner who could steal a base and force defensive mistakes. He plucked Siri off the bench at San Diego after Yordan Alvarez delivered a pinch single and Siri scored an important run. Siri stole 24 bases in 27 tries at AAA.

The Astros had only 44 steals as a team, 17 of them by the centerfielder they traded, Myles Straw. Siri paid off in spades with Baker making moves in a National League ballpark. "He's a tremendous talent. You will see he has good speed, a great arm, which is always needed in the outfield. He was in strong consideration for coming up the whole year, he just wasn't on the roster."

Chas McCormick returned from his hand injury and started in center field. Baker was sending a message that, even though Meyers had played well in his absence, McCormick would still get playing time. Meyers came off the bench and delivered a pinch hit in the game. Baker said he planned to involve both players in future starting lineups based on matchups.

Meyers was one of the biggest discoveries of the 2021 season for the Astros. Most Astros fans had never heard of him. Jose Altuve called him "a five-tool player." The Astros were not even compelled to place him on their 40-man roster the previous winter in order to protect him from being selected by another team in the Rule V draft at the winter meetings.

As it turned out, they were lucky he was not drafted, because he became their starting center fielder in August, hitting .316 with 3 homers and 16 RBI that month. Meyers was also slightly superior defensively in center field to Chas McCormick. McCormick had a bigger major league resume. His .784 OPS in 248 plate appearances gave fans a larger sample size to peruse. Meyers forced playing time after the Straw trade.

"More than anything, he doesn't mind being up there in those situations," said Dusty Baker after Meyers provided a go-ahead eighth-inning single off Joe Smith in Seattle in late August. By then, he had hit 50 balls in play at the average exit speed of 91 mph – above the major league average. "He thinks he's going to come through," explained Baker.

"It's a thought process and a grind and a fight in those situations. That's what stands out. The way he hustles and runs the bases, he's a ballplayer. He works hard and expects to do good things," added Baker.

At the University of Nebraska, where Meyers' father Paul was an All-American, his coach was former Astro outfielder Darin Erstad. "When you have talent with work ethic and are a competitor, it's a pretty good place to start," Erstad told Brian McTaggart of MLB.com. "He's just a pleasure to be around. He's turned himself into a phenomenal ballplayer." The Astros drafted Meyers in the 13th round in June of 2017, their World Series championship season.

Meyers not only hit .307 at Nebraska; he pitched well: 17-4 with a 2.61 ERA. He was named third team All-America by *Baseball America.* He didn't throw hard enough to pursue pitching as a pro, but he improved his power after hitting only three homers in three years at Nebraska. Meyers ripped 16 home runs in 68 games at AAA Sugar Land in 2021.

"Obviously, he's gotten stronger and made some adjustments with his swing and put himself in great position and found that balance between power and contact," said Erstad. "He's just a hard-working kid, works a lot with his dad and they've obviously put together a really good plan. He's in a good spot."

UNHAPPY PITCHER

The 2021 Astros stayed away from controversy until Jake Odorizzi stirred the pot after his September 7 start against Seattle. Odorizzi left that game after throwing 66 pitches with the game tied, 2-2. The Astros won, 5-4 in 10 innings. Odorizzi said "bull----" of the decision to remove him.

"I think it's pretty frickin' obvious. Just go take a look at it. It's not like I just made my debut yesterday. Been doing this for a while. It's extremely frustrating." Odorizzi did not throw more than 5 1/3 innings in a start from July 9 for the next two months. "I'm glad we won," he added.

"If not, I'm sure I would have been the subject of blame for only going five innings." He allowed two hits and two runs in the fifth when Seattle tied the game. "It's not about deserving. It's a situational thing," explained Odorizzi.

"A lower pitch count was a big, glaring thing. I know how hard our guys in the bullpen work. To be able to give them some extra time off is important, especially in a playoff race, and I thought I was in a position to do that."

Statistics showed that Odorizzi was not nearly as effective the third time he faced hitters in a game. Odorizzi had a ten-year career of an .875 OPS allowed to hitters the third time he faced them in a game. In 2021, the OPS was 1.365 in those situations. He was well aware of that. "I know what the numbers are. Everyone acts like I don't understand. I know. The only way to get better at something is by doing it. You can't be better in the sixth if you don't go into the sixth. It's just math." His manager used a fully-rested relief corps in that game. "I understand them," said Baker of Odorizzi's remarks. "We talked about them like men. I want all these guys to go as deep as they can in the games."

Odorizzi texted General Manager James Click the day after he made the remarks, triggering a meeting with Baker, pitching coach Brent Strom and Click. Opinions were aired during the meeting, but no remarks afterwards indicated that minds had been changed.

ALEX BREGMAN

A different Alex Bregman rejoined the Astros August 25. The player who had always approached the game with maximum physical intensity, pushing his body harder and harder, had throttled back his aggressiveness. The new Bregman was determined to play under control rather than throwing caution to the winds regarding his body.

Bregman was the type of player at LSU and earlier in his Astros career who outworked everybody else. There were stories about Bregman taking ground balls an hour after making an error that cost his LSU team a game.

And of Bregman taking batting practice at Baseball USA in Houston alongside aspiring youngsters only a couple of hours after playing a home ALCS game against the Boston Red Sox in 2018.

The ravages of soft tissue injuries took a toll on Bregman's legs and cost him too many games. The third baseman who played at least 155 games in 2017, 2018 and 2019 fought through a right hamstring injury in 2020 and managed to play 42 of 60 games. But when the full schedule resumed in 2021, Bregman was hobbled by a left hamstring injury from winter workouts before the season.

That caused him to back off his usual spring training workouts. Then his left quadriceps muscle was injured. The toll was 59 games. Bregman came to the realization that in order to do what he loves – play baseball as much as possible – he had to change his habits.

"There's only one way to go about it, and that's figure out what the problem is, address it, and try to prevent it from happening again," Bregman told Chandler Rome of the *Houston Chronicle.* "I need to make it to the batter's box as many times as possible every year," said Bregman. "I'm not a burner by any means, so if I'm out by two steps instead of four, I'm out. At the same time, there's something inside of you. I grew up playing the game of baseball. I was taught to play with your hair on fire. It's been an adjustment." Between 2020 and 2021, he spent 90 days on the injured list.

His time from the batter's box to first base slowed from 4.3 seconds in 2016 to 4.48 in 2020 and 4.61 in 2021. "You learn how to rewire yourself," explained Dusty Baker.

"We've all had to do that to find a way to stay in the lineup. I urged him to play smart in the past. If you're out, you're out. If the fans get on you for not hustling, if they don't understand the need for you to stay in the lineup, you have to play another day. There is a need to play smart."

Bregman and the Astros were two outs away from losing to Seattle September 7, trailing 4-2 in the last of the ninth.

This was the type of game Seattle made a habit of winning in 2021. The Mariners routinely won the close games (29-17 in one-run games) and extra inning contests (14-6).

Oddly, they were blown out many times and outscored by their opponents for the season (644-588), but they owned close games.

The Astros, conversely, had a huge scoring advantage over their opponents for the season (726-550) but were nothing special in close games (16-16 in one-run games, 7-7 in extra innings).

Seattle closer Paul Sewald shut them down a week earlier. On this night he was not in his best form.

He walked Jose Altuve on seven pitches and gave up a long fly ball to Michael Brantley. Bregman stepped in the box with Houston 0-for-9 against the Seattle bullpen with men in scoring position.

Bregman ripped a high home run off the wall above the Crawford Boxes in left field to tie the game, standing at home plate for a moment before tossing the bat away in celebration of his first long ball since June 9. He toured the bases with the game tied, 4-4. The Astros went on to win 5-4 in 10 innings when Carlos Correa blasted an RBI double to right field.

This series was the biggest of September for the Astros. A Seattle sweep would have cut their lead to 1 ½ games. By winning the first two, they enlarged their working margin for the division title.

One of those losses came the next day. Seattle mounted a better bullpen effort, handing Ryan Pressly the loss, 8-5 and cutting the Astros' margin to 5 ½ games. Marwin Gonzalez cashed in on his first start at third base for Houston in 2021, nailing a home run. Bregman chimed in with a pinch-hit blast and Jose Altuve also repeated his home run swing from the night before. The Astros failed to hold a 4-2 advantage in the eighth, but they tucked away a series win before their last day off prior to a 17-game September grind.

Shohei Ohtani and the Angels came to Minute Maid Park. Chandler Rome wrote in the *Houston Chronicle*, "Ohtani stopped in Houston this weekend for one final time en route to American League Most Valuable Player honors." Ohtani ripped his 44th home run in the first inning off Framber Valdez. He did win the MVP award in unanimous voting.

Only one other lefthanded hitter had collected an extra base hit against Valdez in 2021. Valdez had allowed only one other home run to a lefthanded hitter in his career. Ohtani was the only player since Babe Ruth a century earlier with those sensational pitching and hitting gifts that attracted baseball fans by huge numbers. He was leading the league in home runs and slugging percentage (.615) and pitching to a 9-1 record with a 2.97 ERA. Most of the time when Ohtani pitched, the Los Angeles Angels declined to use the DH because they needed his bat in the lineup. On this night, he batted second. What was unusual about this game was Ohtani's struggles on the mound. The Astros battered him for nine hits and six earned runs in 3 1/3 innings. In May, he dominated them with ten strikeouts. The relentless Houston attack overcame Valdez' stumbles, 10-5.

The homestand ended with a 4-2 record for the Astros when Lance McCullers, Jr. won his 12th, 3-1. Kyle Tucker's two-run homer provided the difference, but again the hitting attack was not clicking. Bregman was thrown out at home plate when he did not get a good jump off second on a single to right field. His speed was far from normal, but his bat was playing big since his return from the IL. The A's and Mariners both dropped one-run decisions, falling 6 ½ games back. The Astros headed for Arlington with an eight-game home series winning streak intact over the Mariners, Rangers and Angels. Their record within the AL West was a dominant 41-21.

NOTE: It seemed that the decision to have pitchers examined as they left the mound had not only curtailed the flood of no-hitters and strikeouts late in the season, but had brought much more offense back into the game. The unusual mid-season banning of Spider Tack, a substance that aided pitchers' grip on the ball, and other sticky substances worked well for the game.

"SIRI, DO YOU HAVE MORE ANSWERS THAN ALEXA?"

The battle of the voice technology giants could have been decided at Globe Life Field in Arlington September 13. If only Rangers' pitcher A.J. Alexy had been named Alexa! He gave up the second of Siri's two homers.

Jose Siri was the starting left fielder for Dusty Baker because of his speed and strong arm – both valuable tools when the Astros' manager considered a replacement for the injured Michael Brantley. Brantley's troublesome knee led Baker to turn to Siri, which many people do when they're looking for quick answers to a dilemma. Siri provided the answer, becoming the first player since 1920 to hit at least two home runs and drive in at least five runs in his first major league start. Siri had impressed Baker in spring training with his tools.

At AAA Sugar Land, he had hit .321 with 24 steals in 27 tries. Baker noticed his elite speed because it stood out as something lacking in his starting lineup.

The hitters provided the top group in the majors at working counts, reaching base and driving in runs. As a group, they were excellent at running the bases on hits. Often, they were aggressive in going from first to third on singles and scoring from second on hits.

But in September, managers' thoughts often turn to playoff roster composition. The Astros had speedy Jake Meyers and above average runner Chas McCormick, but Siri was in a higher category.

Although he made a baserunning mistake against the Angels a few days earlier when he took off for second too early on a pickoff throw by lefty Jose Suarez, he churned forward and beat the throw from Jared Walsh with a headfirst dive. The Angels did not execute the play well, but Siri helped to force the mistake with his aggressiveness. It was just the kind of play that fired up the Astros and led to thoughts of what kind of impact it could bring to a tight playoff game. Unfortunately, Siri missed the ALDS with a broken finger.

In a 15-1 Houston rout, offense ruled the night against an inexperienced and undermanned Texas team. It masked worry about the starting rotation. Although Zack Greinke was about to return to the rotation the next night, Jake Odorizzi's foot injury prompted his exit in the second inning.

BLACK CLOUD HOVERS OVER ODORIZZI

For Jake Odorizzi, the night was filled with negatives after starting well. Backed by a three-run first, Odorizzi took the mound with a golden opportunity to prove his point from his last start – that he could be effective pitching deeper into games.

He twirled a scoreless first, and the Astros exploded for four more runs in the second. With a 7-0 lead, Odorizzi had the luxury of not needing to be perfect with his pitches.

As he covered first base to take a throw from Yuli Gurriel on a fast-developing play, Odorizzi stutter-stepped close to the base so his footwork would be proper.

He got the out, but he stepped on the base hastily and injured his right foot. A warmup toss verified that he could not put weight on the foot. His night ended abruptly. Just 1 1/3 innings. No victory.

Even worse, the bullpen now was charged with providing 7 2/3 innings of relief, in the fourth day of 17 straight days of baseball.

Fortunately for the Astros, five relievers combined for one-run relief in the blowout win. Cristian Javier was the winning pitcher, but he labored through 2 2/3 innings with 54 pitches. Many of those pitches missed the strike zone by a foot or more. Javier did strike out six, but his pitching line was dressed in a tuxedo compared to the way he delivered the ball. It was Javier under duress and forcing his delivery. To be fair, he was pressed into action suddenly because of the injury. Frequently a former starting pitcher needs more warmup time.

Even with the rules permitting him as much warmup as he wanted, many young pitchers rush that process because the game is stopped while everybody bides time for them to get loose. But given his push into new territory for innings pitched, Javier's situation would have to be analyzed later in terms of what he could provide for a playoff bullpen.

All the stars were in alignment for the bullpen after Javier departed, and the "go-to" top tier of bullpen artists did not have to be pressed into action. They were saved for Greinke's return the next night, when hopefully Brandon Bielak would be back in play as the long man.

When staff ace Zack Greinke returned for his first action since August 29, he thought he would be in the game long enough to get through the lineup twice. That was not the plan, due to the previous night's deep dive into the bullpen.

Former Houston first-round draft choice Jordan Lyles strayed from his fastball-reliant approach that carried him to a 5.43 ERA, mixing in sliders and changeups. He shut out the listless Astros for seven innings in an 8-1 Texas drubbing. The Rangers were 5-3 at Globe Life Field against the Astros. Greinke trailed 4-0 after three innings, holding the line until a four-run sixth blew up his start. He exited after only 75 pitches, but he was pitching without a rehab start due to the urgency of the pennant race. "I felt pretty good," said Greinke.

"Planned on going two times through the order and felt good. For some reason, I went further and did bad after that." He surrendered three bombs to the Rangers, one of them Adolis Garcia's 30th of his fine rookie season.

To make room for Greinke's return to the roster from the COVID list, Odorizzi was placed on the ten-day IL. That took him out of action until a week before the regular season ended, leaving him little chance to be in a postseason rotation. The diagnosis came back as a midfoot sprain. "When we got the diagnosis of no ligament tears or anything like that, it just becomes a soreness thing, and I can play through soreness," said Odorizzi.

Michael Brantley was placed on the injured list September 15 to give his right knee more time to heal. That night's starting lineup was not only without Brantley; Alex Bregman and Carlos Correa were being rested. Dusty Baker's selection of Marwin Gonzalez to play third base resulted in a home run by Gonzalez, back-to-back with Meyers' long ball.

The flow of injuries did not stop. The Astros and injuries were associated like a country song with lyrics about dogs and trucks. About 24 hours before Framber Valdez was due to start against the Rangers, he was shagging fly balls in the outfield in Arlington when he cut the index finger on his pitching hand in a freak accident. Valdez braced himself against the wall when he encountered a sharp object.

There was a chance that the "light slice" could heal overnight, but as a precaution Luis Garcia was informed that he could take the start. Garcia did take the mound for Valdez, pitching on four days' rest. He pitched well in a 12-1 Houston rout, allowing one run in 5 1/3 innings. But the Houston rotation was blown up in the series, losing Odorizzi in the second inning to an injury and necessitating a shuffling of starters because of the Valdez injury.

With Garcia pitching one day earlier than scheduled, the series ended and the Astros headed home for a series against Arizona with two of their three starters for the series listed as "TBA."

The initial plan for To Be Announced #1 was to use reliever Brandon Bielak in a bullpen game. Another option was to recall a rested Peter Solomon from Sugar Land and send another pitcher to the Skeeters to create room for him. The Skeeters had just clinched their East Division title in the Triple A West.

With the magic number for clinching the division standing at 10, the weekend series against Arizona at Minute Maid Park gave the Astros a weak (47-99) National League opponent. But their 7-10 record against NL clubs told the story of struggles in interleague play.

JOSE ALTUVE

Dusty Baker noticed in Jose Altuve's final at-bat September 3 that his frustrations were boiling over. Altuve had slammed down his batting helmet and tossed his bat away in a rare sign of anger after striking out. His power had been missing since the end of July. In August his slash line of .245/.303/.318 with no home runs showed a different Altuve than the seven-time All-Star Astros fans were accustomed to seeing. His return to the leadoff spot in 2021 was necessitated by George Springer's departure via free agency. Altuve had quietly transitioned back to the leadoff spot without any slowdown in offense until the last month. Now he was mired in a long 4-for-37 slump. His OPS was .872 through July, but just .621 in August. Baker gave Altuve the day off September 4.

His resurgence after the extra day off proved Baker's wisdom when it came to dealing with position players. Altuve reeled off 10 hits in his first seven games of September. By the middle of the month, he looked the part of a sparkplug for the playoffs. Altuve also continued his climb up the top rungs of the ladder for all-time Houston hitting records. He moved past Jose Cruz into fifth place in both runs scored and doubles. He was bearing down on Cesar Cedeno for fourth place. Altuve had already reached the status of franchise icon, as did Cruz and Cedeno in their eras. It was a given that someday he would be inducted into the team's hall of fame as they had been.

As a ten-year-old in Maracay, Venezuela Altuve was hitting bottlecaps with a broomstick. The lack of baseball equipment and financial resources to provide it did not prevent him from pursuing what he loved. His nickname, "Gigante," translates to "Giant" in English. That's what he became against all odds. A 5-5 second baseman who was sent home from his first tryout camp with the Astros in Venezuela thought he was finished with the Astros.

His father insisted that Jose return to try out again the day after he was cut, because Al Pedrique had not seen him that day. The next day, Pedrique signed him for $15,000 because that's all he had left in his budget.

"We projected him as a AA or AAA player," said Pedrique. "We knew his hitting had to stand out enough that he would be taken seriously and get an opportunity." Astros farm director Ricky Bennett was impressed early. "For five days I watched Jose, and I couldn't take my eyes off him. He played the game with such flash, such passion. He was always in the right place at the right time. I wanted to take him home with me."

Altuve attracted some attention from Omar Lopez once he started playing professionally in Venezuela. "He has good enough skills, good enough talent to be a ballplayer," said Lopez. "But the problem is he's too short. You need to get glasses to see the kid." Lopez had been watching him and was "sitting on him," in scouts' vernacular, until he turned 16 in 2006. Now Lopez was shaking his hand from the third base coaching box on home trots.

When Altuve belted a high fastball from Madison Bumgarner over the Crawford Boxes to break up a no-hit bid in the sixth inning September 17, he tied Lance Berkman as the all-time hit leader at Minute Maid Park.

He connected for his first major league home run a month after reaching the majors in 2011. The pitcher who allowed the home run was Bumgarner. Now, ten years later, Altuve had three batting titles, a league MVP award, seven All-Star seasons and four 200-hit seasons. He had collected 1,777 hits through the 2021 season.

Did you know...

The 2021 Houston Astros spent a total of 1,428 days on the Injured List. Justin Verlander missed the entire season recovering from Tommy John surgery. He was throwing in the mid-90s after the season and signed a one-year contract to return to the Astros for 2022, with a player option for 2023.

One of the September highlights involved Yordan Alvarez, who became only the third Astro to reach 100 RBIs at age 24 or younger, joining Alex Bregman and Cesar Cedeno. He blasted a 456-foot rocket to center field for a two-run homer.

The Astros took two of three from Arizona to drop their magic number for clinching to eight.

Elsewhere, The Chicago White Sox clinched their first division title since 2008 – the first American League team to clinch its division. The White Sox were ticketed for a Division Series meeting with the Astros, with home field advantage between the two belonging to the Astros as of September 24 but still up for grabs in the remaining ten days of the season.

The Sox had a rotation of Lucas Giolito, Lance Lynn and Carlos Rodon lining up for the Astros. Their lineup was robust. Luis Robert was torrid in September after missing extensive time with an injury.

On the day the Astros started the weekend series in Oakland, they announced that Zack Greinke had been scratched as their starter and placed on the Injured List with a sore neck. Greinke said he started experiencing neck soreness two days earlier. The pain worsened the next day when he discovered he couldn't run or throw.

In his two starts since returning from the COVID IL, Greinke had allowed 12 earned runs in nine innings. The injury, on top of his pitching struggles, cast strong doubts on his availability for the playoffs.

Greinke admitted of his situation since contracting COVID, "It's been kind of a mess since all that, but the important thing now is the season for me is close to over. Just trying to get ready for the playoffs and hopefully help the team out there as much as possible."

His injury shed a different light on Odorizzi, who would have a start against Oakland to prove he was ready for the playoffs. Greinke had allowed 18 runs in his last 13 innings and had failed to deliver more than 76 pitches in a start. Greinke said he "definitely" wanted to pitch beyond his 38th birthday in October 2021. Greinke's teammates had left on the road trip with a "Dress Like Zack Greinke Day," and he mentioned that the 2021 Astros ranked alongside the best groups of teammates he had ever had. Baseball teams have trended toward having "theme road trips" to bring variety to the constant travel of a six-month season. They designate certain road trips for the players to dress alike to enjoy some bonding. This trip was their way of honoring Greinke. Peter Solomon was recalled to replace Greinke.

He followed starter Bielak's three innings with three innings himself, leaving Baker without a long man in the bullpen the next day.

Oakland walked off with a 2-1 win on a Starling Marte hit off Ryan Pressly in the ninth to keep Houston's magic number at three. Pressley and Kendall Graveman both lacked their usual pressure performances. Pressley gave up the winning hit in a 4-3 Oakland walk-off later in the series, but Stanek set the table for the loss after a good relief outing by Javier.

Odorizzi was solid in his next-to-last start, making a bid for the playoff roster.

Greinke threw a bullpen and gave Dusty Baker a chance to consider him for the playoffs. Meanwhile, the Astros still had not clinched a postseason berth and had a four-game losing streak.

Siri made a baserunning blunder in the ninth, getting thrown out at the plate with Alvarez on deck in a tie game. Third base coach Lopez was holding Siri at third, but he was looking at outfielder Seth Brown's casual throw to the infield. Siri had slowed down, and coaches are not inclined to send runners home after they slow down. Siri's age (26) and eight years of professional baseball did not speak well regarding his instincts.

With one week to go, four teams were chasing after two wild card spots in the American League playoffs. There was drama of a different kind in the National League. St. Louis was attracting headlines for its club record 16-game winning streak.

Beyond that, the top two teams in the NL West both had at least 100 wins! The Giants led with 102 and the Dodgers had 100. It reminded some long-time fans of 1993, when San Francisco and Atlanta battled tooth and nail for a playoff spot with more than 100 wins.

But in that case, Dusty Baker's Giants lost to Bobby Cox's Braves, 104 wins to 103, and the Giants did not reach the playoffs!

Tampa Bay, the Chicago White Sox and Milwaukee had clinched their division titles the final week.

The Houston media was focused on the lack of information about Michael Brantley's right knee injury as the Astros met Tampa Bay September 28 to begin the final homestand.

Brantley still had not played since hitting the injured list September 12. The 34-year-old Brantley, hitting .315 and with a shot at a battling title, trailed teammate Yuli Gurriel by two points for the American League lead. Brantley needed nine plate appearances to qualify for the title, but getting ready for the playoffs was the top priority. Manager Dusty Baker told the media two days earlier in Oakland, "He went out to the field one time, and it really didn't work. Right now, he's mostly getting treatment so he can go to work." Speculation was growing that Yordan Alvarez might be the left fielder if the Division Series opened in Houston in ten days.

Alvarez had made 25 of his 35 left field starts with Lance McCullers, Jr. and Framber Valdez on the mound. Those two figured to be the starters in the first two games of the playoffs in Houston.

Alvarez was hitting better when he played the outfield than when he served as designated hitter, with a 1.223 OPS in those 35 games as an outfielder. Brantley could be the DH in those first two games to allow him more time to get his knee ready for playing the outfield. "He's done a great job, probably a better job than any of us counted on," said Baker of Alvarez in the outfield.

Tampa Bay, with the best record in the American League and the best in its team history, needed just one more win to secure home field advantage throughout the AL playoffs. In what could have been a preview of the American League Championship Series, the 2020 ALCS teams met again in the final regular season series. They also had met in the 2019 Division Series.

The Rays were the cutting-edge team in baseball due to their innovativeness with an affordable roster and not many superstars. Their trade for home run basher Nelson Cruz sent their offense to a higher level. Cruz was one long ball away from tying Jeff Bagwell's career total of 449. The Rays had ten players with ten home runs or more. They had set a major league record with 14 pitchers earning saves. In many games they used their starting pitchers only to get them through a few innings at the beginning of the game. They were ready to start firing bullpen bullets early in the game. They could select any one of a number of 95mph pellet-throwers to match up in any inning of a game. There was no team like them, although all teams were headed in that direction in 2021.

Tampa Bay manager Kevin Cash selected righthander Michael Wacha to start the opener of the series. With Houston's magic number to clinch the division at two, Wacha held the Astros hitless for the first five innings. "He was throwing a lot better than a 5.48 ERA," said Dusty Baker of the Texas A&M product. But, customary for the Rays, Wacha came out of the game with the no-hitter alive and Alex Bregman broke it up with a home run off Andrew Kittredge.

Jose Urquidy surrendered a first-inning Crawford Boxes 353-foot homer to Yandy Diaz but kept the game manageable with a 91-pitch effort through five innings, building his stamina for the playoffs. His effort was notable against the best American League lineup in the second half of the season, with a 119-weighted-runs-created-plus figure. Weighted runs created plus (wRC+) is a measurement of a team's offensive production with ballpark factors included.

Tampa Bay had already set a club record with 829 runs, giving credence to Urquidy's performance. Urquidy allowed four hits and one walk through five innings.

Jose Altuve tied his career high with his 31st home run in the eighth off David Robertson, tying the game, 2-2. Tampa Bay took a 3-2 lead with a ninth-inning home run by Randy Arozarena off Maton.

When the Astros came up in the bottom of the ninth trailing by one with a short bullpen if they went to extra innings, they began an improbable rally off lefty Josh Fleming. Yordan Alvarez reached on a rare infield hit, Carlos Correa bounced an infield hit up the middle, stopped by a diving Brandon Lowe but not in time to get an out. Actually, Correa was called out by umpire Rob Drake. But a replay review overturned the call. "We're fighting for our lives," said Baker. "That's one of the few calls that stood in our favor. This place might have come down had they called him out in that situation." The Minute Maid Park crowd was loud. There were 32,297 tickets sold to fans hoping to celebrate a clincher.

With the bases loaded and former Rice University reliever JT Chargois firing 97mph fastballs, Chas McCormick and pinch-hitter Jason Castro had two fabulous at-bats with one out, coaxing a total of 18 pitches before both drew walks to force in the tying and winning runs. The Astros reduced their magic number to one with the thrilling, 4-3 walk-off win.

It was their ninth walk-off win of 2021, and it came against a Tampa Bay bullpen with an American League best 3.24 ERA from a bevy of bullet-throwing relievers who were used interchangeably.

Zack Greinke remained on the 10-day injured list until the final weekend of the regular season, but Baker thought about activating him for the playoffs as a reliever.

Seventh Inning Stretch

Infield Fly Rule

"An infield fly is any fair fly ball (not a line drive or a bunt) which can be caught by an infielder with ordinary effort when first and second or first, second and third base are occupied, before two men are out."

Knowing that rule can make you the hit of any gathering of baseball fans. The infield fly rule can cause havoc, because when an umpire puts his hand in the air to make the call, the baserunners advance at their own risk. The fielder does not have to catch the ball to get the batter out. But if the runners decide to try to advance, they are fair game. If the baserunners panic, the fielders can take advantage to get more than one out. Sometimes the umpire can make a mistake by calling the infield fly rule too soon, and a gust of wind can blow the ball out of reach of the fielder. A runner might think he has to take off for the next base, but he does not have to run. Players are charged with quick thinking on a play of that nature. The infield fly rule is one of the most complicated rules in sports.

Did you know that....

In the first season that saves were an official statistic, the Astros' Fred Gladding was the National League leader with 29.

In Atlanta, former Astro Charlie Morton posted one of the best seasons of any former Astro in 2021. Here's a partial list of former Astros: (*former Astros farmhands when traded in italics*)

Charlie Morton, Atlanta	*Kike Hernandez, Boston*
Gerrit Cole, NY Yankees	*Brett Phillips, Tampa Bay*
Josh Hader, Milwaukee	Jonathan Villar, NY Mets
Adrian Houser, Milwaukee	J.A. Happ, St. Louis
Teoscar Hernandez, Toronto	
Colin Moran, Pittsburgh	
George Springer, Toronto	
Dallas Keuchel, Chicago White Sox	
Myles Straw, Cleveland	
Ramon Laureano, Oakland	
Josh Rojas, Arizona	
Daz Cameron, Detroit	
Jake Rogers, Detroit	
Seth Beer, Arizona	
J.D. Martinez, Boston	
Jordan Lyles, Texas	
Vince Velasquez, Philadelphia	
Corbin Martin, Arizona	

Every team has a list like this. In a sport with frequent trades, prospects either develop into good players in the majors or not. Injuries strike.

Some trades are designed to work in the short term for a contending team but in the long term for a developing team.

Michael Brantley returned to the lineup as the DH after a 16-game absence with a sore right knee. Brantley was 0-for-4. The Astros were 10-6 in his absence while averaging 5.9 runs per game.

As the Astros' September song came to a close, it was not harmonious. On the final day of the month, they had 92 wins but still had not clinched a playoff spot. With four games to go they faced 98-win Tampa Bay.

The Astros had seven opportunities to clinch their division. They could win any of their four remaining games or Seattle could lose any of its three games left.

They could tie Seattle at 92-70 for the AL West title, forcing a one-game playoff the day after the regular season ended.

Former Astro Collin McHugh, now with Tampa Bay, won 19 games in 2015. His career record of 58-35 in Houston coincided with the Astros' improvement, and his own improvement was a perfect match for the team and what it needed from him to reach the playoffs. Houston wasn't a playoff team until the 162nd game of 2015. The man who won that game, Lance McCullers, Jr., was facing McHugh in this game.

McCullers, Jr. had progressed from a number three starter to the ace of the staff. He, like McHugh, developed more expertise and polished more pitches alongside the big names on the staff. He watched proven winners Dallas Keuchel, Charlie Morton, Justin Verlander, Gerrit Cole and Zack Greinke lead the staff and either move on to other teams or drop back in their prominence due to age or injury.

On a night when Greinke went two scoreless innings in relief across Houston for AAA Sugar Land, McCullers, Jr. had the spotlight. He stopped the hot Tampa Bay bats early in the game, starting with four no-hit innings.

Carlos Correa ripped a three-run homer off lefty reliever Ryan Yarbrough. Yarborough entered in the second inning after McHugh worked a scoreless first.

The Rays often started an "opener" who left after an inning or two, yielding to a reliever who might stay in for four or five innings or more. By using this plan, Manager Kevin Cash exploited more favorable matchups.

Dusty Baker had Kyle Tucker batting fifth. He was the first man southpaw Yarbrough faced after relieving McHugh. Another lefthanded hitter, Michael Brantley, was hitting seventh. Yarbrough could use his sweeping slider to advantage against lefthanded hitters. Cash countered with this lefty reliever after the opposing lineup was set up to face a righthanded starter. The Rays were all about matchups, and they often pinch-hit for their position starters for the same reason.

Brandon Lowe's two-run homer off McCullers, Jr., glancing off the foul pole in right field, came in the sixth. It cut the Astros lead to 3-2. McCullers left after six.

The score was still 3-2 when the ninth arrived. Closer Ryan Pressley, 0-2 with a 5.63 ERA in September, walked Randy Arozarena to lead off the inning. Jose Altuve, in his haste to force Arozarena at second on a slow bouncer by Wander Franco, dropped the ball for an error. Slugger Nelson Cruz smashed a grounder at Gurriel, who knocked it down and started a double play.

Then, on the final out, Alex Bregman's throw to Gurriel on Yandy Diaz's grounder came up a little short and Gurriel scooped it out of the dirt to prevent the potential tying run from scoring. The Astros had their clincher, 3-2.

Kendall Graveman pitched a scoreless eighth on the day he returned from the paternity list. He was headed to the playoffs for the first time in his career at age 31.

Starting centerfielder Jake Meyers was on a playoff team in his rookie season. In the remaining three games, the Astros' mission was to win at least one more to secure home field advantage over the White Sox in the Division Series.

Beyond that, Dusty Baker could prepare his pitchers for the postseason and rest his position players if they nailed down the number 2 seed before Sunday.

They were headed to the playoffs for the fifth straight year, four as division winners. During their Golden Era, this was going to be their sixth playoff appearance in seven years.

"We really wanted to get it done maybe a little earlier, but to finish it here against a really good team with a great crowd means a lot," said McCullers, Jr., who won for the 13th time. McCullers, Jr. and Correa called themselves "brothers for life" because they were drafted 40 picks apart at the top of the first round in 2012 and made their major league debuts a month apart in 2015, at the beginning of the Golden Era for the Astros. "He just is never out of big hits or big moments on this team," said McCullers, Jr. of Correa. "We're going to rely on him, we're going to rely on a lot of these guys, but especially him to get us through October."

Beyond October? McCullers, Jr. was set on a five-year contract, but what would Correa choose to do? "I'm hoping there's a way we can retain and sign Carlos, because he's a big part of this team, not only on the field but he's one of the real leaders of this team," said Dusty Baker. Would the Astros make him a big offer to stay in Houston before he became a free agent? That was a question that would be answered later.

As for Dusty Baker, he made history by becoming the first manager to take five different teams to division titles. What was Baker's reaction to the achievement? "I don't really think nothing, other than why was I on so many different teams" he said. "I'm serious. I feel fortunate to have gotten that many jobs, but I feel unfortunate that I shouldn't have lost jobs when I was winning."

Baker had not yet been offered another contract by the Astros. The man who had three Manager of the Year awards was turned away by both Cincinnati and Washington after leading those teams to postseason play. His Hall of Fame candidacy grew stronger with each win.

He was just short of 2,000 career managerial victories. Of the 11 managers with 2,000 wins, ten were in the Hall of Fame. Bruce Bochy was on his way to Cooperstown to make it 11 of 11. "That was the hardest but greatest year ever for me," Baker told his team after the game.

The final weekend brought chaos in the AL wild card race. Fans love chaos! Boston had lost two of three in Baltimore to fall into a tie with Seattle for the second wild card spot. The Yankees were two games in front of them for the first wild card. Toronto was still in the picture, just one behind Boston and Seattle. The Yankees hosted Tampa Bay in a centerpiece series of the weekend. Boston was at Washington and Seattle hosted the Los Angeles Angels. The Atlanta Braves clinched their fourth straight NL East crown September 30, leaving only the NL West battle between the Giants and Dodgers to firm up the playoff picture. The Giants, with 105 wins, led the Dodgers by two games.

Tampa Bay beat the Yankees Friday night while Boston and Toronto won, narrowing the margin to one game between the Yankees and their rivals.

Jake Odorizzi started the next-to-last game of the regular season against Oakland and allowed two runs in the first. Odorizzi and Greinke were the only pitchers on the roster who had thrown more than 130 innings in a major league season prior to 2021, when McCullers threw 162. Odorizzi was ready to go to the bullpen for the playoffs if needed. He had been assigned to the pen for Minnesota against the Astros in 2020 but did not pitch. He had experience against the White Sox and good career numbers. They managed only a .638 OPS against him for his three seasons with the Twins. He had 58 strikeouts in 42 innings against them. "I think, for me personally, I've seen them plenty of times, and I think I have a pretty good idea of how to manipulate facing them over the years." Baker mentioned the possibility of using Greinke as an opener for a couple of innings, since he wasn't stretched out and hadn't pitched in relief since 2007.

Odorizzi allowed three runs in 4 2/3 innings against Oakland and left with a 6-3 lead in his final tuneup. Phil Maton escaped bases-loaded trouble to hold the lead.

The offense kicked in with a strong effort, including four hits from Jose Altuve, in a 10-4 conquest that clinched the number 2 seed in the playoffs.

GURRIEL WINS THE BATTING TITLE

Only five hitters had won batting titles in their age 37 seasons or later: Ted Williams (1957-58), Rogers Hornsby (1911), George Brett in 1990, Tony Gwynn in 1997 and Barry Bonds in both 2002 and 2004 (he was 37 in 2002 and 39 in 2004). Bonds was actually 40 on the last day of the 2004 season, becoming the oldest player in history to win the title. Ted Williams was also 40, but a few days younger than Bonds. Gurriel was the second-oldest first-time batting champ behind Bonds (also 37).

Gurriel had never finished a season above .299. His previous two Septembers brought a fading batting average to the end of the regular season; Gurriel hit .175 in 154 combined at-bats in 2019 and 2020, covering 42 games.

In 2021, he nailed down the crown with two hits in the final Saturday to move 5 points ahead of teammate Michael Brantley. "It's something that's really important," said Gurriel. "I think everybody knows it's a big deal. And it's tough to win a batting title, so it means a lot. I was fine either way with playing today [or not]."

Gurriel did not start Sunday's game. Brantley played, as did Vladimir Guerrero, Jr. for Toronto. Gurriel came off the bench to win the final game, 7-6 in the ninth with a pinch RBI single. He became the second Astro in history to win a batting title, joining Jose Altuve (who has three). Gurriel finished at .319.

Brantley and Guerrero tied for second at .311. Tony Oliva was the only other Cuban-born player to win a batting crown. Gurriel had become a fan favorite in Houston. The difficult decision to leave Cuba for the United States was one he managed well. One of many players who parted with his family after reaching stardom with the Cuban national team, Gurriel was older than almost all of the Cuban defectors who found stardom in MLB.

Gurriel was 32 when he made his major league debut after playing shortstop, second base and third base for the Cuban team. He also played in Japan. Gurriel's father Lourdes was a major star in Cuba.

His younger brother Lourdes Gurriel, Jr. plays for Toronto. The Gurriel brothers defected at the same time, while the Cuban team was playing in the Dominican Republic. Yuli later signed a five-year, $47.5 million deal with the Astros in July 2016 and joined the major league club shortly thereafter.

His transition to first base was not without bumps in the road. Hours of defensive work allowed him to feel comfortable with positioning and the different throwing angles to second base.

Gurriel had just 130 at-bats in 2016 after signing with Houston. Chris Carter had been a good home run hitter for the Astros in previous years, but he hit for a low average and struck out frequently. His defensive skills were lacking. In Gurriel's first full season in 2017, he was a major contributor to the club who hit .299-18-75 for the World Champions.

Gurriel was known as a good-natured, smiling personality whose hair earned him the nickname "La Pina" because of its resemblance to a pineapple. Unlike third baseman Adrian Beltre, who is headed for the Hall of Fame, Pina enjoyed the good-natured fun players had with his hair.

When Gurriel has his cap on, nobody makes fun of his performance. His range and mastery of scoops at first base saved his teammates many errors and helped him win a Gold Glove in 2021, becoming the oldest Gold Glover at first base. His clutch hitting is a strong asset and his bat-to-ball skills result in a tough player to fan. Gurriel's RBI total (345 in his four full major league seasons) is respectable, especially given his placement in the lineup (seventh quite often in 2021).

Gurriel's contract option for 2022, exercised by the team after the end of the season, is worth a modest $9 million for a star player. He and Cuban teammate Yordan Alvarez combined with fellow Cuban Aledmys Diaz.

CORREA FAREWELL?

As the Astros took the field for their regular season finale, all of their starting players knelt outside the dugout so Carlos Correa could be the focus, running onto the field alone in what could have been his final regular season game with Houston. The fans rose in tribute, and they rose again when he was removed late in the game after belting a home run to right field in what could have been his final regular season plate appearance.

If Correa was about to leave Houston, his teammates felt an urgency to win a championship before he departed. "It does mean a lot more because it's the end of an era in a way," said Gurriel through an interpreter. "There's been a lot of time spent together with this group of guys. To break that up, it would be very special to send him off with a championship."

Correa played a career high 148 games in 2021, producing .279-26-92 (BA-HR-RBI) including 75 walks and the best defense at shortstop in MLB. Baseball Reference measured his wins above replacement number at 7.2, tied for the highest in the majors among all position players.

He reached a personal high with 21 runs saved, winning the Fielding Bible award as the top MLB shortstop, the first Astro to win the Platinum Glove as the top individual defender in the sport and his first Gold Glove. His .363 on base percentage was his highest since 2017. His 102 runs scored was a personal high. What was his value on the free agent market? Of the two highest-paid shortstops, Tatis had a huge year, but Lindor suffered through an injury-riddled campaign.

As with George Springer, it is not unusual for highly-paid players on the first years of their lucrative contracts to run into injuries or subpar seasons. Correa was 27, in the prime of his career. But he had a history of injuries.

To his credit, Correa grew into a leadership role and transcended Jose Altuve's stature on the team. He was a prominent weapon defensively with his range, arm and attention to detail on the field.

"He's the leader of the team," said Altuve. "We are where we are basically because of him." McCullers, Jr. also spoke to the statistically unmeasurable qualities of Correa. "He has a lot of grit. I think that may be something that, on the outside, maybe you don't see."

Correa had made it his mission to bring the various factions on the team together. "I make sure on this team everybody gets along and everyone is together. I don't like those separate groups speaking Spanish that never talk to the bullpen guys or the infielders that never talk to the starters," explained Correa.

"I want everyone to create that special relationship. It's just beautiful to see what goes on in this clubhouse, on the plane, whenever we go out to team dinners. Everyone gets along."

"We all needed each other," added bench coach Joe Espada. "Carlos is a big part of the puzzle. He kind of glues it all together."

What was that worth? Could the Astros keep Correa with a multiyear offer and fit it into a $200 million payroll, or could they go higher?

They drew just over two million fans in 2021 – a relatively low number compared to recent championship seasons. Where baseball attendance was headed when the nation moved past the pandemic was difficult to estimate for future payrolls. Zack Greinke and Justin Verlander were coming off the books. Their two salaries combined totaled $57 million. Altuve, Bregman and McCullers were locked up for the next few years.

The other young pitchers were making salaries at the low end of the scale due to their lack of service time. There seemed to be room for $30 million a year for Correa, but how many years would be required to get the total package to a signable figure? 10? 12? 14? That was unknown. How was the Albert Pujols contract regarded now after it ended? Worth the risk? Pujols was 31 when he signed for ten years. Many baseball experts would restrict the largest contracts in the game to players at premium defensive positions, such as shortstop.

If he left Houston, what was Plan B? Signing a free agent shortstop? Which one? Trevor Story of Colorado, Corey Seager of Los Angeles, Marcus Semien of Toronto, Javier Baez of the Mets were the most prominent free agent names. Trade for somebody? Hope that they could patch things together until prospect Jeremy Pena was ready? Move Bregman to shortstop?

Philosophically, is it wise to sign players to gargantuan contracts of $300 million or more for a decade or more? Evidence showed many mistakes made by teams following that pattern. San Diego had Manny Machado and Fernando Tatis, Jr. The Los Angeles Angels had Mike Trout, Anthony Rendon and until 2021 Albert Pujols. Philadelphia had Bryce Harper, the New York Mets Jacob deGrom and Francisco Lindor, St. Louis Nolan Arenado and Paul Goldschmidt to name a few. Tying up such a high percentage of payroll in one player left less flexibility for other moves. One player in baseball could not have the same impact as in basketball or football.

Did you know that....

The Colt .45s' first manager Harry Craft wore the number 1. The last man to wear number 1 before Carlos Correa was interim Manager Tom Lawless in 2014.

Did you know that....

When the Astros moved into the American League, their opening day designated hitter was Carlos Pena.

FINAL DAY DRAMA

The wild card was introduced to the major leagues in 1995. It delivered the drama officials hoped for on the final day of 2021. All of the games started at 3:10 p.m. Eastern time, and the stroke of genius adopted by MLB a few years earlier paid off in spades. The MLB Network bounced from one game to another to track the final-day excitement, and there was plenty of it.

Jose Urquidy delivered a workmanlike six innings. Zack Greinke was perfect for his first two innings in relief before being dinged for his major league high 30th home run in 171 innings.

The Athletics tied the game in the ninth before Gurriel's pinch single provided another walk-off to end the Astros' 95th win. The Astros had three days of rest before meeting the White Sox in Houston.

In the final-day battles, the New York Yankees walked off at home against Tampa Bay, 1-0 to earn one wild card spot. The Boston Red Sox roared from a 5-1 deficit at Washington to clip the Nationals, 7-5 for the second playoff position. Boston had the tiebreaker over the Yankees by virtue of winning the regular season series, 10-9. That gave the Red Sox a Fenway Park wild card meeting with the Yankees. Both teams were banged up and had injured players from their finales, and Boston starter Chris Sale was removed in the third inning after the Nationals roughed him up.

The San Francisco Giants won their club record 107th game to nip the Dodgers by one game for the NL West title. San Francisco prepared to host the wild card winner between Los Angeles and St. Louis. Milwaukee was set to face Atlanta in the other series.

Did you know that….

Jose Lima gave up a franchise high 48 homers in the first year of Enron Field in 2000.

Chapter 2

THE POSTSEASON RIDE

AL Wild Card Game

The playoffs started in Boston, with Nathan Eovaldi starting for the Red Sox against Gerrit Cole. Xander Bogaerts blasted a two-run homer above the center field wall off Cole in the first inning, touching off an explosion of noise at Fenway Park that could have shaken the Old North Church.

The pregame shows featured Bucky Dent's 1978 game-winning home run at Fenway for the Yankees in the Game 163 one-game playoff and Manager Aaron Boone's game-winning 2003 ALCS blast.

Kyle Schwarber lofted a home run to right field off a Cole high fastball in the third. Schwarber started at DH with J.D. Martinez unable to play due to a sprained ankle suffered when he stepped on second base while running to his position in the outfield. Boone pulled Cole after two innings. Baseball's version of the NCAA basketball tournament put the managers through a pressure-packed night. The Yankees started light-hitting catcher Kyle Higashioka and inexperienced shortstop Andrew Velasquez in the last two spots in the lineup. The Red Sox eliminated the Yankees, 6-2.

"I'm sick to my stomach," said Cole after the shortest start of his career. Cole's teams had lost four of his five career "win or go home" games, including Game 5 of the AL Division Series against Tampa Bay – Boston's next opponent – a year earlier.

Did you know that….

Rusty Staub is the only player to collect 500 hits with four different franchises. Staub had 500 hits for Houston, Montreal, the Mets and Detroit during his career.

HOUSTON VS. CHICAGO AL DIVISION SERIES

Much was made in the media of the Dusty Baker-Tony La Russa rivalry before the Astros met the White Sox in Houston to begin their series. La Russa was a Hall of Fame manager; Baker seemed destined to join him some day. Their lengthy careers took many fans back to their battles.

Their story began 50 years earlier in 1971 as teammates with the Atlanta Braves for one game at the end of the season. La Russa had broken into the majors with the Kansas City Athletics in 1963, but he was in the minors until 1968. Atlanta purchased his contract in 1971.

Baker debuted in the majors with Atlanta in 1968 but also was demoted to the minors until he returned in 1971. On the final day of the season, Baker hit fifth and played right field. La Russa batted seventh and played second base. They scored the tying and go-ahead runs in a 6-2 Braves victory.

While La Russa's career ended in 1973, he became a major league manager at age 34 with the White Sox in 1979. Baker moved into the Atlanta lineup in 1972 until he was traded to the Dodgers in 1975. His long career extended through a 1981 World Series championship and two pennants until he retired after 1986 with Oakland. His manager that year was La Russa. In his first managing job in 1993 with the Giants, his 103-win team fell one game short of the Braves for the NL West title.

This was the first time two 70-year-old managers faced off in the playoffs.

Baker told the media stories of his mother making Hank Aaron promise to take care of him when he was a rookie. His father kept some of his signing bonus and invested it, returning it to him a few years later with a sizeable appreciation.

Between Baker and La Russa, they had managed more than 9,000 games in the majors. They had an intense rivalry, highlighted by the battles between La Russa's Cardinals and Baker's Cubs. Their well-documented relationship escalated to a peak in a five-game September 2003 series.

There were staredowns, trash talk and a beanball duel as the Cubs won four times and nailed down the NL Central title. "Dusty and Tony, it was like two boxers going at it," said Cub outfielder Doug Glanville. "We were real cool until we were in the division," recalled Baker. "It got a little testy when we were in the same division playing 18 times. It got even more testy when I got to the Reds and we were a good team. Things kind of deteriorated from there."

When Baker's Giants knocked off La Russa's Redbirds in the 2002 NLCS, a slow home run trot by Kenny Lofton touched off a brawl. Brawls in playoff games are exceptionally rare.

Baker was fired by the Giants after a 2002 World Series loss to the Angels. He joined the Cubs the next year. His last postseason matchup against La Russa was in 2002.

"They're good acquaintances, and when it's time to compete on the field, they're what they should be," said mutual friend Dave Stewart. "I look at them as enemies. I believe they can go have dinner and talk about things outside of the game or inside, but when it comes to the game, I don't think there's any love lost." Their record against each other before this series was 104-104.

Dispassionately measuring the teams by statistics, here's the way some of the most relevant numbers compared:

Houston		Chicago
863	Runs	796
.784	OPS	.758
221	Home Runs	190
3.76	ERA	3.73
1,456	Strikeouts	1,588
1.23	WHIP	1.20

The Astros rated an edge over the White Sox defensively. Carlos Correa was far superior to Tim Anderson at shortstop. Martin Maldonado was a better defensive catcher than Yasmani Grandal, but Grandal was one of the top-hitting catchers in the sport.

With Michael Brantley's knee an issue in left field, Yordan Alvarez was set to play there. His limited range caused some thought to who played center field next to him. Jake Meyers was slightly superior in range and arm to Chas McCormick, but they were equal offensively. Dusty Baker had a decision to make at that position.

Fangraphs rated the White Sox as the best American League playoff team. Chicago was considered to have a superior bullpen. Kendall Graveman was a question mark because of his lack of playoff experience. Graveman had been inconsistent in the last days of the regular season. The White Sox had similar issues with their own top setup man, Craig Kimbrell. The White Sox seemed to rate a slight edge in the starting rotation because of their depth.

Roster decisions put Garrett Stubbs on the team as a third catcher, Jose Siri as a pinch runner/outfielder and sole lefty reliever Brooks Raley in the bullpen.

Zack Greinke and Jake Odorizzi met different fates; Greinke was a long man in the bullpen, but Odorizzi and Marwin Gonzalez failed to make the roster. Cristian Javier was another long man.

Before the start of the afternoon game, Houston owner Jim Crane talked with the media and spoke of his plans to try to sign Carlos Correa. "We'll definitely be in the mix as the season gets over and it's time to address that." His biggest salary expenditure was the five-year, $150 million extension to Jose Altuve.

He referred to that five-year commitment as the organization's history under his ownership on the duration of a contract, but he added that it was not set in stone. "It just depends on where we are with that and what Carlos wants to do," said Crane.

Crane reassured the fans that the organization's "window" for winning in the postseason was not "closing" and that as long as he was the owner the window would remain open.

Correa's representatives had to be hoping that the shortstop could cash in on the playoff run the same way Carlos Beltran did in the 2004 playoffs. After joining the Astros in a three-way trade with Kansas City and Oakland, Beltran sparked the Astros during their regular season second-half run (.258-23-53 in 90 games) to lead them to an exciting finish.

In 2004, Carlos Beltran led the team with eight home runs and 14 RBI in the postseason. After the Astros lost the NLCS to St. Louis, Beltran departed Houston for the New York Mets. The bidding for him reached the $100 million neighborhood, and Beltran's representatives insisted on a no-trade clause in his contract.

The Astros refused to grant that demand and lost him to a slightly higher number from the Mets, but New York's state income tax rendered it a financial wash. The no-trade clause made him a Met.

Beltran had some excellent seasons for the Mets and some disappointing ones over the course of seven seasons. But his 2004 Houston playoff performance was the standout segment of his career. The Astros went to the World Series in 2005 with Willy Taveras as their centerfielder, but they eventually brought back Beltran in 2017 and won the World Series with his help as DH.

Did you know that....

Cliff Johnson slugged nine pinch-hit homers during his time with the Astros. That is the franchise high.

Denny Walling was one of the best pinch-hitters in Astros' history. He has the most at bats (300), hits (82), RBIs (63), and walks (34) in his 13 years with Houston. Walling played for the 1980, 1981 and 1986 playoff teams. He platooned at third base in 1986 with Phil Garner. Walling hit .277 in his career with Houston, .273 as a pinch-hitter. His six home runs rank high among pinch-hitters. Walling's playing time as a starter at first base, third base and the outfield made him a solid contributor in those areas as well.

Game 1

2021 ALDS

Lance McCullers, Jr. heard public address announcer Bob Ford introduce him with the starting lineup as he warmed up in the bullpen. It was the first experience for McCullers as a Game 1 playoff starter. He joined former Houston staff aces such as Nolan Ryan, Mike Scott, Randy Johnson, Roger Clemens, Dallas Keuchel, Shane Reynolds and Justin Verlander on that list of aces. McCullers, Jr. was ready. "I'm much more of a pitcher now than I was in the past," he said. "I feel like I have the ability to fill up the zone with multiple pitches (and) I have the ability to attack different quadrants, whereas maybe in the past I really didn't. I had a curve ball and a fastball."

McCullers, Jr. attacked the White Sox with a lethal combination of sliders and other breaking pitches, depriving them of their favorite pitch to hit – the fastball. He widened home plate by starting his sliders on the outside corner to their righthanded-dominant lineup. They swung at many of those pitches and seldom made solid contact. McCullers, Jr. added the slider in 2021. He left the game after 6 2/3 innings of brilliance leading 6-0. He did not walk a batter and struck out four. "This organization, this city, it means a lot to me and my family," said McCullers, Jr. "They've always treated me with a lot of love and respect, so I always try to give that back." He started Game 7 of the 2017 World Series and Game 7 of the 2020 ALCS as well as five other playoff starts.

McCullers, Jr. tied Greinke for third place in club history with his eighth playoff start. His postseason ERA fell to 2.85 for 17 total appearances. "I have to go out there and just continue being who I've been this season," said McCullers. "I feel like I've added a lot of different layers to my game as far as pitching goes. Physically and mentally, I feel like I'm probably in the best spot I've been."

Dusty Baker went to Kendall Graveman for his postseason debut in the seventh to give him a non-pressure icebreaker. Graveman started his outing well but stumbled and was removed in the eighth. With the score 6-1, Ryan Pressly finished the 6-1 win before a capacity crowd.

Jose Altuve helped to manufacture the second run off White Sox starter Lance Lynn, who was tagged for five earned runs in 3 2/3 innings, by taking off from third on an Alex Bregman smash to third baseman Yoan Moncada. Moncada made a solid pickup to his left, spinning 360 degrees and firing a strong throw to catcher Yasmani Grandal. By the time Grandal could tag Altuve, he had slid past home plate and reached over the catcher's leg to stab the dish with his left hand.

Yordan Alvarez hit a bomb into the Astros bullpen. Jake Meyers picked up hits in his first two at-bats, driving in the first run. Michael Brantley drove in a couple of runs. Chicago starter Lance Lynn, who had a 2.69 ERA during the regular season, ran into a determined lineup.

The Astros approached the game, it appeared, like any regular season game. Their huge edge in postseason experience gave them that focus. Their ALDS Game 1 starting position players had played a total of 327 games in the playoffs, compared to 54 for the White Sox.

"They've been here before," said Baker of the Astros. If you've experienced it, then belief is a big part of this game and belief will take you a long, long ways. These guys, as a unit, they believe."

Did you know that….

Cesar Cedeno is the only Astro player to hit for the cycle twice in the same season.

Game 2

The White Sox had their strength lined up in Game 2. They bashed lefthanded pitching in 2021, and they were facing lefty Framber Valdez. They went right to work in the first inning, loading the bases with one out. Valdez, the top ground ball pitcher in the majors (70%) by far in 2021, needed a ground ball. After surrendering two ground ball hits, he got another grounder from Eloy Jimenez, but it scored a run. Jose Altuve made a diving stop to his left and got the force out at second, but Luis Robert scored from third to put the Sox ahead, 1-0.

Lucas Giolito established a different tone to the series when he struck out the side, whiffing three contact hitters with his full arsenal of a devastating changeup, slider, curve and 95mph fastball.

 Unlike Lance Lynn's trouble with his fastball, Giolito kept the Astros hitters off balance with his infrequent use of that pitch, as he had in a 10-1 win over Houston July 17 in Chicago. Giolito's 2.65 ERA in the second half of the season with a 1.00 WHIP brought him into the game fortified with confidence.

Valdez, whose two starts in the regular season against the Sox totaled 13 1/3 innings with six earned runs allowed, found solid ground in the second inning. He usually had at least one troublesome inning in a start. But for a pitcher who was told by doctors in spring training that his left ring finger was broken and he would miss the season, his 11-6 record and 134 1/3 innings were a godsend to the Astros.

"It's kind of incredible," said Valdez. "A lot of people would think, 'How is that possible he goes from breaking his finger to being available for the first series of the playoffs,' but it's something that I just set my mind on. I wanted to make sure that I could get back as quickly as possible to be ready to help this team out in any way I could." He got back into trouble in the third, but by then he had a 2-1 lead.

The Astros scored twice in the second on walks to Yordan Alvarez and Carlos Correa, a single by Kyle Tucker through the vacant left side and a sacrifice fly by Chas McCormick.

Valdez snapped off a 2-2 curveball to strike out Abreu, who had five straight 30-100 (HR-RBI) seasons, with two men on in the third. That tilted the inning for him, and he stranded the runners.

The White Sox timed some Valdez fastballs in the fifth and tied the game on Robert's RBI single. Baker came out to take the ball from him. "One of my teammates, Tommy John, told me a great pitcher can get out of trouble three times maybe, but a good pitcher, you have to get him after he's in trouble a couple of times." He was replaced by Yimi Garcia, who allowed a line drive go-ahead single by Abreu.

The Sox led 4-2 in the fifth when Giolito, like Valdez, was relieved. "You saw that first inning, he was unhittable," said Correa. "We had to kind of like switch our approach a little bit and make him pitch a little bit more, and we got to the bullpen. That was the key of winning that game." Giolito, who went the distance in his previous two starts against the Astros, lost command and was relieved by lefty Garret Crochet. Yuli Gurriel tagged a fastball from Crochet for a two-run single with the bases loaded and one out to tie the game, 4-4. But Crochet got Correa on a double play ball to preserve the tie after five.

The explosive five-run Houston seventh won the game, 9-4. White Sox relievers Aaron Bummer and Craig Kimbrel surrendered the runs. "This is a big-inning team," said Baker. "Sometimes people wonder why we don't bunt or squeeze or whatever it is, which I believe in also, but you're keeping the other team in the game by keeping the game close. It doesn't always work, but when it works, it works great."

Altuve, Bregman and Alvarez singled off Bummer. Tucker ripped a two-run homer off Kimbrel.

Solid defensive play also was an important component of the win. "We preach that every single day in our clubhouse: Defense wins championships," said Correa. "We take a lot of pride in that. From the moment we showed up in spring training. We said, 'Hey, let's try to be the number one defensive team in the big leagues.'" He explained the mentality required to accomplish that goal. "It's about having that mental approach of being active on every single pitch. Make sure you get that pre-pitch movement on every single pitch, don't take any pitches off, especially now in the playoffs, we're doing a great job with it." La Russa agreed. "They were really good," he said. "I thought we played really well, too, but they played better."

Correa was worth 21 defensive runs saved in 2021- a career best. The Astros led the American League with 78.

Altuve made a diving play in the first to stop a grounder by Eloy Jimenez before it got to right field, turning it into an out. Tucker made two terrific catches in right field, including a leaping catch on a Grandal line drive described by La Russa as "the one that probably crushed us."

The Astros' bullpen decisions were interesting. Ryan Pressly was warming up when the Astros took the lead in the seventh. When their lead grew to 9-4, he entered the game in the eighth and pitched a scoreless inning. Baker decided to use Kendall Graveman, who had been slumping, in the ninth. Graveman surrendered a walk and single to start the ninth. Cristian Javier started warming up. Pitching coach Brent Strom went to the mound. He said after the game that Graveman had been working through some mechanical issues with the lower half of his body. "His post foot, the foot that's on the rubber, he had a tendency to get too quad-dominated instead of maintaining a flat foot on the rubber, which impacts his direction. You're seeing a lot of arm-side misses to righties, and of course with that heavy sink he has, it just exacerbates his movement. So, we had to readjust his sight line, so to speak." The adjustments worked.

Strom added that he and Baker had great faith in Graveman and that he would be fine. But as a key late-inning option, Graveman was in a position to impact the most important games. He needed some confidence that these mechanical changes could work under pressure. He retired the final three batters to close out the game. "It's a matter of one pitch, actually, that kind of has gotten him into trouble or one situation," explained Baker. "I'm very confident in Kendall."

Like Graveman, the White Sox had traded for Craig Kimbrel and thrust him into the role of eighth-inning setup man in front of one of the best closers in baseball, Liam Hendricks. Kimbrel was the active leader in the majors in saves with 372. He never really had adjusted to the change in roles after having a good first half for the Cubs as their closer before the trade. Graveman and Kimbrel were two of the keys to the series.

Game 3

The scene shifted to Chicago, where Guaranteed Rate Park had been close to "guaranteed win park" for the White Sox in 2021. Their home record was 53-28.

Houston lost all of a 5-1 lead in the third. It was 5-3 Houston when Dusty Baker replaced a faltering Luis Garcia with two on and two outs on a 2-0 count. Yimi Garcia faced Leury Garcia, who rocked a three-run homer to straightaway center field for a 6-5 Sox lead.

Yasmani Grandal lofted a changeup for a two-run homer off Luis Garcia earlier in the inning, which began with a leadoff walk to Luis Robert. The White Sox did not have an extra base hit in the series until this inning.

The Astros trailed 1-0 in the first, but Sox starter Dylan Cease could not find the strike zone often enough to be effective, despite his 100mph fastball. Kyle Tucker clubbed a two-run bomb to left field.

Relief protégé Michael Kopech joined Cease in the century club with his electric fastball. With his profile as a starter, he figured to give the Sox as many as five innings if effective. His pitching coach Ethan Katz said as much during an in-game interview. But with two outs in the fourth, Jose Altuve coaxed a walk to change the game for Kopech. With Altuve at first, he went to a slide-step delivery that cost him 4mph on his fastball. Brantley singled to left and Bregman drove in the tying run with a hit to center.

The White Sox continued to tattoo Yimi Garcia. Dusty Baker turned to Zack Greinke under duress, with no outs and runners at first and third. He had wanted to save him for the start of a clean inning if possible, but this game was unraveling and it was still early. It was the first relief appearance in the playoffs in Greinke's 20th playoff outing. A weird play greeted him. Yasmani Grandal bounced to Yuli Gurriel, whose throw home hit Grandal when he ran to the inside of the first base line, allowing Robert to score.

The Astros wanted an interference call on Grandal, but home plate umpire Tom Hallion, the crew chief, ruled no interference. It was 8-6 Chicago. Eloy Jimenez rolled an RBI single and it was 9-6 with the White Sox patrons going bonkers.

The Sox wrapped up a 12-6 runaway to get back in the series. Chicago had a huge margin in hits, 16-6. Houston's lineup struck out 16 times, with nobody reaching base after the fourth inning. Tony La Russa's bullpen stepped up with five hitless innings to end the game, including a key out from slumping setup man Craig Kimbrel. Kimbrel's ERA of 5.63 with the White Sox (including postseason) seemed more irrelevant.

And lefty Carlos Rodon, who shared the staff lead in wins with 13 and led in ERA at 2.37, was set to pitch Game 4.

Game 4 had to wait a day because of rain. Houston native Ryan Tepera, who pitched well in relief in Game 3 for the White Sox, mentioned in a media session that the Astros were doing something "a little different" at Minute Maid Park. The Astros struck out 16 times in two games there; they whiffed that many times in Game 3 in Chicago. "I mean, you know, it is what it is," said the Brazoswood High School and Sam Houston State University product. "They've obviously had a reputation of doing some sketchy stuff over there," said Tepera. "We can say that it's a little bit of a difference. I think you saw the swings and misses tonight compared to the first two games at Minute Maid."

Astros General Manager James Click said, "Unequivocally, nothing untoward is going on here." Manager Dusty Baker: "I haven't heard anybody even talk about it, to tell the truth. You know, he can say what he wants to say. I never even heard his name before until we played the White Sox. I'm not bothered at all by it, really. Most of my life they've been talking stuff on me anyway, you know what I mean? So let them talk."

The Astros had a .787 OPS at Minute Maid Park, where their record was 51-30. On the road, their almost identical .780 OPS figured into their 44-37 record. Ironically, it was the White Sox with the large home-road disparity. Their home OPS was 60 points higher, with their 53-28 record.

White Sox manager Tony La Russa and reliever Aaron Bummer refused to sign on to Tepera's insinuations. "I really try not to get into that," said Bummer.

As for the Astros players, who were booed vociferously in Chicago, their focus seemed to be on the field. "The mentality for us is execution and baseball," said Alex Bregman. "Not anything that's said or written or anything like that. We're focused on playing baseball, the game that we've played since we were 5 years old."

Did you know that...

When the White Sox swept the Astros in the 2005 World Series, they won all four games by one or two runs. Chicago's starting pitchers all went at least seven innings in their starts.

Game 4

Carlos Rodon was at top velocity, hitting 99mph. He beat his chest as he high-stepped off the mound in the first inning.

Rodon got a 1-0 lead when Lance McCullers, Jr. was tagged by Gavin Sheets in the second inning with a home run to center field on a curve ball.

He also hit Jose Altuve with a pitch on the left elbow guard in the third inning. Many rowdy White Sox fans, some fueled by alcohol, cheered loudly in one of the worst displays of sportsmanship by a crowd. Altuve was in pain, but he waved a trainer back to the bench. He began a series of events that turned the game the Astros' way.

Altuve stole second a few pitches later. Rodon walked Bregman and Alvarez on a total of 12 pitches, including two two-strike fouls by Alvarez. Rodon fired two 98mph fastballs for strikes to Correa. He crushed the third one into left field for a two-run double that started a 10-0 margin to the end of the game. Correa reached second and pointed to his left wrist, mouthing the words, "It's my time."

The lead grew to 5-1 by the fourth, but McCullers, Jr. started feeling tightness in his right forearm and left the game. "I felt like I'd thrown the ball really well for the team and figured with the lineup coming around for a third time, I wasn't on short rest necessarily, but my routine was short." He threw his between-starts bullpen and lifted weights later than normal between starts. "Lance is a warrior, and for him to come out of a game of that magnitude, you know it had to be something," said Baker. "We tried to stop it before it got serious."

McCullers left after 73 pitches. His Tommy John surgery in November of 2018 did not concern him.

Baker's next decision shocked some. He called Yimi Garcia out of the bullpen, who had failed miserably in the previous game. Garcia started a chain of five straight scoreless innings to close out the game.

He was awarded the win. Garcia's ERA of 36.00 for his first two postseason appearances was disregarded because of Brent Strom's plan. "He really fits well, especially in the top of the order against those three righthanders." Tim Anderson saw several sliders. He was a notorious fastball hitter who was aggressive on the first pitch. Phil Maton reeled off 1 2/3 innings against some lefthanded hitters, fitting the plan to utilize his specialty.

By the eighth inning, the Astros were pouring it on. If the fans were fueled by alcohol, the Houston players were running on long-lasting adrenaline. Leading 7-1, Kendall Graveman's arm-side control issues resurfaced. He threw one pitch near Jose Abreu's head and then hit him on the left shoulder with another. Tony La Russa left the Chicago dugout and demanded that Graveman be ejected. He was not.

La Russa charged after the game in his press conference that the pitch was intentional. "They did hit him intentionally," charged La Russa. "They should have the guts to admit that they did it. Why they did it, I don't understand." The thought that the Astros would choose to put a man on base leading 7-1 when their mission was to put the game away was questionable. The Sox had exploded for a five-run inning in the previous game.

La Russa's charge that Graveman was throwing at Abreu was baseless, and he had to have been aware of Graveman's recent control issues to the arm side. He would have seen many occasions on video of Graveman's struggles when scouting game footage in his preparation for the series.

La Russa's fixation on being the judge and jury of his opponents' intent to hit his batters was a companion of his competitiveness, even at age 77. His words had no impact on home plate umpire Vic Carapazza or the other members of the six-man crew when they huddled to agree that there was no intent to hit Abreu.

The Astros' passion to beat the White Sox and silence their crowd worked to their advantage. They stole four bases and hammered out 14 hits. When Altuve sent a majestic three-run homer soaring into the left field seats, it traveled on a cushion of finality. It was Altuve's 19th postseason homer, tying him with George Springer and Albert Pujols for fourth on the all-time list. He scored four times to move into fifth in postseason runs with 58. The life had already been sucked out of Guaranteed Rate Field. The fans had lost their bluster and left the building.

Jake Meyers left Game 4 with a left shoulder injury from colliding with the outfield wall on the Gavin Sheets home run. Unfortunately, the injury knocked him out of the playoffs and led to surgery later. Chas McCormick, who took over for him, figured to be the centerfield starter in the ALCS against the Boston Red Sox.

Correa moved into the lead among active players with 54 postseason RBIs, tied for sixth all-time.

Batting champ Yuli Gurriel batted seventh in a rarity demonstrating how stacked the Houston lineup was.

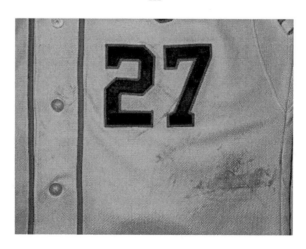

Jose Altuve game used jersey

ALDS DIVISION SERIES HOUSTON STATISTICS

Altuve   .313-1-3   16ab 9 runs 4bb 1.101 OPS

Alvarez   .273-1-3   11ab 4 runs 6bb 1.166 OPS

Brantley   .368-0-4   19ab 0 runs 0bb .789 OPS

Bregman   .375-0-4 16ab 4 runs 2bb .882 OPS

Correa   .385-0-4 13ab 4 runs 4bb 1.068 OPS

Gurriel   .176-0-2 17ab 1 run 0bb .353 OPS

Maldonado .067-0-1 15ab

McCormick .400-0-0 5ab

Meyers   .375-0-2 8ab

Tucker   .294-2-7 17ab 5 runs 0bb 1.000 OPS

McCullers 1-0 0.84 ERA 2 starts 10 2/3ip 1er 3bb 9k

Pressley   0-0 0.00 ERA 3g 3ip 0bb 4k

Maton   0-0 0.00 ERA 3g 3ip 0bb 3k

Stanek   1-0 0.00 ERA 3g 2 1/3ip 1bb 4k

Graveman 0-0 3.00 ERA 3g 3ip 2bb 1k

Y. Garcia   1-1 18.00 ERA 3g 2ip 0bb 2k

L. Garcia   0-0 16.88 ERA 1g 3bb 3k

Valdez   0-0 8.31 ERA 1g 4 1/3ip 1bb 6k

ALCS

Boston was enjoying the underdog's role after being a marked team in 2018. After decades as also-rans, the Red Sox rocketed past the New York Yankees over a 15-year period, winning four World Series.

Manager Alex Cora, the former Houston bench coach, held the World Series trophy high in 2018 after leaving the Astros. He returned in 2021 after his one-year suspension from the cheating scandal to lead his team to prominence again. He had not been a loser as a coach or manager in a postseason series.

"Offensively, we are where we really wanted to be," said Cora before the start of the 2021 ALCS in Houston. "By accident maybe, because this lineup came together after J.D. Martinez got hurt, but now we have this balance, the at-bats are getting better." Martinez said the pressure to win was off. "This year we don't have that," said the former Astro. "None of the media, nobody here, counted on us to be here." After a 24-36 record under Ron Roenicke in 2020, FanGraphs rated Boston's postseason chances at 38.9 percent for 2021. The Red Sox had to come from behind to beat Baltimore the last day of the regular season, putting them in a one-game wild card playoff against the Yankees and Gerrit Cole. Their hitters were hot, and they had great balance. The Red Sox conquered Tampa Bay in four games in the ALDS after being shut out in the opener.

Did you know that...

Third baseman Doug Rader was the first Astro to win a Gold Glove award in 1970.

Yuli Gurriel and Carlos Correa were Gold Glove winners in 2021.

Offense was expected to rule the ALCS, based on the regular season statistics of the two teams and their performances in the Division Series. The Red Sox hit .341 with 26 runs in four games against Tampa Bay, clouting nine home runs. The Astros scored 31 runs in four games against the White Sox while hitting .288.

Boston's offense presented a different challenge for the Houston pitching staff; Alex Verdugo, Kyle Schwarber and Rafael Devers were all excellent lefthanded hitters.

The Red Sox had the best OPS of all teams remaining in the playoffs since the All-Star break at .798. Like the Astros the Red Sox worked counts and drew walks, although Boston's hitters survived a 30 percent chase rate by making contact with pitches outside the strike zone. The hottest hitters in the playoffs for Boston were Devers, Martinez, Verdugo and Kike Hernandez.

Because of the prominence of lefthanded Red Sox hitters, Dusty Baker added lefty reliever Blake Taylor to his 26-man roster for the ALCS. The Boston bullpen had been fortified by using starter Nick Pivetta in relief. He came alive, with playoff adrenaline taking his fastball up to 98mph. Pivetta's body language displayed the extra energy of being assigned to work only an inning or two.

Did you know that....

Yordan Alvarez holds the franchise rookie record with 27 homers in a season

Game 1

Minute Maid Park was jammed with 40,534 charged fans to see the first team since the 1971-75 Oakland A's to play in the League Championship Series in either league five straight years. Oakland advanced to the ALCS by winning its division but did not have to win a playoff series with the postseason format in the 1970s.

Lance McCullers, Jr. was not on the 26-man roster because of a flexor pronator muscle strain in his right forearm. "It's a big blow," said Baker. "You're not going to get any sympathy or pity from anybody, so we just got to find a way." "We're going to try to go out there and win it for him," said Correa. "It's tough, but we're going to have to step up," added Bregman. It was a substantial loss of the de factor ace of the staff, with Greinke now in the bullpen and Verlander recovering from surgery. McCullers' 6.8 hits allowed per nine innings was the lowest in the league during the regular season, and he gave the team its best chance for length from the starting pitcher. The bullpen would become more important. That came into play right away in Game 1.

Framber Valdez threw a first-pitch ball to ten of 16 batters. Only 35 of his 64 pitches were strikes. The leadoff man reached every inning. His 1-0 lead after one quickly disintegrated. Postseason hitting leader Kike Hernandez homered and made a spectacular diving catch with the bases loaded.

Valdez trailed 3-1 when lifted with two men on the third. Chris Sale, like Valdez, accounted for only eight outs. But, like Yimi Garcia for Houston, Adam Ottavino escaped a jam created by the starter and stranded two baserunners.

Jose Altuve made an error on a possible double play ball in the third. Trailing 3-1 in the sixth, he atoned by clubbing his 20th postseason home run on a Tanner Houck pitch, touching off an explosion of noise and a 3-3 tie.

Alex Cora and Dusty Baker kept the bullpen parade coming, with the two of them combining for a record of 16 pitchers in the ALCS. Correa came up with two outs in the seventh against Hansel Robles. When Robles started him with a changeup, Correa saw it well and crushed it, admiring its flight and turning to his bench with his right index finger pointing to his left wrist, mouthing the words, "It's my time." As he put his hand to his right ear rounding third, he was engulfed in a sea of hysteria. His fourth career go-ahead postseason home run in the seventh inning or later was the most in major league history. Each club scored another run, with Ryan Pressly saving the game and Ryne Stanek getting the win. The bullpen allowed only one run in 7 1/3 innings. The 5-4 Houston win included 11 hits. Oddly, Houston was 0-for-7 and Boston 1-for-9 with men in scoring position.

Kike Hernandez set a playoff record for 15 hits in four games, including eight extra base hits, after going 4-for-5 in Game 1. Correa and Chas McCormick had three hits for the Astros.

Tony Eusebio's batting helmet

Game 2

Boston put its 9-5 Game 2 win away early. Luis Garcia could not throw enough strikes to be effective in the first inning, losing Rafael Devers on a walk after jumping ahead 0-2 in the count and then surrendering a grand slam to J.D. Martinez. Houston fans could remember a slam at Minute Maid Park in the 2018 ALCS by Jackie Bradley, Jr. of the Red Sox. After a four-pitch walk in the second, Garcia left with an injury. It was announced as a right knee strain after the game. Garcia was tagged for five runs in one inning.

Dusty Baker made a quick decision to use Jake Odorizzi with as much time as needed to warm up because of the injury. He needed innings from Odorizzi to save his best relievers for Game 3 in Boston. The game quickly got out of hand. Odorizzi seemed to have some rust from being inactive during the Division Series but the real issue, as he revealed after the game, was the lack of warmup time. If he had wanted to take his usual long warmup, he could have taken it. But he took only 14 minutes. That's typical of a starting pitcher used in emergency relief, but Odorizzi was not expecting to pitch at all since he was the planned Game 4 starter.

"You're sitting there pretty much naked to the other team. They get to watch every single pitch you're throwing," explained Odorizzi. He yielded four more runs in four innings in 82 pitches. Boston led 9-0 in the fourth. Rafael Devers added a grand slam in the second, making it the first time in history a team had hit two slams in one postseason game.

Kike Hernandez was becoming the Randy Arozena of 2021, torching the Astros in the American League Championship Series with his fifth home run of the postseason, tying a Boston club record. Hernandez became the top player in postseason history for five games in hits (15), extra base hits (9) and total bases (34).

Boston headed home with a 1-1 split in the series and the next three games at home, giving the Red Sox a chance to clinch the pennant at home by sweeping. The Sox, 16-5 in the playoffs under Cora, were sounding very confident under the manager with the best October managerial mark since early in Earl Weaver's years with Baltimore.

Dusty Baker had a crisis on his hands. His starters covered only 3 2/3 of the first 18 innings in the ALCS. That was an unsustainable pace. There was urgency to get a fresh arm on the roster to replace Garcia. If Garcia went on the injured list, he could not pitch in the World Series. But the World Series was not in focus.

For Jose Urquidy and the pitchers who followed him, Boston had served notice that a heavy diet of fastballs not well located was a red flag. Changeups and breaking balls with a variety of speeds seemed to be the best plan to disrupt the excellent timing of the Red Sox hitters, with Kike Hernandez the prime example.

Did you know that..

Joe Morgan was the first Houston player to be selected to start an All-Star game in 1966. Morgan was unable to play because of an injury.

Game 3

The trend did not change for the Astros in Game 3. Eduardo Rodriguez powered through their lineup, while the torrid Boston hitters pummeled Jose Urquidy in a 12-3 rout.

The crisis for the Houston bullpen got worse. Through three games, the starting pitchers lasted a total of only 5 1/3 innings, posting a 20.25 ERA. That forced the bullpen to cover 20 2/3 innings. Further, Zack Greinke was named the Game 4 starter, and he was not conditioned to go deep into the game.

The Red Sox pounded Urquidy in a six-run second, including a Kyle Schwarber grand slam. "It's kind of like Groundhog Day, a recurring nightmare where you hope to get some innings out of these guys," said Baker. Astros starters continued to repeat mistakes with their fastballs and fall behind in the count because they could not locate their secondary pitches.

Although they trailed only 2-1 in games, the two teams seemed to be separated by the Grand Canyon in their level of competitiveness.

Kyle Tucker, the American League Player of the Month for September-October, ripped a three-run homer. He had little company from the other hitters in the lineup.

The Red Sox became the first team in baseball history to belt three grand slams in one postseason series.

The morning of Game 4, a private MD-87 jet taxied to top speed for takeoff on the Houston Executive Airport runway west of Houston in Waller County with 18 passengers and three crew members headed for Boston for Game 4. But the jet never got airborne. It shot across a road and into a vacant field, bursting into flames. Miraculously, all 21 people escaped the flaming aircraft and survived.

Hours later, with no lives on the line but the World Series hopes of the Astros close to going into flames, highly-charged Fenway Park was energized for a chance to get close to clinching at home.

Cast iron work on selected Minute Maid Park seats

Game 4

Zack Greinke was far from El Cid, the Spanish medieval night who was wounded and went into battle strapped to his saddle. But he was going into a challenging situation with the expectation that he was in the fight of his life.

Greinke made it through only 1 1/3 innings, trailing Boston 2-1 on a first-inning homer by Xander Bogaerts. Like his predecessors in the starting rotation, Greinke failed to reach the strike zone often enough to be effective. The bases were jammed with traffic from three walks. Brooks Raley finished the second inning and gave way to Cristian Javier.

Nick Pivetta allowed an Alex Bregman first-inning Green Monster seats home run but held the lead, 2-1. Cristian Javier led the Houston bullpen effort by keeping the game close, even though at one point the trio of Altuve-Brantley-Bregman at the top of the lineup was hitting a collective .140 in the ALCS. The law of averages was about to hit Fenway Park.

Jose Altuve jumped on a Garrett Whitlock fastball leading off the eighth and sent it over the Green Monster for his 21st playoff home run to become the all-time leader among infielders, passing Derek Jeter. Kendall Graveman mowed down the suddenly ordinary Red Sox hitters, and the game moved to the ninth.

Alex Cora sensed an urgency to the situation and he was right. But his move to insert starter Nate Eovaldi brought a disaster for the Sox. The Astros erupted in a seven-run ninth, all with two outs, for the biggest postseason inning in club history. Carlos Correa's leadoff double was followed by two outs.

Then the gates to Boston Harbor opened.

Jason Castro, who had entered earlier as a pinch-hitter for Martin Maldonado, drove in the go-ahead run with a single and later called it the biggest hit of his career. Castro was the catcher on the three consecutive Houston 100-loss teams 2011-13. A first-round Houston draft choice in 2008, "Castro the Astro" from Castro Valley, California and Stanford University was the lone All-Star on the 113-loss Astros of 2013 when the team reached rock bottom. He left as a free agent after 2015.

Castro had spent most of 2021 as a seldom-used backup to Maldonado. Maldonado was a fabulous defensive catcher who was in a terrible playoff slump on a slumping offensive team. Dusty Baker had no choice when he sent Castro to the plate as a pinch-hitter for Maldonado in the seventh. "What impressed me the most was that he was sitting on the bench for seven innings on a cold night," said Correa. "And you don't have a batting cage nearby to warm up or anything because the ballpark is so old. I don't know how he did it, but I admire that. I can tell you I wouldn't be able to do that." Castro lined out to first base on his first at-bat as a pinch-hitter.

Eovaldi thought he had struck out Castro to end the top of the ninth, but with two outs his 1-2 curveball was called ball two. Castro identified the curve and took it, ripping the next pitch, a split-finger fastball, for the go-ahead single.

Michael Brantley lined a bases-loaded double off Martin Perez, scoring all three runners. The series was tied, 2-2 and it was headed back to Houston for Game 5. It boiled down to the best of three, and Game 4 brought a whole new outlook for the Houston fans.

Game 5

Lefties Chris Sale and Framber Valdez squared off to see which team would move into the driver's seat for the AL title. Both were in top form, to the relief of both bullpens. They became the first two pitchers to start a playoff game and last at least five innings in the 2021 AL playoffs. Valdez had the longest outing of any postseason pitcher to that point.

Valdez became the first pitcher in history to set down the first 12 Red Sox in a playoff game at Fenway. Yordan Alvarez gave him a second-inning 1-0 lead with a Green Monster seat home run off Sale – only the second extra base hit allowed by Sale to a lefthanded hitter in his regular season (nine starts) and postseason in 2021. But it was 1-0 Houston through five, with Sale fired up and firing 97mph darts and sweeping sliders.

When Valdez got a double play ball from Hunter Renfroe in the fifth after the first two Sox reached base the bullpen action stopped. After the first four Houston starters pitched a combined 6 2/3 innings Valdez knifed through eight throwback innings with his two-pitch repertoire. He induced many groundball outs in the 9-1 win, giving the Astros a 3-2 series edge and sending them home for the remainder of the ALCS. Valdez led the majors in percentage of ground ball outs, and he threw 19 straight sinkers to open this game.

Tom Verducci of Fox Sports told the story of his signing at age 21 in the Dominican Republic as the fifth player to try out that day for scout Roman Ocumarez, who had to use his car headlights to throw enough light on the practice field as the sun went down. Valdez signed in 2015 at age 21 – an advanced age for a foreign signing. Luis Garcia signed at 20 in 2017. Jose Urquidy was 19. Most foreign-born players sign when they are 16. As a result of that trio being passed over by other organizations, the Astros spent a total of only $430,000 to sign them. Now the three homegrown hurlers were all keys in the club's postseason drive.

Ryne Stanek worked the final inning going into a day off, giving the bullpen a chance to regroup.

Alvarez was 3-for-4 with 3 RBIs. Since 2019 when he broke into the majors he had the top slugging percentage of any lefthanded hitter against lefthanded pitching. "Nobody else could hit him but Alvarez had him," summarized Dusty Baker. "He was all in on the fastball," explained hitting coach Alex Cintron. Alvarez took Sale's fastball to left field three times for damage. Those were the only hits Sale allowed in 5 1/3 innings. Sale had not allowed three hits in a game to a lefty hitter since 2015 when he faced former Red Sox slugger David Ortiz. Lefty hitters had managed a .271 slugging percentage against Sale in his 11-year career. Alvarez came to Houston in 2016 from Los Angeles in the Josh Fields trade. The Astros now had a 24-year-old superstar on their hands via that trade, after the Dodgers had paid him a hefty signing bonus as a Cuban free agent a few months before trading him.

The sixth inning brought the key rally. Altuve walked and forced an error from first baseman Kyle Schwarber when he went from first to third on a slow roller to third by Brantley. Alvarez drove in both with a hot line drive double to left. One more win and the Astros were World Series-bound.

Game 6

A revitalized Luis Garcia, with his knee feeling much better, took the mound at amped-up Minute Maid Park to try to send the Astros to the World Series. Brent Strom watched Garcia throw a 97.8mph fastball to Kyle Schwarber, then a lethal cutter that struck out Schwarber but darted past Martin Maldonado to the screen. "To take the pain off the knee, we just made an adjustment with the lower half that took the pain away, which probably helped with the velocity," explained Strom. "It's just foot placement, like a golfer who changes his setup a bit." Garcia averaged 95.8mph on four-seam fastballs – about 2.5mph faster than his 2021 average. He took a no-hitter into the sixth inning and left with 5 2/3 innings of one-hit baseball with seven strikeouts.

Alvin, Texas native Nate Eovaldi was on his game as well. The Astros got a first-inning run off him when Yordan Alvarez doubled off the heel of the glove of a leaping Kike Hernandez. Eovaldi whiffed Correa, Tucker and McCormick with runners in scoring position. After Eovaldi departed Kyle Tucker smashed a shot to first base and a run scored when Schwarber stepped on first and tagged Correa for a double play.

With Kendall Graveman trying to protect the 2-0 lead in the seventh, he whiffed Travis Shaw and Maldonado fired a strike to gun down Verdugo trying to steal, stranding a runner at third. The bullpen worked 3 1/3 scoreless innings.

Tucker's three-run homer in the eighth put the game away, 5-0. Alvarez, 4-for-4 with three extra base hits, was the ALCS MVP with a .522 batting average.

Boston scored 25 runs in the first three games and three runs in the last three. Why? Catcher Martin Maldonado discussed a closed-door meeting for the players after Game 3, "Just trying to stay positive with the guys." Exactly what he said did not escape the closed doors, but it was obvious that the pitchers turned around their performances by avoiding fastball mistakes over the middle of the plate and throwing quality breaking pitches inside the strike zone.

"The pitching staff – they threw strikes, they pounded the zone, they limited the walks, and that was the key for us to win the series," said Correa.

The Red Sox hitters pummeled hittable fastballs after they got ahead in counts in the first three games; in the next three, Astros pitchers attacked them with breaking pitches and off-speed stuff that they could not take because the counts were in favor of the pitchers.

As the Astros celebrated their third American League Championship in five years, the city prepared for its third World Series in five years. Dusty Baker was the ninth manager to take a team in both leagues to the World Series.

The Astros scored 27 runs in the ALCS with two outs – a record. They scored 66% of their runs with two outs – an incredible number.

The Astros earned three days off before the World Series started. Atlanta beat Los Angeles in six games to win the NLCS.

Astros Statistics in ALCS

Altuve   .125-2-4 6 runs 3bb   .589OPS

Alvarez   .522-1-6 7 runs 2bb 1.408 OPS

Brantley   .269-0-4 3 runs 0bb   .577 OPS

Bregman   .217-1-1 4 runs 3bb   .656 OPS

Castro   .667-1-2 2 runs 2bb 2.467 OPS

Correa   .250-1-1 5 runs 1bb   .724 OPS

Gurriel   .455-1-6 4 runs 3bb 1.156 OPS

Maldonado   .071-0-0 0 runs 1bb   .307 OPS

McCormick   .286-0-0 1 run 1bb   .619 OPS

Siri   .125-0-2 0 runs 0bb   .250 OPS

Tucker   .261-2-8 4 runs 2bb   .885 OPS

L. Garcia   1-1 6.75 ERA 2 starts   Raley   0-0 3.00 3g

Valdez   1-0 2.53 ERA 2 starts   Taylor 0-0 0.00 2g

Graveman   1-0 0.00 ERA 3 games   Urquidy 0-1 27.00 1g

Javier   0-0 0.00 ERA 2 games   Greinke 0-0 13.50 1g

Stanek   1-0 2.08 ERA 5 games   Y. Garcia 0-0 9.00 3g

Pressly   0-0 3.00 ERA 3 games 1 save

Maton   0-0 2.45 ERA 4 games Odorizzi 0-0 9.00 1g

Chapter 3

2021 WORLD SERIES

Atlanta and Houston were frequent playoff opponents in the postseason in the 1990s. The Braves rolled to 14 straight division titles and eight straight NL pennants, but won only one World Series. The Astros, like those Atlanta teams, were not satisfied with one title.

The Braves typically brushed the Astros aside in the NL Division Series early in their rivalry, beating them in 1997, 1999 and 2001. The Braves won 9 of 10 games in those three series. The Astros bounced back to knock out the Braves in the 2004 and 2005 playoffs.

The Braves played 29 World Series games in the 1990s; none from 2000 through 2020.

The Braves were a rare success story in 2021. Even though they were widely expected to claim the NL East, they struggled most of the season. They became the first team to attain .500 as late as August 6 and make a World Series. General Manager Alex Anthopolous made some impactful trades after mid-season, obtaining a whole new outfield of Eddie Rosario, Jorge Soler, Joc Pederson and Adam Duvall to fill the chasm from losing Marcel Ozuna and Ronald Acuna, Jr. Losing Soler to COVID in the NLCS actually allowed them to rely on NLCS MVP Rosario and Pederson.

The city of Houston embraced the return of the World Series for the third time in five years. Restaurants, hotels and rental car agencies all thrived for the first time in two years. The city got a boost in emerging from the pandemic that only out-of-town visitors could provide.

Lance McCullers, Jr. was unable to recover in time to make the World Series roster for Houston. Jake Odorizzi was added to the roster for the World Series. Marwin Gonzalez replaced Jake Meyers on the roster. Meyers, unfortunately, was to undergo left shoulder surgery soon.

Did you know....

Previous World Series Game 1 starters for the Astros were Roger Clemens in 2005, Dallas Keuchel in 2017 and Gerrit Cole in 2019.

Game 1

Jorge Soler's return to the lineup was momentous. The DH opened the game by cracking a 2-0 pitch from Framber Valdez into the Crawford Boxes for a 1-0 Atlanta lead. Soler made history by becoming the first batter in 117 World Series to lead off the first game of the Series with a home run. Valdez fell behind the first three hitters, and it cost him.

Ozzie Albies singled and stole second, riding home on Austin Riley's double. The Braves led 2-0 after the top of the first. Former Astro Charlie Morton struggled through a 27-pitch first to post a zero when Albies made a good play on Kyle Tucker. Morton was forced from the game and the rest of the Series when a Yuli Gurriel comebacker in the second inning broke his fibula. Lefty reliever A.J. Minter of Tyler, Texas and Texas A&M, got the win with 2 2/3 innings of strong relief.

Valdez continued to struggle, allowing another RBI to Soler in the second on a ground out. When Adam Duvall's two-run homer in the third made it 5-0 Atlanta, the Braves became the first team in history to score in each of the first three innings of Game 1 of the Series. Valdez left after allowing five runs in two innings. Jake Odorizzi picked up the team with 2 1/3 innings of scoreless relief in the 6-2 loss. It was the fifth straight World Series loss at home for the Astros.

Much of the focus was on Valdez's difficulties, but the hitters struck out 11 times and went 1-for-9 with runners in scoring position. Jose Altuve was 0-for-5 with three strikeouts, dropping his 2021 postseason batting average to .178. Alex Bregman was 0-for-4 with two strikeouts.

The Astros were 1-9 in home World Series games.

Game 2

A thunderstorm with tornado warnings began the day in Houston, followed by beautiful clear weather with a cooler night. As in 2005, MLB apparently bowed down to pressure from Fox to force the Astros to open the roof of Minute Maid Park so television could have its blimp shot of the stadium. Astros players liked the roof closed. Jose Urquidy struck out Jorge Soler to end a first-inning Braves' threat.

The Astros scored in their first on a double by Altuve and two fly balls. Bregman's sacrifice fly made it 1-0 Houston. But Atlanta countered with a Travis d'Arnaud home run, 1-1. Houston exploded for four in the second off Max Fried. Jose Siri reached on an RBI infield single for a 2-1 lead. Maldonado struck a single scoring two, one on an error. Brantley's single boosted the lead to 5-1 after two. Fried did stay in the game for five innings. His manager, Brian Snitker, was able to avoid using any of his three talented southpaw setup men.

Urquidy departed with a 5-2 lead after 5, giving way to Cristian Javier. Urquidy's four-pitch mix neutralized the Braves, who flailed many times at his floating changeup. He became the first Mexican pitcher to win more than one World Series game and the first pitcher to win his first two Series games with an ERA under 2.00 (1.80) with ten strikeouts and no walks.

Altuve snapped a 3-for-29 slump by opening with a double and greeting lefty reliever Drew Smyly with his 22nd postseason home run, tying Bernie Williams for second on the all-time list despite having more than 200 fewer at-bats than Williams. The Astros led 7-2 after seven innings and won by that score.

Jose Siri's RBI infield hit gave him a memory of his first World Series start.

Dusty Baker was back in Atlanta, where his career began as a teammate of Hank Aaron 53 years ago. The Braves lost to the Astros, 6-3 September 7, 1968 with a tiny crowd of 6,429 at Atlanta Stadium. His Houston team was working out in the rain the day before Game 3.

Baker was 19 when he made his debut, younger than his son Darren was now. Darren was 3 when he ran onto the field during the 2002 World Series and was swept up by the right arm of J.T. Snow and rescued from possible injury at home plate. That seemed like eons ago.

The next night, 23-year-old Ian Anderson and 24-year-old Luis Garcia would square off in their World Series debuts. Both teams were hoping their starters could give them some length in the game, perhaps five innings or more because their bullpens figured to be headed for the biggest test ever. The Astros were missing Lance McCullers, Jr. and the Braves were without Charlie Morton, leading to the challenges for the relievers. With no designated hitter in the National League games at Truist Park, the Astros were at a disadvantage in the next three games. Their pitchers were not used to hitting and the absence of a DH would force Baker to decide which of his outfielders would not play. If he moved Kyle Tucker to center field to allow Michael Brantley and Yordan Alvarez to flank him in the corners, his defense could suffer. That's what he decided to do. Braves' skipper Brian Snitker was in a quandary with his bullpen. For the three straight nights of games before the next scheduled day off all of the relievers were on alert. During the regular season the longest scheduled series typically is four games. If a World Series goes five games or more, the use of relievers puts them at more exposure to opposing hitters than at any other time.

Game 3

DRAMA stamped Game 3 as a thriller. The Braves had a no-hitter going. Ian Anderson was unhittable through 5 and his bullpen extended the gem with a 1-0 lead. When the no-hitter continued through 7 it was the longest World Series no-hit bid since 1967, when Jim Lonborg of the Red Sox pitched in Game 2 against St. Louis. The Astros did not hit many balls hard. Atlanta won on a two-hitter, 2-0.

The Astros got their first hit from pinch hitter Aledmys Diaz leading off the eighth against Tyler Matzek. His pop fly dropped just in front of a charging Eddie Rosario in left field. Jose Siri was brought into the game on the chilly, muddy night to pinch-run. When Jason Castro struck out and Jose Altuve popped up, Siri took off for second with Michael Brantley at the plate. Travis d'Arnaud was 2-for-43 in throwing out baserunners in 2021. He would have had Siri with a good throw but his throw skipped past Dansby Swanson into center field and Siri sprang up and made it to third. Matzek struck out Brantley to end the Houston eighth, and the crowd was loud enough to be heard in Savannah.

D'Arnaud struck a home run to center field off Kendall Graveman with two outs in the eighth for a 2-0 Atlanta lead. Austin Riley doubled off Luis Garcia in the third, driving in Eddie Rosario.

Alex Bregman got the other Houston hit. He hit a weak grounder through the vacant right side with one out in the ninth.

The Braves took a 2-1 lead in games and showed their bullpen strength with their three outstanding lefties continuing their postseason dominance.

The only time the Astros had fewer than two hits in a playoff game was in 1999, when Kevin Millwood of Atlanta one-hit them. On this chilly, wet night the Braves controlled the game against the offense with the most runs and highest percentage of contact in the majors in 2021. "I think we flush it and move on to the next day and have a short memory," said Bregman. "You give all the credit to them tonight. They pitched their tail off."

The Astros slashed .198/.278/.292 for the first three World Series games.

There was every reason to expect big things from Ian Anderson after he performed so well on the biggest stage. He was a veteran of only 30 major league starts, but Anderson's rare over-the-top delivery with all of his pitches coming from the same release point was impressive. He was among the elite in postseason history for ERA in the postseason with a 1.26 for eight starts. His 35 2/3 innings in the postseason did not seem to be a fluke.

Brian Snitker was all set for his two straight bullpen games, keeping all three of his power lefty relievers available by limiting them to one inning each. A.J. Minter, Tyler Matzek and Will Smith all performed impeccably.

Dusty Baker selected Greinke to start Game 4. Greinke got only four outs in his Game 4 ALCS start against Boston. Greinke hadn't thrown more than 40 pitches in a game since September 19 (about six weeks earlier). With Rosario, Freeman and Albies facing Greinke as lefthanded batters, the Braves posed quite a threat. But Greinke allowed a higher OPS against righthanded batters during the season - .828, compared to .565 vs. lefties.

Game 4

The rain had moved out, but it was still a cool 52 degrees and the Astros had not been able to take batting practice at Truist Park. They faced surprise starter Dylan Lee, who was the first in history to make his first major league start in the World Series. Lee was gone after 1/3 inning, but Kyle Wright gave the Braves a lift by escaping bases-loaded one-out trouble when he allowed only one run to score on a groundout by Carlos Correa. The Braves probably felt that they may have won the game in the first by allowing no more than one run.

Zack Greinke was in the eighth spot in the lineup, only the second pitcher in World Series history along with Babe Ruth not to bat ninth. Greinke got a hit in the second inning. Interestingly, switch-hitter Ozzie Albies decided to bat righthanded against Greinke due to Albies' superiority as a righthanded batter and Greinke's inferiority against righthanded hitters.

Greinke won the first-inning confrontation with Albies. In the top of the third the Braves walked Gurriel intentionally to load the bases and got out of trouble on a Greinke groundout. But Greinke maintained a 1-0 lead through three with a double play grounder off the bat of Freeman.

The Truist Park organist played "It's a Small World" when Jose Altuve came to the plate in the fourth. A few pitches later, the 5-5 second baseman belted a solo homer 434 feet over the center field wall for a 2-0 Houston advantage. It moved him into sole possession of second place on the World Series all-time home run list. It was the hardest hit ball of the night by the smallest player on the field.

Altuve started his second double play in as many innings on a Joc Pederson grounder to keep Greinke in the lead 2-0. But the Astros failed with men on base time after time with Wright escaping jam after jam through his 4 2/3 innings of one-run relief.

Dusty Baker's bullpen door opened for Stanek in the fifth. Raley got into trouble in the sixth, leading to Maton replacing him with two on and one out against Albies.

He got Albies but Riley drove in a run with a single. With the bases loaded Maton surprised d'Arnaud with a fastball for a called third strike to maintain the 2-1 lead.

The Braves got the tying solo home run in the seventh from Dansby Swanson off Cristian Javier, 2-2. Pinch hitter Jorge Soler drilled a line drive home run over a leaping Alvarez in left field for Atlanta's 3-2 lead – its first of the game.

Altuve smoked a line drive to left field in the ninth. It would have been a home run in 26 of 30 ballparks, but Rosario raced back and stopped it from hitting the wall with a fabulous backhanded catch. The Braves held onto their 3-2 lead to grab a 3-1 Series lead. The Astros were 4-for-31 with men in scoring position in the Series.

Did you know...

Former Astros coach Yogi Berra holds the all-time World Series record for at-bats with 259 and hits with 71. Berra's son Dale played for the Astros in 1987.

Yogi Berra holds the record with ten World Championships as a player. He was a three-time MVP and a Hall of Famer. Berra was a gunner's mate in the landings at Normandy Beach in World War II. Many quizzical sayings have been attributed incorrectly to him. As he once summed up, "I really didn't say everything I said."

Among the humorous remarks attributed to Berra was, "When you come to a fork in the road, take it." A friend of Berra's once explained that he was giving directions to his house in New Jersey, which was on a cul de sac. Either way the driver chose to take at the fork, he would arrive at the house!

Game 5

They came in droves to Truist Park to see a celebration of a World Series triumph for the first time in 26 years. They stood for the entire game and filled the air with lusty cheers for the Braves.

Dusty Baker shook up his lineup with justification. Bregman was dropped from third to seventh, while Correa moved up to third and Gurriel was bumped up from seventh to fifth. The Astros were facing another rookie lefthander for the second straight game, Tucker Davidson. Davidson was pitching in a major league game for the first time since June 15. He was the replacement for the injured Morton. This elimination game brought some immediacy to the Astros' plans. Patience was thrown out of the window.

The Braves punched Framber Valdez in the stomach with a first-inning grand slam by Adam Duvall after Valdez fell behind hitters because of curveball struggles. It was the fourth slam allowed in the postseason by the Astros – a new record.

With Braves fans preparing for the winning celebration in the first inning, Houston struck back with two in the second and two in the third for a 4-4 tie. Bregman drove in two with a double. Freddie Freeman cracked a home run in the Braves third on a 3-2 fastball. Valdez's erratic curveball forced him from the game. The game got wilder. The Astros tied it 5-5 in the fifth on a bases-loaded walk to Maldonado after A.J. Minter intentionally walked Bregman. Maldonado moved on top of home plate and faked a bunt on the 3-1 pitch, unsettling Minter into missing badly with the pitch for ball four. Minter was not as effective as in earlier outings, grooving a pitch for pinch-hitter Marwin Gonzalez. Gonzo added to his 2017 World Series success with a two-run single for Houston's first lead, 7-5 in the three-run fifth. The Astros had been 1-for-15 in the World Series with two outs and runners in scoring position.

The Astros spoiled the night and kept the champagne in the bottles outside the Atlanta clubhouse with their 9-5 comeback. They became one of four teams to overcome a four-run deficit to win when playing an elimination game.

The wild game brought a pinch single by Zack Greinke – the first by a pitcher since 1923 in a World Series game. Greinke had the hardest hit ball of the night – 106mph. Dusty Baker used him as his first pinch hitter, saving Marwin Gonzalez for the fifth inning when there was a more important game situation. Gonzalez turned into a World Series standout again just as kids turned into pumpkins for the Halloween game. Gonzalez added the clutch two-run single for a 5-5 tie to his Game 2 2017 World Series home run off Dodger closer Kenley Jansen in Los Angeles.

Six Houston relievers kept the Braves down after the fifth, with starter-turned-reliever Jose Urquidy earning the win with one scoreless inning.

Maldonado drove in three runs after entering the game with an .098 batting average for the 2021 postseason. The teams headed for an off day in Houston.

Did you know?

George Springer hit .379 with 5 homers and 7 RBIs in the 2017 World Series to lead the Astros to their victory over the Los Angeles Dodgers. His OPS was 1.471.

Springer scored six runs to lead Houston in the 2019 World Series loss to Washington in seven games. His OPS was 1.108.

Game 6

Jorge Soler's tape measure home run off Luis Garcia over the railroad tracks at Minute Maid Park gave Atlanta a 3-0 lead in the third. Dansby Swanson added a two-run laser off Cristian Javier in the fifth to lift the Braves to a 5-0 cushion. They cruised to a 7-0 victory and finished their climb from a .500 record in early August to World Series winners for the first time in 26 years. Lefthander Max Fried was the personification of Sandy Koufax, Steve Carlton and Cole Hamels with his dominance.

The Braves continued the recent trend of parity in the sport. They were the 14th different team to win the World Series since 2000. They won in the 44th week of the year after winning 44 games before the All-Star break and 44 after in the year that they lost their icon Hank Aaron, number 44. Some 21 different teams of the 30 in the majors reached the World Series in the last 22 seasons.

The Astros could console themselves with their strong season followed by outstanding success in the playoffs against the White Sox and Red Sox. They ran into a team playing at its peak and fell short of their goal, but they continued to excel in their culture of excellence.

The Astros became the first team in history to win three games in a row after trailing in a postseason series in four different series over a three-year period.

Alex Bregman underwent right wrist surgery a few days after the end of the World Series. Jake Meyers had shoulder surgery. Brent Strom resigned as pitching coach, saying that Josh Miller and Bill Murphy were ready to be promoted. He later decided to take a pitching coach job with the Arizona Diamondbacks near his home.

Justin Verlander signed as a free agent to return to Houston.

The Astros' Golden Era became the best for any Houston professional team. The Astros had made five straight trips to the ALCS and three World Series appearances in five years.

100

2021 World Series Statistics

Altuve   .222-2-2 1bb .731 OPS

Alvarez   .100-0-0 5bb .508 OPS

Brantley   .333-0-1 3bb .824 OPS

Bregman   .095-0-2 2bb .343 OPS

Correa   .261-0-4 1bb .624 OPS

Gonzalez   .250-0-2 0bb .500 OPS

Greinke   .667-0-0 0bb 1.333 OPS

Gurriel   .273-0-2 2bb .606 OPS

Maldonado .235-0-4 1bb .498 OPS

McCormick .000-0-1 0bb .000 OPS

Siri   .167-0-1 0bb .333 OPS

Tucker   .286-0-0 3bb .756 OPS

L. Garcia   0-2 5.68 ERA 2 starts   Stanek 0-0 4.15 ERA 5g

Y. Garcia   0-0 0.00 ERA 4 games   Taylor 0-0 13.50 ERA 2g

Graveman 0-0 2.25 ERA 3 games   Urquidy 2-0 3.00 ERA 2g

Greinke   0-0 0.00 ERA 1 start   Valdez 0-1 19.29 ERA 2g

Javier   0-1 12.00 ERA 3 games

Maton   0-0 0.00 ERA 5 games

Odorozzi 0-0 0.00 ERA 1 game

Pressly   0-0 0.00 ERA 3 games

Raley   0-0 2.70 ERA 4 games

Chapter 4

THE GOLDEN ERA

How long is an era? It can't be defined until it ends.

In the context of the 60 years of Houston Astros history, the era that started in 2015 is the best. Entering the 2022 season, the era is still alive. With six playoff appearances in seven years through 2021, the Astros have fielded their best teams of any era over the longest current stretch.

Reviewing the loosely-structure eras of the team's history lends perspective to the present by using the past as prologue. Since the New York Mets entered the major leagues in 1962 alongside the Astros, those two teams are often compared to each other. Through their total history, the Astros have a better winning percentage, .498-.480 (through 2021). The Mets have more highs and lows than the Astros. In their expansion season of 1962, they were 40-120. They won the World Series in 1969, 48 years earlier than the Astros. The Mets repeated as World Series champions in 1986. (1973, 2000 and 2015 brought losses). The Astros lost the World Series in 2005, 2019 and 2021, with their title in 2017.

2015

The fruits of General Manager Jeff Luhnow's master plan to rebuild the Astros arrived in 2015. After focusing their attention on a restructuring of the entire organization in 2011 when Jim Crane's group bought the team from Drayton McLane, Jr., the Astros used the draft choices they accumulated by trades and by drafting high to put together a surprise year in 2015. With homegrown players Jose Altuve, George Springer, Carlos Correa, Dallas Keuchel and others, the Astros lost a hotly-contested playoff series to Kansas City. Their attention to development yielded eye-popping results. This playoff appearance began their current string of success.

Keuchel won the Cy Young Award. Correa was Rookie of the Year. Luhnow acquired Scott Kazmir, Mike Fiers and Carlos Gomez in stretch drive trades to nail down a wild card playoff spot.

Luke Gregerson, Pat Neshek and Will Harris delivered after Luhnow added them to the mix for the late innings. Free agent outfielder Colby Rasmus belted 25 home runs. Evan Gattis paid off in a trade with Atlanta for Mike Foltynewicz with 27 bombs, mostly in the DH role.

Luis Valbuena surprised with 25 homers, and Jose Altuve blossomed at second base. Altuve joined Keuchel on the All-Star team and hit .313. Valbuena came from the Cubs in the Dexter Fowler trade.

New manager AJ Hinch took the team from a 70-92 record in 2014 to 86-76, blending players together from a roster that included Chris Carter, Jason Castro, Preston Tucker, Jed Lowrie, Hank Conger and Marwin Gonzalez. Lowrie and Jonathan Villar held down shortstop until Correa arrived in June.

Keuchel parlayed his sinker and changeup with a rangy infield to win 20 games, followed by Collin McHugh's 19 wins. Lance McCullers, Jr. was promoted from the minors to give the pitching staff another power arm.

The Astros led the AL West for a good portion of the season until fading in the final days and finishing two games short of the Texas Rangers. But Keuchel shut out the Yankees in Yankee Stadium in a breakthrough Wild Card playoff win for the franchise, pitching on three days' rest.

The Kansas City Royals had all they could handle in Houston for the ALDS, but the Royals prevailed and won the series in five games. The Astros blew a 6-2 lead late in Game 4, leaving them with confidence that they could play with the best. They were to build on that when they returned to the playoffs in 2017.

Did you know that....

Both Joe Morgan and Roger Metzger of the Astros tied for the National League lead in triples in 1971 with 11.

2017

After missing the playoffs in 2016, a powerful team blew out of the starting blocks and went on to dominate the American League on its way to Houston's first World Series title. With American League Most Valuable Player and batting champ Jose Altuve putting together a banner season, the Astros made a key trade for Justin Verlander minutes before the August 31 deadline for playoff eligibility. Verlander was a difference-maker, helping the team grind through a difficult playoff run to knock off the Los Angeles Dodgers in the World Series.

Dallas Keuchel, Charlie Morton and Brad Peacock led the staff in wins with 14, 14 and 13 respectively. Mike Fiers was the only Houston starter to escape injuries, but by the time the World Series arrived he was not on the roster.

The 2017 season was singular in its crisis management. Dealing with the effects of all the pitching injuries that led to an 11-17 record in August, the Astros traded for Verlander and then turned their attention to Hurricane Harvey. They plunged into the community to help those in need. The community rallied around them, and the baseball team's success was a needed diversion from the struggles of hurricane relief efforts.

Verlander's arrival took them to new heights and convinced them that they had everything they needed to win a championship.

The memorable 2017 ALCS was the best example of home field advantage in recent years. The home team won each game, with the Astros taking Games 6 and 7 to slay the Yankees and punch their ticket to their second World Series. Their 101-61 regular season record was the second best in club history at that time. Nobody was predicting that the next two seasons would both produce better records.

Marwin Gonzalez led the club in RBIs with 90. As with the pitching staff, the team succeeded because the whole was better than the sum of its parts. The team's strength came from its balance, with eight players driving in at least 50 runs. Altuve finished at .346-24-81.

The incredible 2017 World Series matched two teams with at least 100 wins for the first time since 1970. Clayton Kershaw whiffed 11 in seven innings in Game 1, a 3-1 Dodgers win. On a 103-degree night, Kershaw took a 144-64 record to the mound and stopped the Astros on three hits. One was a homer from 23-year-old Alex Bregman. Kershaw was in his prime at age 29. Even though he missed weeks with a back injury, he went 18-4 with a 2.31 ERA.

A classic Game 2 at Dodger Stadium brought the Astros their first World Series win. They would not forget how hard they had to work to earn it. Justin Verlander took a no-hitter through four and a 1-0 lead over Rich Hill, who got an early hook from Manager Dave Roberts. Joc Pederson tied it with a home run and Corey Seager sent the Dodgers in front 3-1 with another. Dodger closer Kenley Jansen was brought in earlier than usual in the eighth inning. Carlos Correa singled in a run. Jansen came back for the ninth with a 12-for-12 record in postseason saves. A slumping Marwin Gonzalez ripped an 0-2 pitch from Jansen for the biggest home run in Houston history to tie the game, 3-3. Jansen had not allowed a home run on an 0-2 count in 82 at-bats. The game went to the tenth, with former Astro Josh Fields allowing back-to-back home runs to Altuve and Correa. It was still tied after the Dodgers scored twice off Ken Giles in their half of the tenth. George Springer homered in the 11th off the last reliever remaining for the Dodgers, Brandon McCarthy. Chris Devenski survived a Charlie Culberson blast to win the 7-6 thriller. Never had there been five home runs in extra innings of a World Series game until this night. Or in any game in the history of baseball, covering 214,000 regular season and 1,334 postseason games!

In Houston, the Astros claimed Game 3, 7-5. Lance McCullers, Jr. had a 5-1 lead when he left in the sixth. Reliever Brad Peacock allowed two inherited runs to score, but his 53-pitch outing got him a rare save of 3 2/3 innings.

The Dodgers squared the Series 2-2 when Alex Wood throttled the Houston hitters in a 6-2 game that erupted late for Los Angeles. Charlie Morton also pitched well for Houston, keeping the game close.

It was tied 1-1 going to the ninth when Ken Giles of the Astros failed to retire a batter and allowed three runs. That threw the closer role wide open for AJ Hinch for the rest of the Series.

Game 5 was the game to top all World Series games. Kershaw was spotted with a 4-0 lead over Keuchel. Yuli Gurriel's three-run homer created a 4-4 tie. The Dodgers regrouped to give Kershaw another chance, leading 7-4. The three-time Cy Young winner also gave up two more, and Altuve's homer off Kenta Maeda tied the game, 7-7. The five-hour, 17-minute marathon was getting more interesting. The Dodgers rallied for three in the ninth to tie it, 12-12. That's what the score was when the clock struck 12 midnight. Just 12 minutes earlier, Kellie Price turned to her husband and said, "I think this game is gonna end on the 30th." It did end October 30th, one year to the day after Kellie's son, Joseph Fleming, died of cancer at age ten. Lance McCullers, Jr. had tossed a World Series ball to Joseph's parents before Game 5 as a memento. Lance had become a family friend after spending hours with Joseph in his final year and speaking at his memorial service on the baseball field where he played for the Blue Chips select team in League City, Texas. Joseph wore uniform #21. So did Derek Fisher. Fisher went in to pinch-run at second base in the 10th inning and raced home with the winning run on Bregman's single to left field. It was his fifth straight World Series game with an RBI, and the Astros won, 13-12. It was a game for the ages.

Back at Dodger Stadium, the 3-1 Dodger victory in Game 6 sent the Series to the limit of seven games. Rich Hill pitched well and gave way in the fifth to the Dodger bullpen. Verlander lost it despite allowing two runs in six innings.

Series MVP George Springer delivered a big blow in Game 7. His fifth home run of the World Series off Yu Darvish helped the Astros to 5-0 lead, with McCullers, Jr. pitching on fumes and Morton setting down the final 11 to secure Houston's first ever World Series Championship.

Manager AJ Hinch stepped away from analytics with his use of the bullpen in the World Series. He and his team had come a long way from 2015 to the ultimate moment in baseball.

The 2017 World Series parade in downtown Houston

Fans jamming into a parking garage above the World Series parade in 2017

Did you know that….

Nolan Ryan hit a homer in his first game with the Astros.

2018

Another powerful regular season sent the Astros into the 2018 playoffs. They lost to the eventual World Series champion Boston Red Sox in the American League Championship Series.

Fueled by the addition of Gerrit Cole to the starting rotation in a January trade, the Astros set a new club record with 103 regular season wins. Cole joined Verlander, Keuchel, Morton and McCullers, Jr. in the rotation. Following the lead of the 2017 team, the Astros were incredibly successful on the road with a .704 winning percentage, finishing 57-24. But statistically there was a major difference in how the two teams went about their business of winning. The 2017 team was much better offensively; 2018 brought much better pitching.

A major league strikeout record (1,687) fell to the 2018 Astros. Verlander and Cole were the first two major league pitching teammates to reach 250 k's in modern baseball (since 1900).

Alex Bregman led the club in home runs with 31, RBIs with 103 and many other categories such as on base average (.394) and slugging percentage (.532). He finished second to Mike Trout in AL MVP voting.

Another major difference between the 2017 and 2018 teams was postseason performance. After dispatching Cleveland in three ALDS games, the banged-up Astros position players struggled to hit against 108-win Boston in the ALCS in 2018.

Verlander pitched a fine game in Boston to claim the opener, but the Red Sox struck back and beat Cole in Game 2. In Game 3, Boston's Steve Pearce homered off Joe Smith in the sixth and the Red Sox added five in the eighth against Roberto Osuna, including a grand slam by Jackie Bradley, Jr. Charlie Morton lasted only 2 1/3 innings in Game 4. Josh James lost the 8-6 contest, with Bradley adding another home run.

David Price dazzled the Astros in Game 5 with a strong dose of changeups, winning 4-1 to give the Red Sox the title on their way to a World Series win.

A limping Jose Altuve hit .250 in the ALCS and headed for the operating room to repair a broken kneecap. He was denied a home run at Minute Maid Park on a controversial call by umpire Joe West, who ruled Altuve out on fan interference when Mookie Betts tried to catch the ball reaching over the right field wall. Bregman hit .133 with seven walks in the series. Relievers Nate Eovaldi and Craig Kimbrel had starring roles for Boston. Andrew Benintendi's great diving catch on Bregman's line drive to end Game 5 was the biggest play of the series.

2019

After the 2018 season ended, the Astros lost three starting pitchers who combined for 499 innings. Charlie Morton and Dallas Keuchel became free agents and Lance McCullers, Jr. underwent Tommy John surgery. Nonetheless, they were still favored to win the American League West when 2019 arrived. They added free agents Michael Brantley, Robinson Chirinos, Aledmys Diaz and Wade Miley.

Justin Verlander opened the 2019 season with a strong effort to earn his eighth Opening Day win. The Astros stumbled out of the gate, though, with a 2-5 road trip to open the season. By midseason, the Injured List was populated by such prominent players as Carlos Correa, George Springer and Aledmys Diaz. Their twin ten-game winning streaks sustained them through the bumps in the road. They had a 30-15 start to the season. Reliever Ryan Pressly smashed a club record with a 32-game scoreless streak. He joined closer Roberto Osuna and setup man Will Harris to form a trio reminiscent of Octavio Dotel, Brad Lidge and Billy Wagner many years earlier.

Cuban rookie Yordan Alvarez slugged his way to the majors by June 9, and provided a dynamic impact player in the lineup. Alvarez belted 23 home runs and drove in 71 runs. Alvarez went on to win unanimous AL Rookie of the Year honors. He had a major league rookie record OPS of 1.067 for the Astros in 87 games.

The 2019 Astros were on a par with the 2017 club offensively. Their pitching was superior to 2017 statistically, but fell short of the 2018 staff in ERA and strikeouts.

The Astros had four starters in the All-Star Game for the first time in club history. Alex Bregman, Michael Brantley, George Springer and Justin Verlander all started the game.

At the trade deadline, General Manager Jeff Luhnow dealt a large package of prospects to Arizona for former Cy Young winner Zack Greinke. Greinke joined a Houston rotation with these statistics for the top four at the July 31 deadline:

Justin Verlander 14-4, 2.73 ERA 0.81 WHIP 151 IP 31BB 196 K's

Gerrit Cole   12-5 2.94 ERA 1.00 WHIP 143 IP 37 BB 212 K's

Zack Greinke   10-4 2.90 ERA 0.95 WHIP 146 IP 21 BB 135 K's

Wade Miley   9-4 3.06 ERA 1.12 WHIP 126 IP 40 BB 106 K's

Aaron Sanchez, who joined the Astros in a deadline day trade with Toronto, pitched a no-hitter August 3 in his Houston debut. In one of the most memorable days in the team's history, Sanchez walked to the bullpen to warm up while ceremonies on the field honored the 2019 Houston Astros Hall of Fame class. Included in the group on the field were members of the inaugural class of the Astros Hall of Fame in 2018.

Three of them had pitched no-hitters for Houston: Larry Dierker, Nolan Ryan and Mike Scott. The karma in Minute Maid Park surrounded Sanchez in a special moment. He was 3-14 with a 6.07 ERA for Toronto in 2019. During his All-Star year of 2016, Sanchez blazed to a 15-2 record with a 3.00 ERA. Since then, blister problems on his pitching hand and ineffectiveness had dogged him. On this night, Sanchez mystified the Seattle Mariners for six innings of no-hit ball. He came out of the game because he had reached a pitch limit forced by inactivity in the previous ten days. Three relievers combined with Sanchez on a four-pitcher no-hitter.

Verlander twirled his third career no-hitter at Toronto September 1. The game was scoreless until the ninth, when Abraham Toro belted a two-out, two-run homer off former Astro Ken Giles in the 2-0 win. Toro also made a good play at third base for the final out.

By the time another milestone regular season ended, the Astros had piled up 107 victories. They joined a small group of elite teams who won at least 100 games for three straight seasons. There were only six.

Team		Season by Season	Total Wins
Philadelphia Athletics	1929-31	104-102-107	313
St. Louis Cardinals	1942-44	106-105-105	316
Baltimore Orioles	1969-71	109-108-101	318
Atlanta Braves	1997-99	101-106-103	310
New York Yankees	2002-04	103-101-101	305
Houston Astros	2017-19	101-103-107	311

The Astros led the majors in wins for the first time in their history. They became the first team in history to lead the league in pitching strikeouts with the fewest strikeouts by their hitters. They led the majors in batting average (.274), slugging percentage (.495) and on base percentage (.352). They outscored their opponents, 920-640. The run differential of +280 was the third highest in the majors since 1961. Their offense was on a par with the 2017 World Championship team. Their run differential was the best of their 100-win clubs.

Offensively, Alex Bregman led the way with 41 home runs, 122 RBIs, 122 runs and 119 walks. Jose Altuve enjoyed his best home run season with 31. George Springer delivered 39 long balls and 96 RBIs. Yuli Gurriel drove in 104 in his best season. Michael Brantley checked in at .311 and was the picture of consistency, even against the toughest pitchers he faced.

The Astros set a new club record for grand slam home runs with 11, breaking their own club record for total home runs in a season as well with 288. They were one of 15 teams to set new club records in that department in a major league record year for home runs with 6,776.

Gerrit Cole constructed a powerful and remarkable season with a 20-5 record, leading the American League with a 2.52 earned run average. He finished second to Verlander in the Cy Young Award voting.

In the American League Division Series, the Tampa Bay Rays were in a decided underdog role against the Astros, who had the best record in the majors. The Rays had won the regular season series from the Astros, 4-3.

Verlander shut out the Rays while he was in Game 1, leading Houston to a 6-2 win. Verlander was 8-0 in his career in the Division Series, setting a record for wins in that round of the playoffs. Jose Altuve belted a home run for the third straight year in Game 1 of the ALDS.

Cole followed Verlander's lead by pitching shutout ball while he was in the game (7 2/3 innings). Cole broke Mike Scott's Houston postseason record for strikeouts with 15. He threw a 100mph fastball on his 115th pitch. No two pitchers in history had put together consecutive games like Verlander and Cole. Alex Bregman homered in the 3-2 win.

With the series shifting to St. Petersburg for Game 3, the Rays found their stride behind Charlie Morton, and Kevin Kiermaier's three-run homer off Zack Greinke lifted them to a second-inning lead on the way to a 10-3 blowout.

AJ Hinch returned to Verlander for Game 4 on three days' rest despite his limited experience on short rest and the large body of statistics pointing to more failures than successes for all starting pitchers working on short rest in the postseason. Verlander ran into a 32-pitch roadblock in the first inning. The Rays took the game, 4-1, calling on ace Blake Snell to close out the game and square the series.

The Astros had the home field advantage for their ninth winner-take-all game in club history. Their record in the first eight was 4-4. The day before, both Washington and St. Louis won Game 5s on the road – in Los Angeles and Atlanta, respectively.

"The pressure is awesome. And it's on both of us," said AJ Hinch the day before Game 5. "I love it. I love that we're here. And the way that we got here is nerve-racking, just because you don't want to get to a Game 5. We fought all year to have a better record and to win our division to get this particular game at home. And they've got to come into our house and beat us again. I don't know who could be confident than us." The players knew that a huge roaring crowd would be an asset to them, and it was. "They came out all year to support us," said Gerrit Cole. "They're a baseball-savvy town. They understand big pitches. They understand big plays. And they love to bring the energy."

Cole established a powerful tone in the first inning. The Astros' hitters clicked in their half of the first against Tyler Glasnow's 98 mph fastballs and snapdragon curves. George Springer led off with a single and advanced to third on Michael Brantley's hit. Jose Altuve rifled a single to score Springer and get Brantley to third.

Alex Bregman drove a curve to right center, scoring both runners for a 3-0 cushion before Glasnow could get an out. The Astros became the first team to open a deciding playoff game with four straight hits. Yuli Gurriel singled in Bregman and it was 4-0 Houston after one.

The Fox Sports studio broadcasters thought the Astros hitters knew what was coming. They did. Alex Rodriguez, David Ortiz and Frank Thomas reviewed the video highlights of the hits and agreed that the Astros took confident swings as if they expected what pitch Glasnow was about to throw them. One tipoff was Bregman waiting back and lining the curveball to right center.

The former players nailed their analysis by explaining that a pitcher might start his hands higher on a fastball than on a curve, and the hitters could pick up the difference quickly. They showed video clips of Altuve talking to Carlos Correa after he scored the third run. He seemed to be passing along scouting information. After the game, Bregman denied that contention. But Glasnow told reporters after the game that he thought he was tipping his pitches by doing exactly what the studio analysts said.

Altuve hammered a high 98mph fastball for a home run and Brantley added his first postseason extra base hit of 2019 in the 6-1 Houston win. Cole struck out 10 to set a record with 25 strikeouts in a division series. He extended his winning streak to 18 games – a major league record for the live ball era (since 1920). The Astros had not lost a Cole start since July 12. "The run he's been on is second to none," said Tampa Bay skipper Kevin Cash. "Elite pitching like that can really quiet good offenses."

All five of the games in the division series were won by the home team. "Really, honestly, now that we won it, it was good to get hit in the mouth twice," Cole analyzed. Altuve (.350-3-5) and Cole (2-0, 2.57) were eye-popping in the series.

The New York Yankees, with 103 wins in the regular season, were next for the Astros. The Yankees rolled over the Minnesota Twins in their division series in a three-game sweep. That bought them four days off before the ALCS. But the Astros conquered them in six games.

Did you know that....

Juan Agosto appeared in 82 games out of the bullpen for the Astros in 1990. That is the club record for a left-handed pitcher.

The Washington Nationals snatched the World Series from the Astros by winning Games 6 and 7 in Houston. The Nationals came from behind in the late innings of Game 7, fueled by a Howie Kendrick home run off the right field foul pole off Will Harris in the 7th inning.

The visiting team won all seven games in the 2019 World Series. Washington's dynamic duo of Max Scherzer and Stephen Strasburg topped Houston's 1-2 of Gerrit Cole and Justin Verlander in the first two games at Houston, 5-4 and 12-3. Ryan Zimmerman and Juan Soto clobbered Game 1 home runs. Five Nationals players had two hits in their 14-hit attack in Game 2.

In Washington, the Astros rebounded with 4-1, 8-1 and 7-1 wins with their pitching bouncing back to shackle the Nats' hitters. Zack Greinke started Game 3 with five relievers backing him up. Jose Urquidy won Game 4 with able support from five relievers. Cole took Game 5 with home run support from Alvarez, Correa and Springer.

The Astros could not solve the mystery at home, losing Games 6 and 7. Strasburg topped Verlander 7-1 with 5 RBIs from Anthony Rendon, and Scherzer turned Game 7 over to Patrick Corbin, whose three shutout relief innings gave Howie Kendrick a chance to knock a game-deciding home run off Will Harris in the seventh off the right field foul pole.

The Astros fell just short despite winning 107 games in the regular season.

Here's the statistical comparison of the 2017, 2018 and 2019 seasons for the Astros:

	BA/OBA/SL	OPS	Runs/Opp	Run Diff.	ERA	Strikeouts
2017	.282/.346/.478	.823	898/700	+196	4.12	1593
2018	.255/.329/.425	.754	797/534	+263	3.11	1687
2019	.274/.352/.495	.848	920/640	+280	3.66	1671
2021	.267/.339/.444	.783	863/658	+205	3.76	1456

2020

The beginning of 2020 brought an earthquake of major proportions to baseball.

The Houston Astros were punished by MLB Commissioner Rob Manfred for cheating by stealing signs electronically during games in 2017 and 2018. Their general manager, Jeff Luhnow, and manager, AJ Hinch, were suspended for one season and the team was fined $5 million and stripped of draft choices in the first and second rounds for 2020 and 2021. Carlos Beltran and coach Alex Cora also were suspended for one year and lost their jobs. Cora was set to manage Boston and Beltran had been hired to manage the New York Mets.

In the report made public January 13, MLB's investigation revealed a player-driven sign stealing system utilizing decoding signs in the team's video replay room in the clubhouse and relaying them to players on the field. The findings were that the live game feed from the center field camera allowed employees in the replay room to see what signs were given from the catcher to the pitcher by magnifying the camera shot to show the catcher's fingers. The signs were relayed quickly to the batter, who could know what pitch was about to be thrown to him.

Early in the season, bench coach Alex Cora called the replay room to obtain the sign information, according to the report.

Sometimes the employees in the replay room sent a text to a staff member on the bench via a smart watch. In other cases, the text went to a cell phone stored nearby.

The coronavirus pandemic sweeping across the world early in 2020 made it a year unlike any other. With the season reduced to 60 games, the season began.

A Dose of Normalcy

July 23, 2020   Finally the 2020 Major League Baseball season started, after the minor league seasons had been cancelled. Some 119 days after it was supposed to begin, the long-awaited campaign got underway. Instead of the usual 162-game marathon, it was a 60-game sprint. That's all the world would allow in 2020.

The last time major league baseball had a 60-game season was 1878. Professional baseball started in 1869, but the National League was not formed until 1876. That season had a 70-game schedule. The Chicago White Stockings, managed by Albert Spalding, went 52-14 that year to win the National League title. There was no World Series, because the American League had not been formed yet. Spalding was the starting pitcher (called bowler) in 60 games, with a 47-12 record. The White Sox actually played 66 games. Ross Barnes led the White Sox in batting average with a .429 mark for 322 at-bats. The ball was pitched underhand from 45 feet then, with the batter instructing the bowler where he wanted the ball pitched! The fielders did not use gloves.

July 24 The usual buzz for Opening Day in Houston was missing. There were no public functions, such as the normal pep rallies leading up to the game. No need for traffic control. The Seattle Mariners were in Houston to start the 2020 campaign.

Former Astro catcher Scott Servais was managing the only team in the American League West not given a chance to at least make a splash.

The Astros and Oakland were both highly regarded. Texas was credited with the best pitching rotation in the division.

Many fans who had not stayed in touch with baseball during the pandemic would be watching on television, but the media hype was nowhere near the norm for Opening Day in Houston.

Baseball itself was the one thing that WAS normal. There were no fans – only about 1,500 cardboard cutouts picturing fans who paid $100 to the Astros Foundation to be represented in the seats. There was some piped-in crowd noise from the Ballpark Entertainment booth. Much had been made in the media about the Astros getting a "pass" in road venues from booing fans. Those fans who had reacted all winter long after the cheating scandal had been active on social media, but their presence at the ballparks would not be felt. A challenge still existed when it came to dealing with angry opponents on the field, though. Yet, in what seemed like such a different world altogether, even that emotion might be dampened by the strangeness of what the players encountered.

The Astros ripped a club record 288 home runs in 2019 while leading the majors in on base average (.352) and slugging percentage (.495). They scored 920 runs to rank third in the majors. That seemed irrelevant as the 2020 season commenced.

Opening Day Game

With some pregame pageantry, including a flyover, the players of the Astros and Mariners knelt before the national anthem in tribute to racial injustice and deaths caused by the coronavirus. The player introductions of the starting lineups seemed strange, with the players standing in place instead of running from the dugout as they customarily have done through the years.

When Justin Verlander took the mound and fired 96mph fastballs and hard-breaking sliders, normalcy set in for the young Mariners. Verlander made his 12th Opening Day start, topped by only five pitchers in the history of the sport. He led the Astros to their eighth straight Opening Day win, 8-2.

Alvarez, Urquidy cleared to join team

On the COVID-19 front, Yordan Alvarez and Jose Urquidy were cleared to resume baseball activities. They remained on the Injured List, but they joined the alternate squad at Whataburger Field in Corpus Christi for workouts.

721-day Wait for McCullers

Game 2 for the Astros brought Lance McCullers, Jr. to the mound for his first start in 721 days. Tommy John surgery ended his 2018 season early. He missed all of 2019 recuperating. If he had faced a full season in 2020, McCullers may not have been allowed to pitch more than about 120 innings or so. In a short season of 60 games, there would be no need for restraints. McCullers looked sharp late in a 92-pitch 7-2 win.

Verlander Out with Forearm Strain

Reports on Twitter during the Astros 7-6 loss to Seattle July 26 indicated that Justin Verlander had an elbow injury that would require him to miss the rest of the 2020 season.

Pitching Emergency

Not only was Brandon Bielak needed desperately in Houston, but more reinforcements were needed as well. Ryan Pressly and Chris Devenski reported elbow soreness. Austin Pruitt was shut down from throwing after suffering a setback. Reliever Joe Smith opted out of the season under the COVID rules. The pitching staff was in a shambles.

New Astros Manager Dusty Baker said it was his decision to leave the San Francisco Giants after their Game 7 World Series loss in 2002. Baker said he was shocked to be released by the Cincinnati Reds after leading them to the playoffs three times in four seasons. The Washington Nationals did not tender him a contract after his two seasons with 95 and 97 wins. "That's the one that really hurt, because I thought we did a great job," said Baker. "Sometimes your feelings are hurt, but you've got to continue on in life and continue on in living."

Brent Strom, who joins Baker in the Seventies Club among managers and coaches, presided over Cy Young winners Dallas Keuchel and Justin Verlander in Houston. He also was instrumental in helping Gerrit Cole, Charlie Morton, Collin McHugh and Will Harris reach new heights in their careers. Strom stepped down after the 2021 season, but his impact on the organization will be felt for some time to come.

Dodger Retaliation

The highly-ranked Los Angeles Dodgers had no such problems. They had the game's best bullpen depth, and they flaunted it by opening the two-game series at Minute Maid Park with a 5-2 come-from-behind win. Walker Buehler left the game in the fourth inning trailing 2-0, but the Dodger bullpen choked off the Astros after that.

In the sixth inning, Dodger reliever Joe Kelly took the mound with a 5-2 lead. He walked two, and when covering first base to take a throw he put his foot in the middle and just in front of the first base bag. Batter-runner Michael Brantley stepped on it. Brantley's ankle rolled over slightly, causing him to leave the next night's game when he was not running well. Kelly fell behind Alex Bregman and uncorked a fastball over his head and slightly behind him on a 3-0 count. He struck out Carlos Correa to end the inning on a slider.

Earlier, he threw a slider that did not break and wound up near Correa's head. When he struck out Correa, Kelly and Correa exchanged looks and Kelly yelled, "Nice swing, b—tch!" according to Dusty Baker. He then threw back his head and stuck out his tongue as he walked to the dugout. Correa took a few steps toward him and the benches emptied.

The umpires were able to cool down emotions and did not eject any players, but they warned both teams. The warning prevented the Astros from retaliating if they did not want to risk any of their pitchers from being ejected.

Given the warning that all teams had been given before the season by Commissioner Rob Manfred about throwing at Astros hitters, Kelly stepped out into clear danger with the commissioner's office.

Kelly was suspended for eight games. Manager Dave Roberts got a one-game suspension and Baker was fined for violating the 2020 rule prohibiting anybody in uniform from coming within six feet of an umpire on the field.

The Other Side of the Field

Dusty Baker had been worried about this kind of retaliation for the cheating. His opinion was that Kelly crossed the line when it came to striking back. "I didn't anticipate that," said Baker. "I didn't anticipate throwing over somebody's head three balls and no strikes. One of our more important guys. If you're going to throw at somebody, you don't throw at the head."

"Joe Kelly threw a ball behind Bregman's head on 3-0 on purpose," said Lance McCullers, Jr. "Not only did he take it upon himself to, I guess, send a message, but he wasn't even part of the team during that (2017) season. We knew coming into the game that he likes to go off script. It is what it is. It was done unprofessionally. What he did after he punched out Correa was unprofessional. Running into the dugout was unprofessional. So, it is what it is."

Altuve Demotes Himself

Before the August 15 game, Jose Altuve asked Dusty Baker to move him down to seventh in the batting order. His message to Baker was that his teammates were hitting better than he was and that he should not be hitting third. Baker told reporters that only one other player had done that in his entire managerial career. He refused to name the other player because the player lied to the media about the conversation. Altuve had not hit seventh since his rookie season of 2011.

Altuve was hitting .181/.253/.313 in his first 20 games. His strikeouts were uncharacteristically high: 19 in 83 at-bats. That was a 23% strikeout rate. His career rate was just 13%. Since he was healthy, this unusual slump had people mystified. It was based on issues with his hitting mechanics. Dusty Baker mentioned his pitch selection and timing. His high leg kick and stride toward home plate was not in synch. He was not meeting pitches squarely.

He was guessing, resulting in swinging at bad pitches because he guessed wrong or taking good pitches to hit because he guessed wrong. To his credit, he put the team ahead of himself when he asked to be demoted.

When the series at Coors Field opened the next night, Yordan Alvarez was declared lost for the season. A partial tear in his right patella tendon had been discovered, and surgery was scheduled for the next week.

Luis Garcia, pitching above Class A for the first time, saved the bullpen in his major league debut with 4 1/3 innings of one-run baseball. With a doubleheader looming the next day, Dusty Baker credited Garcia's work for providing a major lift for the pitching staff.

Jose Urquidy waited a long time for his 2020 debut. He spent 35-40 days alone in his Houston apartment after testing positive for COVID-19. His symptoms were not extensive, but he lost strength and had to regain it before he could get himself in shape to pitch again. "I started from zero," said Urquidy. "I had to do a lot of stuff to build the strength in my arm to be able to throw the way I want to, so it wasn't a normal rehab for me."

He was unable to throw during the quarantine. When he went to the alternate training site in Corpus Christi, he began the long process of throwing again.

"Win of the Year"

Baker called it the "Win of the Year." The Astros, trailing 5-1 in the eighth, came to bat in the ninth against one of the top closers in the game, Kenley Jansen, down 5-2.

It was a scene similar to Game 2 of the 2017 World Series, when Marwin Gonzalez blasted a home run off Janzen to prevent the Astros from falling into an 0-2 hole to open that World Series. They rallied to win that game in 11 innings and went on to win Game 7 of that Series at Dodger Stadium.

Carlos Correa led off the ninth with a single. When the dust cleared, the Astros had struck six straight hits off Jansen and defeated the 32-14 Dodgers, 7-5.

The next night, the Dodgers unleashed their high-powered relievers in a bullpen game and blasted the Astros 8-1. Zack Greinke took a beating. The road trip ended 2-9 and sent the Astros to Houston for their final homestand of the season searching for enough of a rebound to get them into the playoffs.

Framber Valdez won Game 2 of the series in Seattle September 21 by showing his poise and allowing his hitters time to break through. Valdez, at times laughing and smiling when he gave up a hit or threw a pitch past catcher Martin Maldonado, displayed the mental improvement he made over the winter through visits to a psychologist in the Dominican Republic. "It doesn't matter what the situation is, if they scored five runs on me, six runs on me. I'm out there and I'm laughing, I'm staying loose because I know that's the only way I can execute a good pitch the next time – if I have a good attitude above everything else."

The Astros clinched a playoff spot in the worst possible way. They blew a one-run lead on a home run one pitch away from winning, then lost in ten innings after scoring in the top of the frame. In a late game on the West Coast, the Angels fell to the Dodgers and Houston's spot was secured. Could a team have felt more unworthy of a playoff spot?

Dusty Baker managed a record fifth different team to the playoffs. For the first time in their 59-year history, the Astros made the playoffs four years in a row. As the most hated team in baseball, they made it to the finish line without their staff ace, Justin Verlander, who pitched in one game. They patched together the bullpen without their closer, Roberto Osuna.

They fielded a lineup without their DH, Yordan Alvarez, for all but two games. They debuted nine rookie pitchers. They lost relievers Chris Devenski and Brad Peacock. They had six rookie pitchers on their playoff roster.

The Astros lost their final tune up, 8-4 to finish 29-31 - the first American League team to reach the playoffs with a losing record.

WILD CARD PLAYOFF ROUND

For the first time, 16 teams entered what was expected to be a truly unpredictable month-long marathon. The Wild Card round was best-of-three, with the extra-inning format reverting back to the traditional format used before 2020. During the 2020 regular season, a runner was placed at second base to begin each extra inning. That was not the case for the postseason.

After that, the remaining eight teams would enter Division Series playoff bubbles in Houston, Arlington, San Diego and Los Angeles.

HOUSTON (8) AT MINNESOTA (3)

Houston was 9-23 on the road in 2020. Minnesota was 24-6 at home. The Twins had not lost back-to-back games at home all season. Until this series.

In Game One, Kenta Maeda proved to be as tough to solve as the numbers indicated he might be. Maeda left with a 1-0 lead after five innings. The Twins got a run off Zack Greinke, who was pulled after four innings. Greinke threw 79 pitches.

Framber Valdez reprised the role of Charlie Morton in Game 7 of the 2017 World Series. He entered the game in the fifth and finished it. Like Greinke, he allowed two hits. The Twins could not solve his biting curveball, and Houston won 4-1.

Tied 1-1 in the ninth, closer Sergio Romo almost escaped bases-loaded trouble. Shortstop Jorge Polanco made an error and Jose Altuve took a 3-2 pitch for ball four with the bases loaded to send home the go-ahead run.

Justin Verlander underwent Tommy John surgery the next day. Verlander had one more year on his Houston contract, but he would miss that year in 2021 undergoing rehab. The two-time Cy Young Award winner with a 2.74 career ERA in 74 starts as an Astro was out for all of 2021.

In Game 2, Jose Urquidy gave the Astros an excellent start, leaving with a 1-0 lead in the fourth inning. Javier followed suit with what Framber Valdez did in Game 1, emerging from the bullpen after being in the rotation to provide solid relief and cover for the lack of depth among the team's relievers. Ryan Pressly saved the 3-1 win to sweep the brief series.

Carlos Correa addressed the media after he snapped a 1-1 tie with a long home run in the seventh inning. "I know a lot of people are mad, I know a lot of people don't want to see us here, but what are they going to say now?"

Correa unashamedly took on the ABC-TV broadcast team of Karl Ravech, Eduardo Perez and Tim Kurkjian for their treatment of the Astros cheating scandal during a sizeable portion of the Game 1 telecast. "I feel like on the broadcast yesterday you guys were too focused on the cheating scandal and now that we won the series, I think we deserve a little credit."

Did you know....

The Astros were a wild card playoff team in 2004, 2005 and 2020.

ALDS

HOUSTON VS. OAKLAND

Entering the playoff bubble at Dodger Stadium, both the Astros and Oakland Athletics were about to go into a grudge match. Oakland rated the favorite's role after winning the AL West and winning the season series from Houston, 7-3.

Emotions bubbled over when Ramon Laureano started after Houston hitting coach Alex Cintron following a hit batsman. The most outspoken Oakland player was pitcher Liam Hendricks.

Houston had a spotty bullpen, racked by injuries and an opt-out by Joe Smith. The Astros did not have the luxury of keeping Framber Valdez and Cristian Javier in the bullpen for the ALDS. "We're getting it done with an oddball group," said Brooks Raley. "Everybody knows we don't have Verlander or Cole, but we're finding guys to step up in Framber and Javier and the offense is coming through."

Game 1 brought the Houston offense back into prominence. After trailing 3-0 with Lance McCullers, Jr. on the mound, the Astros went to work against Chris Bassitt and turned the game into an offensive battle. They strung together several hits to score four times in the sixth for a 7-5 lead and went on to claim Game 1, 10-5.

Game 2 brought the focus to George Springer, who blasted two home runs to pass Babe Ruth on the all-time postseason home run list with 17. He tied Nelson Cruz, David Ortiz and Jason Werth for seventh on the all-time list. Springer's postseason history included a major chapter at Dodger Stadium in Game 2 of the 2017 World Series. Springer lit up the night with two home runs that night as well, one day after striking out three times.

Many were questioning AJ Hinch's decision to keep Springer in the leadoff spot for that 2017 game. Some were even questioning why Springer was in the lineup at all, given his four strikeouts in Game 1.

Oakland drilled breaking balls from Jose Urquidy on the way to a Game 3 triumph. Oakland's 9-7 decision sent the series to Game 4.

The Astros did not announce their Game 4 starter until a few hours before game time, settling on Zack Greinke because a doctor's exam revealed no structural damage and Greinke's arm felt much better after playing catch. Greinke had been battling shoulder issues. Carlos Correa drove in five runs in the game, and the Astros won, 11-6.

Oakland scored first in all four games, but the Astros rode power hitting that had been absent for much of 2020. Each team belted 12 home runs. The total of 24 set a new record for a Division Series. Houston pounded Oakland pitching for a .322 Division Series average, embellished by a .333 mark with men in scoring position. The Astros scored 33 runs in 35 innings.

Did you know that….

Former Astro first baseman Bob Watson is the only player to hit for the cycle in both the American and National Leagues.

Death of Joe Morgan

The baseball world mourned the death of Hall of Fame second baseman Joe Morgan, who passed away of a nerve condition. Morgan was the third Astro former All-Star to pass away in 2020, following Bob Watson and Jimmy Wynn. He was traded in 1971 from Houston to Cincinnati in the final building block to the Big Red Machine, earning MVP awards in their back-to-back World Series years of 1975 and 1976.

The list of Hall of Famers who died in 2020 grew longer. Whitey Ford, Bob Gibson, Lou Brock, Tom Seaver and Al Kaline preceded Morgan in death.

"Most people think of me as being part of the Big Red Machine, which I'm very proud of," said Morgan in 2019 at his induction into the Houston Astros Hall of Fame. "But I try to tell people that I learned to play baseball in the Astros organization. When I went to Cincinnati, I already knew how to play. All the things I did blended well with that team, but I learned the things I learned in Houston."

His teammate with Houston, Hall of Fame second baseman Nellie Fox, suggested that he flap his left elbow in his batting stance as a reminder to keep it higher so he wouldn't hit under the ball. One Hall of Famer mentored another.

A native Texan from Bonham, Morgan endured racism while playing for Durham, North Carolina. He was the only black on that team. First baseman Walt Matthews, who went on to become one of the most important scouts in the organization, warned the white racists to stay away from Morgan.

He convinced Morgan not to quit baseball when he was treated roughly by some of those fans.

2020

ALCS

At San Diego

It was no big surprise that Tampa Bay was one of the teams in the ALCS. The surprise in this series was Houston. "We need to make sure that we prioritize flexibility and being reactive to game situations," said General Manager James Click before the series. Click said of his experience with Tampa Bay, "My focus right now is putting the Astros in the best position possible to beat them, which on a scale of zero to weird is pretty weird."

The Astros got only 4 1/3 innings from Jose Urquidy, 4 2/3 from Zack Greinke and 4 from Lance McCullers, Jr. in the Division Series against Oakland. Greinke hadn't made it past the fifth inning in more than a month. Tampa Bay was better equipped in depth for a longer series, with a high-octane bullpen.

Tampa Bay players fed off being lightly regarded by the media. They beat the Yankees in the ALDS, winning the final game against $324 million Gerrit Cole.

Game 1 started well for the Astros, with Jose Altuve belting a first-inning home run off Blake Snell. Altuve became the all-time home run leader among second basemen in playoff games. He also ranked fourth in hits among second basemen. Diego Castillo ended the Rays 2-1 win by striking out Altuve with a runner at second.

Lance McCullers, Jr. was on his game in Game 2, striking out 11 in seven innings. Except for a 454-foot bomb by Mike Zunino, he allowed no earned runs. But three unearned runs in the first on Manuel Margot's home run to center field after a throwing error by Jose Altuve gave the Rays a 3-0 lead. The Astros were 1-for-8 in those situations and left 11 men on base in the 4-2 loss to Charlie Morton.

The Astros, who led the league in fielding percentage during the regular season, endured another Altuve error later in the game. Dusty Baker mentioned the word "yips" when talking about Altuve's two errant throws. Former Astro Charlie Morton won the game, with a save from Nick Anderson.

Game 3 starter Jose Urquidy had a quick first inning. Jose Altuve spotted him a 1-0 lead after one when he took Ryan Yarbrough deep to left field on a cut fastball. Altuve made his third throwing error of the series, bouncing a throw into left field, to lead to the pitching change. Baker probably would have been justified pulling Altuve instead of Urquidy! The Rays went on to win, 5-2 and Hunter Renfroe added two dazzling diving catches.

Altuve and "The Thing"

Throwing problems can be termed "the thing" or "the yips." Jose Altuve was in the throes of the mental stigma that triggers bad throws. He had made three in two games after making none in two months during the regular season. Some observers expected Dusty Baker to move Altuve from second base to designated hitter for Game 4, but he did not.

Baker was known as a players manager who supported his men and stood up for them publicly when they went through tough times. He was seen walking alongside Altuve during pregame workouts with his hand on Jose's shoulder, apparently laughing as they talked.

Two second basemen who had experienced major throwing problems, Steve Sax and Chuck Knoblauch, both went through extended periods without being able to make accurate throws on routine plays.

Sax made 24 errors before the All-Star break in 1983. "I would come off the field cursing myself," said Sax. "It's the worst thing you can do to yourself. I can see it in Jose's eyes. No one feels worse than he does, and this is happening to him at the worst time."

Altuve smoked a 400-foot home run to left center in the first inning off Tyler Glasnow, the 6-8 righthander whose fastball was sitting at 101 mph through the early stages of the game. Then he smacked a high curveball to right field for his second RBI in the third, giving Zack Greinke a 2-0 lead.

Randy Arozarena lined a 3-2 curveball into the left field seats to tie the game, 2-2 in the fourth.

The Astros answered in the fifth, turning around some of Glasnow's fastballs on a single by Martin Maldonado and a tape measure blast by George Springer. Springer found the fourth and highest deck of the Western Metal Supply Company behind the left field stands for a 4-2 Houston advantage. It was his 18th career postseason home run.

The Rays mounted a sixth-inning threat, loading the bases with two outs. Greinke allowed two runs in six innings and won the game. Cristian Javier made his first ALCS appearance, mowing down six Rays. Ryan Pressly survived a Willy Adames RBI double in the ninth, getting the final three outs for his first save of the ALCS in a 4-3 win.

Greinke met with General Manager James Click shortly after making these comments after Game 4: "It was nice having someone have confidence in me. Because since I've been here, they haven't seemed to have confidence in my ability." Greinke was pulled while dominating Washington in Game 7 of the 2019 World Series for 6 1/3 innings. He felt that in addition to that game "there's probably a dozen examples if you look back at it." Click said Greinke "wanted clarity on his role going forward." Greinke had one more year on his contract.

Game 5 brought a bullpen day for both teams. Dusty Baker was forced to use his bullpen as Tampa Bay often did due to Framber Valdez needing one more day of rest to give him his usual four days between starts. He selected Luis Garcia as his starter. It was Garcia's first playoff appearance. Garcia had not pitched since September 27.

He opened a parade of five rookie pitchers for Houston – tying a playoff game record. After Garcia's two scoreless innings, Blake Taylor, Enoli Paredes, Andre Scrubb and Brooks Raley followed. The five combined for 6 2/3 innings and allowed only two runs.

George Springer homered off the balcony on the third deck of the Western Metal Supply Company on the first pitch from Tampa Bay starter John Curtiss.

Carlos Correa ran off the field toward the dugout after the top of the ninth, telling Jose Altuve he was "about to end it." He repeated that prediction to Dusty Baker before stepping up to the on-deck circle. Then Correa ended the game with a 416-foot home run to center field off Tampa Bay closer Nick Anderson with one out in the ninth, 4-3. It was Correa's second career postseason walk-off home run, and he stood at home plate to watch the ball carry 416 feet.

It was the first time a team had started and ended a postseason game with home runs. Springer and Correa were playing their 61st playoff game together. Both players pointed up to a suite at the top of the stadium, where their third base coach was applauding. Gary Pettis, despite getting treatments for multiple myeloma blood cancer, was allowed to attend the game.

Correa's walk-off home run went in the team's record books behind Alan Ashby in 1981 against the Dodgers in the Division Series, Jeff Kent against the Cardinals in the 2004 NLCS, Chris Burke against Atlanta in the 2005 Division Series, Altuve against the Yankees in Game 6 of the 2019 ALCS, and Correa's own blast in extra innings in Game 2 of that ALCS against the Yankees. The Astros became only the fourth team to force a sixth game after trailing 3-0 in a postseason series. Only the 2004 Red Sox came all the way back to win in seven games.

Game 6: Old school manager, old school call. Sacrifice bunt in the fifth inning, trailing 1-0. Martin Maldonado, batting ninth, sacrificed the runners to second and third for the first out in the inning.

Maldonado informed Dusty Baker before he batted that he would be putting down a bunt if the first two batters reached base. George Springer punched a two-run ground ball single through the right side off Diego Castillo to give the Astros their first lead, and they went on to win, 7-4.

Castillo had not allowed a run in 13 career postseason innings, but the Astros scored four times in their biggest inning of the series. Coach Gary Pettis had challenged Springer every day during the season in batting practice to hit a ground ball to where Pettis was standing, to the right of second base. Springer could not do it in batting practice. But he did it against a mid-90s sinker at a crucial time in a playoff elimination game.

Blake Snell had a 1-0 lead in the fifth despite struggling to find the strike zone. With no outs, Manager Kevin Cash walked to the mound and took Snell out of the game. The Rays bullpen had not allowed any inherited runners to score in the entire postseason. The 2019 Cy Young winner was enraged, shouting toward the center field wall when he saw Cash coming to the mound and again yelling as he walked to the bench. Cash brought in Castillo, and the game changed.

Winning pitcher Framber Valdez threw 52 curveballs of his 101 total pitches. The Rays swung at 24 of them, missing 15 entirely. The 15 swings and misses on a curve were the most in the pitch-tracking era (since 2008). He allowed one run in six innings.

Although the Astros had become only the second major league team in history of 39 to force a seventh game after losing the first three in a best-of-seven series, they still had to win one more.

Did you know...

Mike Scott would have been the Game 7 starter if there had been a seventh game in the 1986 NLCS between the Astros and the Mets. The Mets avoided Scott, who had dominated them in the series, by winning Game 6.

Game 7

Charlie Morton vs. Lance McCullers, Jr. Both had a history of Game 7 excellence. McCullers started Game 7 of the 2017 World Series at Dodger Stadium. Morton relieved him. Together, they stopped the Dodgers and won a World Series. McCullers pitched in relief in Game 7 of the ALCS that year against the Yankees, saving the game for Morton in a 4-0 shutout. In the process, he threw 24 straight curveballs. Given the Rays' struggles hitting that pitch, there was a chance something like that could happen again.

Morton had beaten McCullers, Jr. in Game 2 of this series, 4-2.

Since the ALCS went to a best-of-seven format in 1985, this was the eighth Game 7. Each of these teams had won its only ALCS Game 7. Tampa Bay beat Boston in 2008, 3-1. Houston beat the New York Yankees, 4-0 in 2017 on the Morton-McCullers collaboration.

Houston's Game 7 History

2004 NLCS

St. Louis 5, Houston 2

The Astros led 2-1 in the sixth with Roger Clemens on the mound. Scott Rolen turned the game around with a three-run homer. Jim Edmonds made an incredible diving catch in left center field on a drive by Brad Ausmus with two men on base. The Astros had led the series, 3-2 but lost the final two games at St. Louis.

2017 ALCS

Houston 4, New York Yankees 0

Charlie Morton and Lance McCullers, Jr. shut out the Yankees. McCullers went four innings for the save. Evan Gattis provided a fourth-inning home run. Brian McCann drove in two insurance runs.

The Astros had trailed in the series, 3-2. They won all four of their home games. In a combined 108 pitches by Morton and McCullers, 65 were curveballs.

2017 WORLD SERIES

Houston 5, Los Angeles 1

Houston jumped on the scoreboard with five runs in the first two innings. George Springer opened the game with a double off loser Yu Darvish. Springer added a two-run homer in the second, his fifth of the World Series. McCullers was pulled after 2 1/3 innings after setting a World Series record by hitting four batters. Five pitchers worked in the game, with Morton sealing the win with four innings of relief. He was the winning pitcher.

2019 WORLD SERIES

Washington 6, Houston 2

Houston took a 2-0 lead to the seventh behind a dazzling Zack Greinke. Anthony Rendon homered for Washington to cut the lead to 2-1. Juan Soto walked, prompting a pitching change by Manager AJ Hinch. Will Harris entered the game and allowed a home run off the right field foul pole to Howie Kendrick. Washington took a 3-2 lead and went on to win to complete a rare World Series with the road team winning every game.

ALCS 2020 Game 7

Charlie Morton established control of the game early. He took the mound with a 3-0 record and an ERA of 0.69 in playoff elimination games. Morton had a 2-0 lead by the end of the first inning. Randy Arozarena struck again, bashing a two-run homer off Lance McCullers, Jr. after Manuel Margot was hit by a pitch.

Mike Zunino added a solo shot on a high curveball in the second, giving Morton a 3-0 lead that looked more like 9-0 the way he was mowing down the Astros.

Morton retired 14 in a row through 5 1/3 innings. The Astros trailed 4-0 in the seventh but made a late rally with a two-run single in the eighth by Correa off Pete Fairbanks. Fairbanks whiffed Bregman with two on to keep the Rays in front, 4-2. The Rays won Game 7 by that score and headed for the World Series for the second time in their history.

The Astros headed into the offseason with big decisions to make.

"The industry has sustained $2.7 billion to $3 billion worth of losses and it may take us years to try to recover from this," said GM James Click. "Our spending is going to be dependent on what we think 2021 is going to look like operationally and what the market bears out as a result of that."

Postscript

Jose Altuve had a spectacular postseason with his bat, despite his throwing troubles. He ripped five home runs during the 13 postseason games, hitting .375 with 11 RBIs and a 1.229 OPS. Altuve boosted his career total through 2020 to 18 postseason long balls – tied with Reggie Jackson and Mickey Mantle for fifth place on the all-time list. He is the all-time leader among second baseman in the postseason in hits (92), home runs (23) and RBIs (49) through 2021.

George Springer continued his postseason explosiveness, driving in 10 runs to pass Derek Jeter as the leadoff man with the most RBIs in postseason history (34). Springer's total of 19 career postseason home runs tied Albert Pujols for fourth place on the all-time list through 2020, behind Manny Ramirez (29), Bernie Williams (22) and Derek Jeter (20). Carlos Correa (.362-6-17) led the club in home runs and RBIs during the postseason in 2020.

Did you know that.....

The first playoff game won by the Astros was in 1980 and Frank LaCorte was the winning pitcher.

Chapter 5

TRACKING HISTORY

Baseball Comes to Houston

Although the history of major league baseball in Houston started with the first game of the Houston Colt .45s in 1962, the acquisition of a franchise to enter the National League years earlier was a fascinating story by itself.

The saga of baseball in Houston begins prior to 1861. *Houston Baseball: The Early Years 1861-1961* did exhaustive research but was unable to pinpoint the exact date of organized baseball's beginnings in the city. Baseball had been played for quite some time in the Bayou City before 1861. There were reports dating to 1838 of various ball games in the area. Baseball or "town ball" had been played in some form in America since around 1735. The first mention in print of baseball in Texas involved the formation of a club at Galveston February 24, 1859. New Yorker Abner Doubleday was stationed there several years later.

There was a newspaper report about a meeting April 11, 1861 hours before the firing started at Fort Sumter to begin the secession of Southern states from the Union.

By the mid-1880s, baseball took a turn into the professional level in Houston. The Texas League was formed. It included teams in Houston, Galveston, San Antonio, Ft. Worth, Dallas, Austin and Waco. They played a 30-game schedule. One of the biggest challenges at the professional level was the constant presence of gamblers who would pay players to fix games. The new league was supposed to police bribing players to fix games, but it didn't.

By 1888, a new Texas League brought a full-time professional team to Houston and cleaned up the gambling issues. The Houston Babies were born. The Babies won the Texas League championship in 1889 – the first professional sports title for the city. The Texas League ceased play in 1900 and 1901, but reformed in 1903. By 1896 the team's name changed to Buffaloes. That name stuck.

By 1921, the St. Louis Cardinals formed an alliance with the Houston Buffaloes that was to last for decades and benefit both organizations. The Buffs had a working agreement with the St. Louis Browns earlier in the century. After winning four Texas League championships, the team was sold for more than $200,000. Houston fielded subpar teams after that through 1920, when they were sold again to a local group headed by John Crooker.

About the time that Houston was upgraded to Class A status in 1921, St. Louis Cardinals General Manager Branch Rickey was setting up a minor league system that would become the industry standard. The Cardinals bought the Buffaloes around 1922, although the arrangement was kept quiet until about 1925. The Texas League threatened to intervene in the sale until the Cardinals agreed to build a new stadium in Houston. At the time, Commissioner Kenesaw Mountain Landis was attempting to prevent major league clubs from establishing farm systems. But Rickey prevailed in a precursor to his involvement in Houston's successful effort to secure a major league franchise 35 years later!

The Cardinals started an affiliation with the Buffaloes that would last until 1958. A long string of championships and development of major league stars who climbed the farm system ladder through Houston began.

In the winter of 1927 architects designed a 12,000-seat stadium on Cullen Boulevard. Buff Stadium, a couple of miles east of downtown Houston, was ready for the opening of the 1928 season. Setting the tone for Colt Stadium in 1962, Buff Stadium became known as a hitters' graveyard.

The star players moved through Houston on their way to major league excellence. Jerome "Dizzy" Dean, Joe "Ducky" Medwick, Howie Pollet, Wilmer "Vinegar Bend" Mizell, Enos Slaughter, Ken Boyer and Solly Hemus all entertained the Houston fans.

In 1946 Houston advanced to AA status under new owner Allen J. Russell. Russell had worked his way up from parking attendant. The Buffs even outdrew the St. Louis Browns in 1947. The Buffs drew 401,282 fans in 1948. When the Chicago Cubs placed their farm club in Houston, Billy Williams and Ron Santo played there.

Sportswriter George Kirksey arrived in Houston in 1946 after World War II. He opened a public relations firm and met many of the power brokers of the Houston economy. Among them were Craig Cullinan and R.E. "Bob" Smith. Kirksey was interested in financial backers for a Houston major league franchise. He immersed himself in the Houston Little League program as he did promotional work for the Houston Rotary Club.

Kirksey made an early bid to purchase the St. Louis Cardinals in 1952, nearly landing the team from financially troubled owner Fred Saigh for $5 million. Word of the negotiations leaked in St. Louis, and August A. Busch stepped in to buy the team and keep it in St. Louis. He changed the name of Buff Stadium to Busch Stadium, moving the fences in 20 feet closer. By 1958, attendance was down in the Texas League and in Houston. The Cardinals sold the Houston Buffs and Buff/Busch Stadium. Houston had new independent ownership and moved up to AAA status in the American Association. There was speculation that a major league team might be on the horizon for Houston.

Kirksey was still hopeful of attracting a team to move to Houston after the St. Louis Browns moved to Baltimore in 1954. He aligned with Cullinan, an heir to Texaco. The two of them campaigned tirelessly for major league baseball in Houston, forming a syndicate of 17 investors to pursue their dream. They named the company the Houston Sports Association in 1958 when their investors grew to 28. The HSA made a $4 million bid to buy the Cleveland Indians, but were turned away again.

Rebuffed by major league owners unwilling to expand to Houston, the HSA attracted Harris County Judge and former Houston Mayor Roy Hofheinz to its group. Hofheinz was a dynamic orator and well-connected politician who had campaigned for Lyndon Johnson. Hofheinz and R.E. "Bob" Smith were close friends. Smith had a net worth of nearly a billion dollars, according to some reports. He and Hofheinz controlled real estate holdings in Houston.

Did you know...

After Dizzy Dean left Houston and became a star for the St. Louis Cardinals, he pitched in the 1934 World Series. Dean was struck in the head by a throw while sliding into second. The next day Dean told reporters, "They X-rayed my head and found nothing."

R.E. "Bob" Smith and Judge Roy Hofheinz (L-R)

The Houston group continued to meet with major league owners, showing off a scale model of an air-conditioned, domed stadium to demonstrate that the hot weather could be defeated in Houston. That was one of the concerns in the offices of Major League Baseball. Another was the doubt that a city in the South would support baseball. St. Louis was the furthest major league city west of the Mississippi River prior to the late 1950s. A team in Houston would cut into the vast territory of the Cardinals. But several other cities were mounting bids for their own teams – New York, Denver, Minneapolis and Toronto among them. New York attorney William Shea was pushing hard for a National League team.

The Continental League

Turning elsewhere, the HSA aligned itself with a group threatening to form a new third league, the Continental League. By 1960 Branch Rickey had left St. Louis and joined the Continental League as its prospective president. His clout and the threat of a legislative assault on the antitrust exemption of Major League Baseball threw a scare into the major leagues. Toronto, New York, Minneapolis and Denver joined Atlanta, Dallas-Ft. Worth and Buffalo in the proposed league.

Senator Estes Kefauver of Tennessee chaired a subcommittee investigating the application of antitrust laws to all professional sports. With the political clout of Texas Senator Lyndon Johnson also a factor, the National League caved in to the pressure and awarded two new franchises to begin in 1962. Houston and New York got the expansion teams. National League baseball returned to New York for the first time since 1957, when the Brooklyn Dodgers and New York Giants moved to the West Coast.

The official announcement about the National League expanding to Houston and New York came October 17, 1960. The teams were named the Houston Colt .45s and the New York Mets. They were scheduled to start in 1962.

The American League expanded to Los Angeles and Washington in 1961. The old Washington Senators moved to Minneapolis-St. Paul to become the Twins while Washington gained an expansion franchise and named it the Senators. Again. The HSA bought out the Buffs' ownership group, ending minor league baseball in Houston for decades.

The Continental League dissolved. George Kirksey said, "If the Continental League is dead, it is the livest ghost walking the baseball orchards. It was a wonderful solution to a difficult problem and reflects credit to the men of three leagues."

The HSA turned its attention to building a temporary stadium on South Main for the Colt .45s in 1962. The hook that landed them the franchise, the domed stadium, was on the drawing board for the future.

It would not be ready until 1965 because of construction delays. Gabe Paul of the Cincinnati Reds was hired as the first general manager of the team.

Roy Hofheinz became the key decision-maker for the Colt .45s. He overrode some of Paul's decisions, leading to Paul's quick exit from Houston. Paul had informally offered broadcast rights for the team for $375,000, but Hofheinz nullified that effort and set a figure of $1,500,000 without Paul's approval.

Hofheinz also steamrolled Paul over the first home for the team. Paul wanted to use old Busch Stadium, but Hofheinz opted for a temporary Colt Stadium so the fans could see the construction of the domed stadium while they watched the team play. After Paul departed, Paul Richards took over as general manager.

Colt Stadium

The expansion draft in October of 1961 was rigged by baseball authorities to prevent the Colt .45s and Mets from acquiring many respectable players from the player pool stocked by all of the established teams in the National League.

Bob Aspromonte of the Los Angeles Dodgers was considered to be the best player picked by the Houston franchise. He turned out to be one of the best players on the team and a fan favorite, but many of the other expansion draft choices were simply placeholders. Richards emphasized pitching and defense with his player acquisitions. He ordered the grass on the field to be grown long and the fences to be distant with lights dimmed to suppress offense, because the Colts were lacking in that category.

In the expansion draft with the Mets, the Colt .45s went heavily for more inexperienced players. In later drafts, the expansion teams were able to fill out their rosters entirely.

More of the expensive veteran players were selected by the Mets. The team started with four picks at $125,000 per player. In the first Houston group were Phillies pitcher Dick "Turk" Farrell, Giants second baseman Joe Amalfitano, Pirates catcher Hal Smith and Braves outfielder Al Spangler. The Colt .45s then picked sixteen players at a cost of $75,000 each. Three more players were added at $50,000 each. Amalfitano was impressed at the cost of his contract. He told a reporter, "I will have to go out and get another life insurance policy. I am worth more than I thought." The player pool draft cost the Houston team a little over $1.8 million.

Both the Mets and Colt .45s were concerned about the draft process that was announced by National League President Ford Frick. General Manager Paul Richards said he was happy with the results of the draft. After complaining about the process at the end of the season, Richards had a change of heart about the draft. "If I had known it was going to be this, I wouldn't have said a word." Richards said the team focused on a strong defense.

Did you know that....

The Colt .45s played in 21 doubleheaders in their first season in 1962.

1962-64 Colt .45s home uniform

COLT .45s ERA

The Colt .45s hired a former member of the Cubs' College of Coaches, Harry Craft, to be their first field manager. The Chicago Cubs rotated their managers between the major league club and the minor league teams, concentrating on a program of consistent instruction at all levels.

Craft had most recently been the manager of the Houston Buffs minor league team in the American Association, the Cubs' top affiliate. Craft previously had been the manager of the American League Kansas City Athletics.

The Cubs rotated Craft from the major league roster down to their triple A team in Houston July 15, 1961. The Cubs had an interesting leadership approach for a couple of seasons but they abandoned this practice. Craft was the manager of the Cubs for 16 games in 1961. Craft was named manager at Houston in mid-September 1961.

1962

With the initial group of players from the expansion pool supplemented by some free agent signings, the Colt .45s were handicapped. While they shocked the Chicago Cubs by sweeping them to open their inaugural season at Colt Stadium, the season was a long one. Outfielder Roman Mejias provided some power, beginning with a pair of three-run homers in the first game. Bob Aspromonte provided some thrills with his power hitting and excellent glovework at third base. He got the first hit and scored the first run for the Colt .45s.

GM Paul Richards was looking beyond 1962, dealing Opening Day starter Bobby Shantz to St. Louis May 6 for outfielder Carl Warwick. Shantz, who beat the Cubs 11-2 in the opener at Colt Stadium with a complete game, was pitching on fumes near the end of his career, and Warwick was 25 years old. Dick "Turk" Farrell took over as the team's ace pitcher

Roy Hofheinz, who celebrated his 50th birthday with the Opening Day win, insisted that the Colt .45s players wear specially tailored western suits on road trips. They had tooled leather boots, western slacks and jackets and Stetson hats – all in powder blue. The players soon grew tired of the traveling garb, with constant comments from airport passersby about being part of a rodeo or a cowboy singing group. A fan stole Bob Lillis' hat off his head on a road trip. After that, other players claimed their hats had been stolen also. Finally, Hofheinz gave in halfway through the 1962 season, and the cowboy suits disappeared almost as fast as the Edsel.

One oddity on the field involved catcher Hal Smith, who was wearing a huge mitt to catch the knuckleball of Bob Tiefenauer against the Pirates. With the game tied 6-6 in the seventh inning, Smokey Burgess hit a fly ball to left field and Roberto Clemente tagged at third to score. Roman Mejias caught the ball and Smith tossed his mitt away and quickly put on Tiefenauer's glove after the pitcher tossed it to him.

He tagged out Clemente, explaining afterwards that he never would have been able to catch the throw from Mejias in the oversized catcher's mitt.

The heat and humidity of Colt Stadium wore on the players. The outfielders carried mosquito repellant spray cans in their back pockets. The nearby domed stadium construction had a huge hole in the ground for the playing field, which was below ground level. It filled up with rain water, forming a breeding ground for mosquitoes known as "Elliott's Lake," named after county judge Bill Elliott. Players estimated they lost several pounds during some of the games. Spectators were being carried off into ambulances with heat exhaustion. The extreme heat caused the National League to approve Sunday night games in 1963 to avoid more problems.

The Philadelphia Phillies rolled over the Colt .45s 17 times in a row before Houston finally won the final game of the season series. The Colts finished with a record of 64-96. The lackluster Houston offense provided only 464 runs. Turk Farrell was 10-20 despite a 3.02 ERA! Roman Mejias was the club's home run leader with 24 and RBI leader with 76. The Colts finished ahead of the New York Mets (40-120) and the Chicago Cubs (59-103).

1962 MVP

Bob Lillis was named the first MVP of the Colt .45s. Lillis was a veteran infielder who played for the Dodgers before spending the end of the 1961 season with the Cardinals. Nicknamed "Flea", Lillis was a steady presence for the team at shortstop, playing 99 games at the position along with significant action at second base as well. Lillis hit .249 for the team with one homer after gaining a regular job in June.

General Manager Paul Richards described him as "not only an outstanding player and great hustler, but he is a great inspiration to our younger players. He has a quiet leadership quality that is rare among ballplayers." Those leadership qualities served him as he joined the team's front office in player development following his playing career. Lillis joined the major league coaching staff and was the first former franchise player to become manager of the team in 1982.

1963

The 1963 season did not finish much better for Houston. The Colt .45s were 66-96. Turk Farrell led the club with 14 victories. Tough-luck Ken Johnson finished 11-17 despite a 2.65 earned run average. Don Nottebart pitched a no-hitter against the Phillies, winning 4-1. Juan Marichal of San Francisco no-hit the Colts, 1-0. The Colts made major league history by putting an all-rookie lineup on the field September 27, 1963.

Here is their lineup with the ages of the players:

P-Jay Dahl   17

C-Jerry Grote   20

1B-Rusty Staub   19

2B-Joe Morgan   20

3B-Glenn Vaughan   19

SS-Sonny Jackson   19

LF-Brock Davis   19

CF-Jimmy Wynn   21

RF-Aaron Pointer   21

Rusty Staub, Joe Morgan and Jimmy Wynn gave fans a preview of three superstars for the future during their debut seasons. Staub was Houston's first "bonus baby." GM Paul Richards braved Hurricane Carla to sign 17-year-old Staub in New Orleans for $132,000 in September of 1961.

1963 MVP

Hal Woodeshick was named the team's MVP following the 1963 season. Woodeshick won 11 games in relief with a stingy 1.97 ERA. He also picked up ten saves, although saves were not yet recognized as an official statistic. He became the first franchise member to receive consideration for the Cy Young Award, but it went to Sandy Koufax.

Woodeshick lost 16 games in 1962 as a member of the Colt .45s starting rotation. He found his place in the bullpen in Houston, getting 36 unofficial saves in his seasons in Houston.

1964

As the domed stadium continued to rise beyond the right center field fence at Colt Stadium, the 1964 season began on a sober note. Just before the opener, pitcher Jim Umbricht died of cancer.

Aging veterans Pete Runnels, Nellie Fox and Don Larsen were former star players who were added to the youthful group pushing its way to the majors. Fox tutored fellow second baseman Joe Morgan, decades before both of them became Hall of Famers. The Colts finished 66-96 again, and original Manager Harry Craft was fired. In April, Ken Johnson pitched a no-hitter but lost 1-0 to Cincinnati when the Reds scored their run on two errors. Johnson finished 11-16 despite a 3.63 ERA.

151

Strapping first baseman Walt Bond bashed 20 home runs and drove in 85 runs, but leukemia claimed him a few years later in 1967. Larry Dierker made his major league debut on his 18th birthday, striking out Willie Mays and Jim Ray Hart.

In the last game at Colt Stadium, Bob Bruce blanked the Dodgers, 1-0 in 12 innings for his 15th win, setting the club record.

1964 MVP

Third baseman Bob Aspromonte was voted the Colt .45s MVP following the 1964 season. Aspromonte led the team with his .280 batting average and was second on the team with a dozen homers. He also led the National League in fielding percentage at third base. Aspromonte finished ahead of future Hall of Famers Ron Santo of the Cubs and Eddie Mathews of the Braves. The 12 home runs were a career high. Aspromonte set a franchise record by appearing in 157 games. Following the season at the winter meetings, Aspromonte was popular in trade talks. He was mentioned in several rumors swirling around the Dodgers massive slugger Frank Howard. Colt .45s owner R.E. "Bob" Smith squashed any movement of Aspro and Howard was traded to the Washington Senators.

Aspromonte developed a special friendship with a nine-year-old fan from Arkansas named Billy Bradley, who was blinded by lightning as he ran off the field to a water fountain during a Little League game.

When Bradley met Aspromonte at a Houston hospital in 1962 before the first of his three surgeries to restore his sight, he requested a home run that night. Aspro the Astro, as he was later called, was reluctant to promise such a gift but he delivered. He later came through on two more occasions for Bradley with grand slams upon request before games. Bradley eventually regained his sight and pitched a no-hitter in amateur baseball, dedicating it to Aspromonte.

Aspromonte held the club record for career grand slams with six until Carlos Lee broke it in 2011.

Did you know...

Bob Bruce had a winning record (30-27) for the three years of the Colt .45s despite the team's 196-288 history, including 96 losses in all three seasons. Bruce was 15-9 in the final year (1964) of the Colt .45s with a 2.76 ERA.

1965

EARLY ASTRODOME YEARS

The building known as "The Eighth Wonder of the World" opened to great fanfare in 1965. Now it sits empty, with an uncertain future. Many would prefer that it be demolished, but that is not allowed for a building on the National Register of Historic Places. Houston is a modern city, by some measurements the most diverse in the United States. Few residents in 2021 were in the city in 1965, and many do not study the history of buildings. There are few historic buildings remaining in Houston. The usual treatment is to knock down an old building and replace it with something much larger.

The Astrodome, originally known as the Harris County Domed Stadium, changed sports stadiums for decades to come, introducing a sports palace with air conditioning and allowing the scheduling of events throughout the calendar with no concerns about weather. The moveable seats allowed them to be repositioned from a baseball configuration to a football field alignment. The Houston Livestock and Rodeo Show flourished for decades in the Astrodome, with the vast parking lot outside expansive enough to allow room for a carnival, the rodeo cook-off and parking for patrons. Concerts, the UCLA-Houston basketball game in 1968, the Bobby Riggs-Billie Jean King tennis match, heavyweight fights and many other historic events graced the Astrodome, which put Houston on the international map.

Tal Smith, who spent almost 60 years in professional baseball, joined the Houston organization in 1960. Gabe Paul asked Smith to accompany him from the Cincinnati Reds to the Colt .45s when Paul accepted the general manager position. By 1963, Paul had left for Cleveland. Smith was about to join him there when Judge Roy Hofheinz asked him to stay and serve as the liaison and project manager for the HSA during the domed stadium construction project. Smith reminded Hofheinz that he was not an architect or engineer. Hofheinz convinced him that he could do the job. Smith wrote in SABR publication *Dome Sweet Dome*, "Air-conditioned, covered stadiums with upholstered seats and unobstructed sight lines, entertaining video displays, restaurants and clubs, luxurious suites and other amenities are the norm today, but who knows when they might have come about if not for Judge Hofheinz's novel concept and those who carried out his vision."

Former Astros President and General Manager Tal Smith

Courtesy Houston Astros Baseball Club

Walter O'Malley, Craig Cullinan, Gabe Paul and R.E. "Bob" Smith (L-R)

Walter P. Moore and Associates engineered the roof, selecting steel trusses to support the roof structure with a lamella structure chosen because of its spider web network of trusses. The roof had to handle sustained wind velocities of 135 miles per hour with gusts up to 165. Kenneth E. Zimmerman devised a pair of innovations that set the Astrodome apart from any long-span structure. Zimmerman used the "knuckle" column and the "star" column to solve some complex problems.

Hofheinz was possessed by a vision of the Colosseum in Rome from his visit there. The ancient Romans constructed a tent-like covering above the Colosseum to shield spectators from the sun's heat. "Looking back on those ancient days, I figured that a round facility with a cover was what we needed in the United States, and that Houston would be the perfect spot because of its rainy, humid weather," said Hofheinz.

Roy Hofheinz at the Colosseum in Rome

The execution of Hofheinz's dream was not without drama. Hurricane Cindy hit the Texas coast in 1963, with 90mph winds in Victoria, 125 miles southwest of the construction site. Houston did not feel the effects of the hurricane to that extent, sparing Hofheinz from considerable embarrassment if the project had to be scuttled.

In February of 1964, all of the dome's spans had been completed and all the trusses and frameworks were in place. The roof was liberated from the erection towers, and the 7.5-million-pound lamella dome came to rest entirely on the stadium walls. All was well. The stadium had sunk 4 inches, as predicted by the engineers, under the combined weight of the roof and the frameworks. As the jacks were removed atop each of the 37 erection towers, the engineers got varying results from the daily tests they performed to check the structural soundness of the building. The County Commissioners began to doubt the design.

There were some anxious moments until Kenneth Zimmerman realized that the differences were caused by the different temperatures of the frameworks as they moved from sunshine into shadow. The problem was solved by making the checks at the same time of day.

When Hofheinz and his partner, Bob Smith, were trying to decide what the team's new nickname would be, they narrowed the choice to Stars or Astros. The NASA program in Houston was developing astronauts, and the two men saw a natural association. Hofheinz told Smith to pick a name and Smith chose Astros.

The Colt .45s nickname had to be shed anyway because Colt Industries, the conglomerate that included the gunmaker for the Colt .45 revolver, was threatening to obtain royalties for official Colt .45 merchandise.

When the newly-named Astros moved into the newly-named Astrodome, Larry Dierker was a part of the team. He had grown up in Los Angeles, and when he went to Dodger Stadium he thought it was heaven.

When he and his teammates got their first look at the Astrodome after spring training in 1965, nobody said anything for a while. "Dodger Stadium was a relic; it was old Colt Stadium," wrote Dierker. "We were in the 21st century."

They were looking at a building made with almost 10,000 tons of steel! The tension ring at the heart of the structural design weighed 750 tons.

Dierker pitched in an intrasquad game the next day, and his fielders had a hard time catching pop flies. The glare of the sun through the Lucite panels of the roof made it next to impossible for the fielders to track fly balls. This was the first indication that changes would have to be made in the playing conditions.

The roof panels were painted off-white to block the sun from streaming through.

That tactic worked, but the grass was dying on the field because the sunlight was not reaching it. With the grass getting scarce, the dirt around it was spray-painted green for cosmetics. But the surface of the infield was not up to major league standards. The Astros got through the 1965 season, but Hofheinz was scrambling to find artificial turf to replace the grass.

Tal Smith studied Monsanto's "Chemgrass" that had been developed in 1964 at Moses Brown School in Providence, Rhode Island. It was tested and found acceptable for use in the Astrodome for baseball, football and other purposes. Astroturf was born, and it swept through the world of multipurpose stadiums just in time to provide solid playing conditions through rain. The Astros played on it to open the 1966 season.

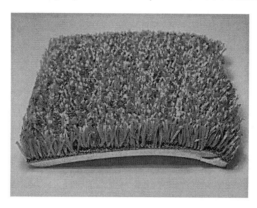

Lawnmowers were out. Brooms and vacuum cleaners were in.

After a season playing on painted dirt in the Astrodome, the team played its first games in 1966 on the Monsanto-invented "Astroturf". The players universally noticed that the turf made the ball play much faster than they had experienced playing on natural grass.

The Astros and Dodgers played an exhibition series on it in mid-March. The Astros scheduled seven games in the Astrodome to try to get the new surface in ready shape for the National League season. Dodger second baseman Jim Lefebvre said that they had made lots of improvements on it since the spring training game. "The ball still comes off of it very fast. But I've noticed lots of improvement off of the dirt. They've done a lot of work on that."

In the first series, there were a few problems. Bunts usually rolled toward the mound, since the field wasn't crowned.

The first hop had lots of top spin on it, making it more difficult to field. And the dirt in the infield tended to be lumpy since it was not very deep.

Astros officials had worked on creating a softer surface underneath the green carpet to reduce the speed of ground balls through the infield. Another mat was laid down on the cement floor before the Astroturf was laid down for the regular season.

Veteran infielder-turned-coach Nellie Fox liked the new surface and predicted correctly that lots of stadiums would use it. The Astrodome still at this point had a Bermuda grass outfield. The plan was to put Astroturf there by mid-season if the turf was successful, and it was.

It was so successful, in fact, that the carpet in Manager Grady Hatton's office was removed. Astroturf also found a home there.

Tal Smith had to swing into action with some innovative people who developed Astroturf. It became the model for athletic fields of the future for decades. Stadiums in Pittsburgh, Philadelphia, Cincinnati and St. Louis turned to Astroturf.

The turf could be adapted from baseball to football to accommodate both sports, relieving ownership of the need to care for grass fields.

After piloting the club through its first three seasons, Harry Craft was dismissed as manager in 1964 and replaced by Luman Harris. Harris presided over a slightly worse season than the .45s had in their three 96-loss campaigns, finishing 65-97 in his only full season as skipper. Grady Hatton took the reins for the next two and a half seasons.

With all of the focus on the Dome, the team's 65-97 record in 1965 was secondary. Naturally it was a big hit at the box office – but the hit was the building. The team itself was weak, but the attendance was more than two million! The deadening influence of an indoor stadium with air conditioning robbed many players of home runs and extra base hits. Mickey Mantle of the Yankees led off the April 9 exhibition opener before a packed house and got the first hit.

Catcher Ron Brand, who got the first hit for Houston, asked Mantle to take the first pitch so the ball could be sent to the Hall of Fame in Cooperstown, New York.

Mantle said he was too nervous to swing anyway. Mantle also hit the first home run in the Astrodome, but Houston won 2-1 in the 12th when Nellie Fox singled in Jimmy Wynn.

When National League play began there, Richie Allen swatted the initial long ball in a 2-0 shutout by Chris Short of the Phillies.

Bob Aspromonte hit the first Houston home run in the Astrodome in regular season play April 24th off Vernon Law. Turk Farrell was able to get by with an 11-11 record with a 3.50 ERA. Willie Mays clouted his 500th career home run in the Astrodome September 13 off Don Nottebart, a massive blast estimated at 440 feet into the centerfield bleachers. Joe Morgan set a longstanding club record with a six-hit game July 8 against Milwaukee.

1965 MVP

The Astros MVP in 1965 was the Toy Cannon, Jimmy Wynn. Wynn was a catalyst for the Astros offense and settled in centerfield for the team. Wynn spent most of the season in the third spot, but Manager Luman Harris moved him all around the lineup. Wynn slugged 22 homers to lead the team, becoming the third member of the franchise to hit 20 homers. He also finished third in the National League after Maury Wills and Lou Brock with his 43 stolen bases. Wynn's stolen base number was even more significant because it equaled the previous record for the entire team!

Only 23 years old, Wynn became one of the young stars in the league. Teammate Joe Morgan led the National League in walks, but Wynn was fourth in the league with his 84 bases on balls. Surprisingly, this was the only time that Wynn was selected team MVP.

Jimmy Wynn grew up near Crosley Field in Cincinnati, waiting outside the stadium for home run balls from Reds sluggers Frank Robinson and Vada Pinson. He signed with the Reds, but Houston acquired him in the November 1962 first-year draft, one of the best moves in franchise history.

Wynn hit a home run onto the freeway outside Crosley Field as an Astro.

1965-70 Houston Astros home uniform

Did you know that….

Catcher Johnny Edwards played in a franchise record 151 games behind the plate in 1969. That still stands as the Houston record. Brad Ausmus caught 143 games in 2006. Craig Biggio caught 139 games in 1991.

Houston's Amateur Draft History

Baseball instituted the amateur draft in 1965. Before the draft, teams had been in bidding wars with other franchises to try to sign the best amateur players. In the few years after baseball's first expansion, the price tags rose for the number of players who were signed as "Bonus Babies." Rick Reichardt signed with the Los Angeles Angels as a 21-year-old from the University of Wisconsin for a reported $200,000.

The game's top player, Willie Mays, made only $85,000. Baseball decided to join the other professional sports leagues with a draft for new talent for the 1965 season, using the team won-loss records to determine the draft order. Until the 21st century, the worst team in each league alternated with the first choice.

Five times in franchise history, the Astros were awarded the first pick in the draft with mixed results. After the decline of the team in 1975, the Astros picked atop the board and selected a college pitcher. Floyd Bannister, a left-handed starting pitcher from Arizona State, was their pick. Bannister made only six minor league starts for the team before making the team in the spring of 1977. Bannister started at rookie ball, and was moved to Double and Triple A during his quick run through the farm system.

Bannister made 363 starts in his 15-year major league career, but only a handful were in Houston. He won 11 games over two seasons but was traded to the Seattle Mariners for All-Star shortstop and former Houston high school star Craig Reynolds after the 1978 season.

The Astros next picked atop the draft board in 1993. They selected the college player of the year, Phil Nevin of Cal State Fullerton, as their top pick. The Astros are remembered for passing on Michigan high school star Derek Jeter, but four other teams passed also. He lasted until the sixth pick. Nevin went to AAA Tucson. After being called up in June 1995, Nevin was put in the fifth spot in the Astros' lineup behind Jeff Bagwell.

In his first major league at-bat, Nevin knocked in James Mouton and it looked as if the Astros had found a new third baseman.

By the end of the month, Nevin's average had dropped to .073 after a rough 0-for-26 stretch and he was returned to Tucson. He reacted angrily when told of his demotion. He was traded the next season to the Detroit Tigers in a deadline deal for closer Mike Henneman. Nevin played for several seasons in the majors but never reached the stardom that was projected for him.

The Astros hit paydirt with their next top draft choice. In 2012 in new General Manager Jeff Luhnow's first draft, the Astros selected Puerto Rican shortstop Carlos Correa. Many draft lists had Georgia high school outfielder Byron Buxton as the top player, but the Astros found the future All-Star and Rookie of the Year in Correa. Correa signed below his assigned slot value for the first overall pick, which allowed the Astros to use some of the savings to sign another pick they had later in the first round - Lance McCullers, Jr. Both were integral parts of the Astros' championship teams. Under the new slotting system, players were assigned monetary values, but teams could sign them for less if the players agreed as long as the team did not exceed the total allotted it for the entire draft class.

The Astros also had the top choice in 2013. They took Stanford senior pitcher Mark Appel. Appel had grown up in southwest Houston, and had rejected the Pirates' offer as a junior the year before. Appel progressed up the Astros chain but never made it to the majors, advancing as high as AAA. He was dealt after the 2015 season to the Philadelphia Phillies in a deal that gave the Astros closer Ken Giles. Appel pitched six seasons in the minors.

The final top choice for the Astros was a high school left-hander from California, Brady Aiken, in 2014. Aiken had agreed to a contract with the team, but in the usual pre-signing physical possible elbow issues were discovered and the Astros moved to lower the signing bonus due to the injury risk.

Aiken and the Astros were not able to work out their differences, and he failed to sign. The Indians used their first-round pick in 2015 on Aiken, who needed elbow surgery and never made it to the majors. The Indians released Aiken following the 2021 season.

Since the Astros did not sign Aiken, they received a make-up pick in the 2016 draft. This pick turned out to be a bonanza, when the Astros selected Louisiana State's Alex Bregman.

1966

Astroturf was installed in 1966. Grady Hatton took over as the new manager after Luman Harris was fired. Jim Wynn missed the last two months of the season with an injury, with Rusty Staub stepping up to lead the team in RBIs with 81. Dave Giusti won 15 games, including two one-hitters, for a 72-90 team. Giusti also set a club record that stood for 23 years by driving in six runs in a game, pitching a shutout in that all-around effort. The youthful core of the team was making its impact. Joe Morgan and Sonny Jackson were on the cover of *Sports Illustrated.* Bob Aspromonte cranked his sixth grand slam to beat the Cubs in the last of the ninth, 7-4.

1966 MVP

In 1966, another youngster won the team MVP, Rusty Staub. The New Orleans native had 81 RBIs as a 23-year-old. Staub was already in his fourth season with the Astros. Staub hit a lofty .280, finishing just out of the top ten in the National League in that category. Staub joined Jimmy Wynn in the Astros' young outfield. Staub became a force in right field and picked up 13 outfield assists, which was third among the league's outfielders.

1967

The Astros slid to a 69-93 mark in 1967 – their sixth straight season below a .450 winning percentage. Rookie Don Wilson won ten games, including a Father's Day no-hitter against Atlanta with 15 strikeouts. Cuban Mike Cuellar led the staff with 16 wins, including a 16-strikeout game, and pitched in the All-Star Game.

Jim Wynn launched tape-measure home runs at Cincinnati and Pittsburgh on his way to club records in home runs (37) and RBIs (107). Wynn ripped three home runs in the Astrodome June 15, a franchise first, in a 6-2 win over the Giants. Rusty Staub hit .333 with a league-leading 44 doubles.

Wynn battled baseball's soon to be all-time home run leader, Hank Aaron, for the National League title in 1967. Wynn lost the title by two homers, but it was an impressive performance for the Toy Cannon with 37 homers while playing in the spacious Astrodome. Wynn had missed the end of the 1966 season with a broken wrist, and the power explosion came suddenly.

Wynn hit three homers in the month of April, missing some time with injuries. By the final week of the June he had tied Aaron at 18.

But in Houston there was another home run story. Eddie Mathews slugged the 500th homer of his career that July. The homer off the Giants' Juan Marichal at Candlestick Park made Mathews just the seventh member of the exclusive 500-homer club.

By August 13, Aaron and Wynn continued to pace the league at 29 homers. Wynn had a big weekend series at Dodger Stadium, connecting for four homers. Aaron and Wynn were tied at 37 homers on September 17, but Wynn did not homer again. Aaron hit homers on the 20th and 26th and won the home run title with 39. Orlando Cepeda won the RBI title with 111 and won the league MVP.

Wynn established himself as a power source with the league's best, but he never repeated those numbers in Houston.

The luster of the new Astrodome was no longer enough to draw big crowds for the team. Veteran faces were brought in to try to generate more wins.

1967 MVP

The 1967 team MVP was Rusty Staub again. He hit .333, finishing fifth in the National League behind future Hall of Famer Roberto Clemente. Staub also led the league with 44 doubles. Wynn finished 11th in the league in MVP voting while Staub was a distant 22nd. It was, however, the first time that the team had two players place so high in MVP voting. Mike Cuellar was a force, finishing 16-11 with a 3.03 ERA in 246 innings.

After the 1967 season, the Astros traded a couple of their prospects for established players, sending shortstop Sonny Jackson and first baseman Chuck Harrison to the Braves for veteran starter Denny Lemaster and shortstop Denis Menke. Lemaster provided a durable arm in the 1968 season when pitchers dominated hitters. Lemaster joined Don Wilson, Larry Dierker and Dave Giusti in the starting rotation.

1968

The Astros sank to last place in the ten-team National League in 1968, hitting only 66 homers and batting a poor .231 in Harry Walker's first half season as manager. The Astros had lost John Bateman and Ron Brand in the expansion draft to Montreal.

24-inning game

In "The Year of the Pitcher," 1968, Tom Seaver of the Mets and Don Wilson hooked up in a Tax Day pitching duel that turned into a 6:06 marathon, with the Astros winning 1-0 in the 24th inning.

Seaver gave up only two hits to the Astros, a second-inning double to catcher Hal King and a tenth-inning single to Rusty Staub.

The only early chance the Astros had was denied when Mets second baseman Ken Boswell nailed King trying to score on Aspromonte's grounder in the second. Seaver finished his night with ten innings pitched, only three strikeouts and no walks.

Wilson was almost as impressive. Beyond a Seaver single, Wilson also yielded two singles to Ed Kranepool and Art Shamsky.

The bullpens then came into play. Mets Manager Gil Hodges summoned seven relievers to the hill over the next thirteen innings. Astros Manager Grady Hatton made use of four relievers. Before the night was over, Astros reliever Jim Ray pitched seven innings and gave up only one hit while striking out 11 Mets.

Finally, in the 24th inning, Norm Miller led off with a single to right. Bob Aspromonte hit a bases-loaded grounder to Al Weis that went between his legs to allow the game to end. Miller crossed the plate and the latest night game ever played to that point ended at 1:37 a.m. The game was the longest game played without any scoring. It was also the most innings ever played in a night game. It tied the mark for the longest game played with a decision, equalling a record set in 1906.

The Mets utilized 22 of their 25 players, with Tommy Agee and Ron Swoboda going 0-for-10 at the plate. Aspromonte went 0-for-9 for the Astros.

The Astros actually have been part of two of the longest baseball games in major league history. In addition to the 24-inning marathon, the Astros and Dodgers battled for 22 innings and well into the morning hours in 1987.

Bob Gibson led the majors in ERA with a 1.12 record in 1968. Denny McLain won 31 games for Detroit. Houston hosted the All-Star Game.

The National League won the All-Star Game, 1-0 at the Astrodome. Willie Mays scored the only run when he singled in the first inning and came home on a Willie McCovey double play ball.

Grady Hatton was fired mid-season and replaced by Harry "The Hat" Walker. The Astros again limped home with a 72-90 record, in last place.

1968 MVP

Newly acquired shortstop Denis Menke was the Astros MVP for the 1968 season. Menke was moved to second base in the second week of the season after former All-Star Joe Morgan was injured. Menke was a steadying influence on the team, but he hit only .246 with six homers, while both Rusty Staub and Jim Wynn had much better seasons at the plate.

General Manager Spec Richardson went out to acquire more veterans. Right after the World Series, the Astros moved Dave Giusti and catcher Dave Adlesh to the Cardinals for veteran catcher Johnny Edwards.

Edwards proved to be an outstanding handler of the pitching staff and was a welcome addition after being displaced first in Cincinnati by Johnny Bench and then in St. Louis by Tim McCarver a year later.

At the 1968 winter meetings in San Francisco, the Astros were busy trying to get more offense. Mike Cuellar was traded to the Orioles in a deal for former American League Rookie of the Year Curt Blefary. Blefary was slotted to be in one of the corner outfield spots for the next spring.

1969

In January 1969, the Astros sent Rusty Staub to the Montreal Expos for first baseman Donn Clendenon and outfielder Jesus Alou. Clendenon had played for Walker when he previously managed the Pirates. Clendenon refused to report to spring training in Cocoa. He did not want to play for a team in the South. The Astros attempted to have the deal voided and have Staub returned to the Astros. Dodgers owner Walter O'Malley lobbied Astros owner Roy Hofheinz not to pursue it. Reluctantly, the Astros ended up taking pitchers Skip Guinn and Jack Billingham right at opening day. Billingham pitched three seasons for the team, but found his greatest success with the Reds.

The expansion draft and some aggressive trades cost the Astros some excellent players for 1969. In a period of 18 months, the Astros lost such mainstays as Bob Aspromonte, John Bateman, Dave Giusti, Sonny Jackson, Mike Cuellar, Rusty Staub and Claude Raymond. The trade of Cuellar to Baltimore for Curt Blefary was one of the worst in the team's history.

The deal for Rusty Staub to the Expos was equally destructive. The season got off to a disastrous 4-20 start.

Don Wilson, angered by a 10-0 beatdown by Cincinnati in Jim Maloney's April 30 no-hitter, took the mound fired up the next night and shoved a no-hitter down the Reds' throats. Wilson was angered by the Reds' aggressiveness in running up the score, and he let them know he would be going after them.

Despite Cincinnati Manager Dave Bristol shouting from the dugout at him and trying to break his concentration, Wilson maintained his poise and delivered the payback. The Astros regrouped by going 20-6 after their 4-20 start and finished 81-81, with Denis Menke driving in 90 runs as a shortstop.

The player shuffle left the Astros with a hole in the middle of their lineup and at first base. They moved Blefary to first base and had Norm Miller play more in the outfield. The Expos moved Clendenon at the June trading deadline. He became a large piece of the success of the New York Mets and a key contributor to their first championship.

The Astros were also more aggressive targeting players during the season. They made a pair of waiver deals with the expansion Seattle Pilots, receiving pitcher Jim Bouton and former batting champion Tommy Davis to slot into the outfield. The team rallied and was in the hunt until the final days of the season when the Atlanta Braves swept the Astros. After their fifth-place finish, the Astros moved Blefary to the Yankees for another veteran, first baseman Joe Pepitone.

The 1969 season was the first time baseball was played in a split division format. The Astros were assigned to the National League's Western Division. For Houston it was rare to be in the hunt late in the season. The 1969 team was led by a group of potent starting pitchers. Larry Dierker became the team's first 20-game winner and earned an All-Star birth. He had 20 complete games and threw 305 innings!

He was joined by Don Wilson and Denny Lemaster at the top of the rotation and rookie Tom Griffin burst onto the scene to win 11 games. By the last week of August, five teams were within two and a half games of first place Los Angeles. The Astros had never been this close so late in a season.

Two Slams in One Inning

One of the biggest events of the season was the Astros' National League record of two grand slams in the same inning. They took a 5-2 lead into the ninth inning in their game against the Mets at Shea Stadium. Shortstop Denis Menke cleared the bases with a grand slam to open up a 9-2 lead off Cal Koonce.

The Astros continued to rally, sending fourteen men to the plate. Mets skipper Gil Hodges brought on another reliever, Ron Taylor. Houston reliever Fred Gladding got a second at-bat that inning and blooped a single over third baseman Wayne Garrett's head for an RBI single. It was the only hit of Gladding's 13-year career. Jim Wynn took aim at history, hitting his own grand slam. The Astros ended up scoring 11 runs in the ninth and winning the game, 16-3.

The Astros weren't finished. They beat the Mets in the second game of the doubleheader, 11-5. That game was also noteworthy as Astros starter Larry Dierker hit the only homer for the team in the nightcap. Dierker hit his homer off a young reliever from Texas for the Mets, Nolan Ryan.

Previously, only once had a single team hit two grand slams in the same inning. The Minnesota Twins had accomplished it in 1962 by Bobby Allison and Harmon Killebrew against the Cleveland Indians.

Seven Double Plays in a Game

A pitching matchup in 1969 between veteran Denny Lemaster and future Hall of Famer Juan Marichal produced a record-setting performance, with the Astros topping the Giants 3-1. The win completed a three-game sweep.

The Astros turned a National League record-setting seven double-plays, which also tied the Major League mark.

The fielding fest got started when Lemaster loaded the bases in the first inning. He was relieved by Manager Harry Walker. Dooley Womack induced a grounder to shortstop Denis Menke. He went to Joe Morgan at second and on to Curt Blefary at first to retire Jim Ray Hart and end the inning.

In the third, the Giants started another rally with singles by Willie Mays and Jack Hiatt. Dick Dietz hit a grounder to Doug Rader at third. Rader started the around-the-horn double play to stop another San Francisco rally.

The Giants leadoff man Hart reached on a single to start the fourth. Third baseman Bobby Etheridge bounced to Menke at shortstop and the Astros had their third double play grounder in four innings.

 The Astros did it again in the fifth. Marichal led off the inning with a single but was quickly erased by a grounder to Joe Morgan. Morgan then threw to Blefary to retire Frank Johnson and again stop the Giants rally.

In the seventh inning, Astros closer Fred Gladding came in after an error and a walk had put two on for the Giants. Marichal grounded to Menke for another twin killing and the Astros clung to a 2-1 lead.

Giants' pinch-hitter Bob Burda led off the eighth with a single to right. But Ron Hunt hit a grounder the other way, and Blefary turned that into a double play as well.

 Gladding remained in the game in the ninth as the Astros increased their lead to 3-1. Gladding gave up a double and single to put runners on the corners. This time, Gladding got Etheridge to bounce to Morgan at second base. Menke and Blefary completed the turn and the Astros were able to set the double play record and get the win.

The decades of the Sixties closed with only one .500 season for the Colt .45s/Astros.

1969 MVP

In 1969, **Larry Dierker** was selected by the local baseball writers as the team MVP. Dierker was an All-Star for the first time and posted a fine 2.33 ERA that was fifth in the National League. The Astros posted their best record ever at 81-81 for Manager Harry Walker. Dierker was still only 22 years old for most of the season.

174

1970

The Seventies began with a black cloud over the team. Judge Hofheinz had built an amusement park, a convention hall and a hotel to fill out his "Astrodomain." He also bought the Ringling Brothers Barnum and Bailey Circus. With those financial commitments, the baseball team was struggling. Then Hofheinz suffered a stroke.

Spec Richardson made one deadline deal, picking up swingman George Culver from the Cardinals. Richardson made only minor moves as the Astros regressed slightly.

The arrival of 19-year-old superstar Cesar Cedeno lifted spirits. He ascended to the major leagues and showed his exciting promise by hitting .310 at age 19. Cedeno is considered by many Astro historians to be the best athlete in the team's existence. He had blazing speed, a solid arm and tremendous bat-to-ball skills. Cedeno hit for average and power.

Bob Watson moved from left field to first base and made an impact. Denis Menke had another tremendous year at shortstop, pacing the club with 92 RBIs. But the pitching staff slipped, and the team finished 79-83.

Jimmy Wynn became the first player to hit a regular season homer into the upper deck or yellow section of the Astrodome. Wynn connected for the long home run off the Braves knuckleballer Phil Niekro. The homer landed in the third row of the yellow section, only a few seats over from where teammate Doug Rader had connected during the exhibition season a few weeks earlier.

More remarkably, in the first inning, Wynn had hit a homer off Niekro into the purple seats, just below the upper deck. Wynn's third inning blast landed even farther into the upper deck. First baseman Joe Pepitone said, "It was quite a show today."

1970 MVP

Joe Morgan was voted the Astros MVP for 1970. Morgan was an All-Star and scored 104 runs batting second. Morgan stole 42 bases hitting ahead of slugging outfielder Jimmy Wynn. Morgan was a very patient hitter, drawing 102 bases on balls.

Morgan ended the season fourth in stolen bases and fifth in walks. He started the season slowly but raised his average 60 points and finished at .269.

1971

The 1971 team also went 79-83. Towering 6-8 righthander J.R. Richard made his major league debut in September by striking out 15 Giants. In the early years of the franchise, the team had never had a player burst onto the scene like James Rodney Richard.

Richard was the Astros top draft choice in the June 1969 amateur draft. After a dominating career at Lincoln High School in Ruston, Louisiana, Richard became the prize of the Astros farm system. Richard was one of the sport's tallest pitchers when the Astros summoned him from AAA Oklahoma City in September 1971.

Richard received four starts and in his major league debut in San Francisco he made his mark. Richard was given the ball for the second game of a doubleheader and struck out 15 hitters, tying the Major League record of Karl Spooner of the 1954 Brooklyn Dodgers. Spooner also struck out 15 Giants, but they were the New York Giants before their move West. Richard pitched a complete game and got the win in the Astros 5-3 victory.

Richard split time between Triple A and Houston in 1972 and 1973. He was called up at the June trade deadline in 1973 and inserted into the starting rotation a week later. Dominance was on display!

By 1976, Richard had supplanted Larry Dierker as the ace of the staff. The towering righty also became the second member of the franchise to win 20 games. Richard's height created a big advantage for him, giving enemy batters a shorter time to decide whether it was a fastball or slider. Richard became the first Astro pitcher to lead the league in strikeouts when he fanned 303 in 1978. He struck out 313 in 1979. In 1980, Richard was chosen to start for the National League in the All-Star game. He was the first pitcher in franchise history to be given that honor.

Richard began the 1980 season with ten wins by the All-Star break but he was shut down due to arm problems. A few weeks later, Richard was attempting a throwing session at the Astrodome but collapsed and was rushed to the hospital for what was determined to be a stroke. Richard was never able to regain his form and return to a major league mound after that, despite several seasons of working his way back.

With Cedeno, who led the club with 81 RBIs and Richard, the Astros featured two players who became among the best in baseball. Unfortunately, the supporting cast was not deep enough.

General Manager "Spec" Richardson compounded the difficulties by trading away Joe Morgan, Cesar Geronimo, Jack Billingham, Denis Menke and Ed Armbrister to Cincinnati for Lee May, Tommy Helms and Jimmy Stewart. Although May produced for Houston, the loss of Morgan and the others was devastating.

Those players completed the components of one of the most dominant teams of the Seventies. The Reds went to three World Series in the Seventies and made two other playoff appearances. Morgan became a two-time National League Most Valuable Player in 1975 and '76. The trade did not backfire on the Astros immediately.

After acquiring May, the Astros moved their top position playing prospect, John Mayberry to Kansas City for reliever Jim York.

These deals provided the Astros with veterans at the middle or end of their careers, while the Reds' and Royals' hauls allowed for their success later in the decade. The Astros also dealt three more prospects to the Padres for Dave Roberts, who had burst onto the scene and was inserted into the starting rotation behind Dierker and Wilson. The Astros won 84 games in the strike-shortened 1972 season, but the fall came quickly as the veterans aged.

1971 MVP

For the 1971 season, starting pitcher Don Wilson was selected as the team's MVP. Wilson was a 16-game winner and had the best season in his career. Wilson was named an All-Star for the only time in his career and he pitched two scoreless innings in the game.

Wilson was thrust into the staff ace role after Larry Dierker went down in August with elbow trouble. Dierker had been injured since the All-Star break and the Astros needed help in the rotation. Wilson won eight of his nine starts from August to mid-September. Wilson authored 11 complete games in his final 14 starts. He dropped his ERA from 3.00 in early August to 2.69 for the season. One of his top outings was in late September when he spun a one-hitter against the Reds and won 4-1.

In that win over Cincinnati, Wilson was a recipient of the Astros second triple play in franchise history. Manager Harry Walker had high praise for Wilson. "Right now, I would rate Wilson in a class with Bob Gibson, Tom Seaver, Ferguson Jenkins and even Sandy Koufax," said Walker.

1972

The Astros put together the best record in team history in 1972, finishing 84-69 in a strike-shortened season. But in the same division with Cincinnati, they were consistently beaten in the next several years by players they traded away. GM Spec Richardson hired Leo Durocher to lead the team.

Leo Durocher

Durocher led the Astros from late in 1972 through the end of the 1973 season. The Astros had finished second to the Cincinnati Reds in 1972 after he replaced Harry Walker. Bolstered by more veteran acquisitions, the team fell to fourth place in 1973. The 67-year-old Durocher left as the oldest manager of the team until Dusty Baker was brought in to manage the team in 2020. "For someone who's been in baseball as long as I have, it is time to rest," said Durocher. He never managed again. Durocher began his managerial career with the Brooklyn Dodgers back in 1939. He later managed the New York Giants and Chicago Cubs before being hired to lead the Astros.

Durocher led the Giants to their improbable four-game sweep over the Cleveland Indians in the 1954 World Series with the young budding superstar Willie Mays. He never returned to postseason play.

Durocher managed the Cubs from 1966 to 1972 after the end of the "College of Coaches" experiment and got the team back into the race, thanks to a star-studded infield of Ernie Banks and Ron Santo, both Hall of Famers. He is remembered for the crash of the Cubs down the stretch in 1969, when the eventual World Champion New York Mets overcame his team.

Durocher was known for his fiery temper and getting into arguments with the umpires. Durocher was only ejected twice in his tenure with the Astros.

Durocher is remembered for his comparison of Astros star Cesar Cedeno to Mays. Cedeno was never quite able to live up to Durocher's comparison.

The Astros' mix of young players was probably not the best fit for Durocher. Second-year starter Jerry Reuss was given a heavy workload of 40 starts, still a franchise record. The team had problems finding a strong arm at the back of the bullpen to close out games. The Astros had tried to find a couple of veteran arms, finding Juan Pizarro and Cecil Upshaw available, but they were never quite able to fill the void.

The entire experiment lasted just thirteen months. The Astros immediately promoted third base coach Preston Gomez to manager after Durocher retired. Gomez had previously managed the expansion San Diego Padres and had filled in for Durocher when he had been ill during the season. Durocher walked away after 45 years in the game.

1972 MVP

The Astros 1972 team MVP was Cesar Cedeno. Cedeno was in his third season with the team and was one of the budding stars in the National League. Cedeno was an All-Star selection and finished sixth in the National League in the MVP race.

He placed fourth in the National League with a .320 batting average while slugging 22 homers. Cedeno also stole 55 bases, finishing third in the league. He also became the first Astro outfielder to win a Gold Glove.

1973

The Astros again played winning baseball (82-80) in 1973. Lee May delivered a big year, driving in 105 runs. Cedeno blossomed, hitting .320 with 25 homers and 56 stolen bases to set the club record. Bob Watson drove in 94 runs, and third baseman Doug Rader added 89.

1973 MVP

The 1973 Astros team MVP was shortstop Roger Metzger. Primarily known as a defensive player, Metzger provided one of his top offensive campaigns. Durocher moved Metzger into the second spot in the lineup at the start of May, but he was only hitting .088. Metzger started an 11-game hitting streak and finished at .250. Hitting in front of emerging star Cesar Cedeno proved to be a big help. Metzger stayed in the second spot. He also played stellar defense and joined Cedeno and third baseman Doug Rader as Gold Glove winners. It was the only Gold Glove of Metzger's career. He also set the franchise record with 14 triples, a record that still stands.

1974

Preston Gomez took over as manager in 1974 and guided the Astros to a .500 season, 81-81. Another ill-considered trade removed Jimmy Wynn from the Astros and sent him to Los Angeles for lefty starter Claude Osteen. Osteen replaced Jerry Reuss in the rotation after Reuss went to Pittsburgh for lefthanded-hitting catcher Milt May.

May joined a strong lineup. Cedeno had another banner year, belting 26 home runs and driving in 102 runs. Lee May, Bob Watson and Doug Rader all had excellent statistics.

Tommy Helms hit well, as did May. Pitchers Larry Dierker and Don Wilson both reached the 100-win plateau. Tom Griffin led the club in wins with 14.

Nearly a Third No-Hitter for Wilson

Don Wilson is the only Astros pitcher to hurl two no-hitters in an Astros uniform. Wilson came very close to getting a third, only to be pulled after eight innings through some bizarre twists of fate. In the 1974 game, reliever Mike Cosgrove gave up a ninth-inning single up the middle to Reds first baseman Tony Perez, the first batter he faced, and the no-hitter was lost. Wilson had previously no-hit the Braves in 1967 and the Reds in 1969.

Wilson gave up a pair of unearned runs to Cincinnati in the fifth inning. He walked two hitters. Pitcher Jack Billingham bunted them over to second and third with two outs. Reliable shortstop Roger Metzger fielded a soft grounder by Pete Rose, then threw it high over first baseman Lee May's head to allow both of the runs to score.

The Astros collected seven hits and scored once on an error by Reds third baseman Dan Driessen in the seventh inning, but couldn't get any closer to home plate.

Wilson was scheduled to lead off in the bottom of the eighth. Fans at the Astrodome were disappointed to see Gomez tab Tommy Helms to hit for him. Helms grounded out to shortstop and Cosgrove came out to pitch the top of the ninth inning.

Cosgrove told reporters after the game, "Wilson had to be disturbed. He had to be mad. If he wasn't, he wouldn't be much of a ballplayer. It didn't make me feel good to go out there and pitch with all of those fans booing."

Gomez said, "You have to try and win. I made my own decision," pointing to his heart. "I get paid for winning baseball games, not no-hitters."

Wilson's gem was the third one-hitter for the Astros. Tom Griffin and Dave Roberts pitched the others.

Wilson won one more game. The near no-hitter was even more difficult for Astros fans to handle when Wilson died in that off-season of carbon monoxide poisoning in an accident in his home that winter. Wilson's young son also died in that accident.

If Wilson had completed the no-hitter, he would have tied Hall of Famer Cy Young for second place all-time in no-hitters. He would have been one no-hitter behind then all-time leader Sandy Koufax with four.

It was the second time in his managerial career that Gomez had pinch-hit for a pitcher throwing a no-hitter. While managing the expansion San Diego Padres in their second season of existence, Gomez lifted his ace, Clay Kirby, after eight no-hit innings.

Padres reliever Jack Baldschun gave up a hit, and then two more and the Mets beat the Padres 3-0. Kirby never threw a no-hitter in his ten-year career. The Padres waited until 2021 for their franchise to have a no-hitter. Former Astro Joe Musgrove threw that no-hitter for the Padres against the Rangers in 2021. Musgrove nearly reached perfection, only hitting slugger Joey Gallo with a pitch.

Longest Astrodome Single

Mike Schmidt of the Phillies ripped the longest single Astrodome observers ever saw in 1974, a soaring drive that hit a speaker attached to the ceiling in center field and fell to the field while the stunned Phillies baserunners advanced only one base. Centerfielder Cesar Cedeno retreated to the wall and looked up when the ball hit the speaker 117 feet above the playing field. Later projections placed the estimated distance of the drive at about 500 feet if it had not struck the speaker.

The ground rules of the Astrodome provided for any such batted ball to be in play. Schmidt led the league anyway with 36 home runs that year.

Cliff Johnson

Cliff Johnson's first full season with the Astros was 1974, after limited opportunities in the two previous seasons. Johnson spent the first six years of his 15-year career in Houston. He had his best seasons with the Astros as measured by on base average and slugging percentage. But he was helpful to the team only on offense.

183

He caught 66 games in 1976 but still led the league in passed balls. First base and the outfield were not adequate positions for him either. Johnson hit five pinch home runs in 1974 and wound up his career with 20, more than any other player at that time.

Johnson caused his teammates an extra morning workout when Bill Virdon punished the entire team for Johnson's unwillingness to run out a pop fly in one game. The next day, all of the players had to line up at home plate and run to first several times to reinforce the need to run out all batted balls in a game.

1974 MVP

Greg Gross was selected as the Astros team MVP for the 1974 season. Gross had a brief September trial with the Astros the previous year but took over the vacant right field spot for the team fulltime following the trade of Jim Wynn to the Dodgers.

Gross finished second in the Rookie of the Year voting to the Cardinals Bake McBride, and won *The Sporting News* award for the National League. Gross was a fourth-round draft choice of the Astros in 1970. He rose quickly through the farm system and hit .314 as a rookie in 1974. He had three hits on Opening Day out of the leadoff spot. By the time the Astros returned home from opening on the West Coast against the Giants and the Padres, Gross was hitting .589 and had 11 hits. Gross stayed in the leadoff spot for the rest of the season and he collected 185 hits.

1975

The Astros cratered in 1975 in their new orange-striped uniforms. Lee May was traded to Baltimore for Enos Cabell and Rob Andrews. Bob Watson took over at first base for May and drove in 85 runs.

It was a disastrous 64-97 season, but out of the ashes rose two important future acquisitions. The Astros purchased pitcher Joe Niekro from Atlanta and outfielder Jose Cruz from St. Louis.

Pitcher Jose Sosa became the first Astro to homer in his first major league at-bat. Preston Gomez was fired and replaced by Bill Virdon.

The Astros were taken into receivership in 1975 by Ford Motor Credit Company and GE Credit Company. Roy Hofheinz and Bob Smith paid an initial expansion franchise fee of $1.85 million in 1962. Hofheinz bought out Smith's share for $7.5 million in 1967. With the expansion of Hofheinz's holdings into the Astrodomain and Barnum and Bailey Ringling Brothers Circus, financial difficulties caused the receivership move. For the next four years the team was under severe budgetary constraints.

General Manager Tal Smith emerged to lead the franchise back to respectability, taking it from last place in 1975 to a championship. He had departed Houston in 1973 to join the New York Yankees before returning to mastermind the massive rebuilding project.

1975 MVP

The Astros team MVP was first baseman Bob Watson in 1975. Watson gained some notoriety May 4 when he dashed home from second base on a homer by Milt May and beat the Reds' Dave Concepcion to make his way into the record book. He was known as the man who scored the one millionth run in baseball history. It was Watson's work in the remainder of the season that propelled him to the team MVP award.

Watson hit .324, which was the second highest mark in Astros history to that point.

Watson, nicknamed "Bull," seized the cleanup spot at the start of May and earned his second All-Star nod. He was moved to first base by Manager Preston Gomez after the off-season trade of Lee May to the Orioles. Watson hit 18 homers and knocked in 85 runs and combined with Cesar Cedeno to be the dynamic pieces in the middle of the Astros lineup.

There was another important development. Tal Smith built the Arm Farm.

The Arm Farm

During the 1975 season, the Astros had bottomed out with many of their veteran players. Management began a concerted effort to look at their major league pitching and organizational depth to determine the next best steps.

New General Manager Tal Smith found a core to build around in longtime starter Larry Dierker and young veterans Ken Forsch and James Rodney Richard.

With this core intact, the Astros began the search for young pitchers. Smith used the veteran position players on his team to expedite the process of getting major league-ready arms.

Smith sent minor league outfielder Mike Easler to the Cardinals for a player to be named later. That turned out to be reliever Mike Barlow.

The biggest move was a deal moving three players including starting catcher Milt May and lefty starter Dave Roberts to the Tigers for two young pitching arms, Gene Pentz and Mark Lemongello. The Astros also acquired catcher Terry Humphrey and outfielder Leon Roberts.

Left-handed reliever Fred Scherman, a 30-year-old-middleman, went to Montreal.

The Astros spent their top draft choice on Bo McLaughlin, a tall right-hander who pitched in parts of four seasons with the team.

Right after the World Series, the Astros started to get busy. They dealt with the World Champion Cincinnati Reds and got pitcher Joaquin Andujar for two minor league pitchers.

The makeover was just getting started. In the Rule V draft, the Astros selected Gil Rondon from California. Two days later, the Astros sent longtime third baseman Doug Rader to the Padres and got Joe McIntosh and Larry Hardy. McIntosh was injured during a lockout and never appeared in a game for the Astros.

When the off-season ended, the team had acquired seven young arms with less than a year's experience. The previous management group had claimed 30-year-old knuckleballer Joe Niekro off waivers from Atlanta at the end of spring training and plugged him into the bullpen.

The Astros focused their 1976 draft on the rebuild as well. Arizona State left-hander Floyd Bannister was the Astros' choice with the first pick in the draft. Dave Smith and Bert Roberge followed.

The trade acquisitions began to make their mark. Starter Tom Griffin was allowed to go to the Padres on a waiver claim in August of 1976. Joe Niekro remained in the bullpen, but Bo McLaughlin came up and was inserted into the rotation by Bill Virdon.

Joaquin Andujar was one of the first acquisitions made by Tal Smith with the Astros. Andujar came to Houston in an off-season trade with a live arm but erratic control. In 1974 while at Triple-A with the Reds, Andujar walked one more batter than he struck out.

The Reds could not risk putting Andujar in big game situations on the Big Red Machine as it plowed through National League competition, but he was exactly the kind of player the rebuilding Astros were looking for. Andujar had a high leg kick and lots of moving pieces in his delivery, which made his delivery difficult to duplicate. But the Astros welcomed him in 1976.

Andujar began the season in the bullpen but was moved quickly into the rotation. By mid-summer, he was very solid and in July beat both the Mets and the Expos in 1-0 complete games.

He had an outstanding start in 1977, going 10-5 with a spot on the National League All-Star team. He was injured in his final start before the break and didn't return until September. He won only one more game, but was one of the most entertaining players to watch. Andujar loved to hit and had three homers in his first tour of duty in Houston, including an inside-the- park effort against the Montreal Expos.

Andujar was also known for his antics, such as switch-hitting on the wrong side of the plate or wearing a warm pitching sleeve on his left arm. He traded punches with Ray Knight, his former minor league roommate, in a Reds-Astros game.

Andujar became a sold third starter behind J.R. Richard and Dierker. Joe Sambito also came onto the scene. At that time, six of the Astros' ten-man pitching staff were 25 years old or younger.

On the Arm Farm, 21-year-old Dan Larson also was a key in the rotation. Nearly half of the Astros' starts in 1976 came from pitchers who were 25 years old or younger. The Astros pitching staff became the land of opportunity.

Bill Virdon brought the Astros back with an 80-82 record in 1976. Cesar Cedeno, Bob Watson and Jose Cruz all had fine seasons, and J.R. Richard won 20 games. Larry Dierker stopped Montreal at the Astrodome with a no-hitter.

The oddity of the season was a postponement at the Astrodome because it rained so hard, accumulating more than seven inches, that the stadium employees and the fans could not overcome the flooding to get to the stadium! It was the only baseball postponement at the Astrodome.

Only about 20 fans made it to the game. They were treated to dinner by the Astros. The players from both teams actually ate on the field, served on tables set up near second base.

The umpiring crew checked in with the team at about 4 p.m. and couldn't make it out of their hotel, the Shamrock Hilton, which was in the Texas Medical Center and only a couple of miles away.

The street flooding continued, but the Pirates' team bus was able to make it to the stadium through the high water. After spending the evening at the stadium, the bus was able to return to the hotel very slowly. Former Astros star Bob Watson told Brian McTaggart of MLB, "It was a typical summer afternoon with a 10% chance for rain or something like that."

Tal Smith recalled to team historian Mike Acosta in 2014 that it wasn't a difficult decision. "On that day, June 15, it was the trading deadline, and Joe Brown was the general manager of the Pittsburgh club at the time. I conferred with him, told him what I was going to do, which was fine."

The concession staff that made it to the field set up tables on the Astroturf infield. A buffet line was made and players and staff ate on the field around game time. Enos Cabell recalled that a steak dinner was served. Most of the players were dressed in uniform and were joined by stadium workers and front office personnel marooned at the stadium.

Some of the players decided to remain at the stadium and stayed in the suites in the outfield section. Cabell decided to brave the trip and headed out with J.R. Richard and Cesar Cedeno. They plowed through the water.

All of the ticket holders were given refunds for the game. There had been a game in 1975 that had been delayed nearly an hour due to heavy rains in Houston, but never again was there a rain in.

1976

Manager Bill Virdon retooled the lineup for the 1976 season. Exciting outfielder Cesar Cedeno was a featured performer, with a .297-18-83 season as the team improved dramatically to 80-82. Virdon had a no-nonsense approach to the players. Everybody ran hard. The players showed up with a lunch pail and prepared to give everything they had physically. That was perfect for 1976 in the Astrodome, where the wide-open spaces and Astroturf demanded all-out sprinting to run the bases and cover the territory. Cedeno was perfect for this type of baseball.

Bob Watson had a big year: .313-16-102.

Joe Niekro was one of 11 starting pitchers used by Virdon. His rebirth with the knuckleball was a critical beginning of the 1980 playoff team. Niekro was encouraged by his brother Phil, a Hall of Famer, to use the knuckleball their father taught them in the back yard in Lansing, Ohio after their dad got home from working in the coal mines. Joe had been reluctant to rely on that pitch, but his career had bottomed out with Atlanta because his fastball-slider-curveball-changeup mix was below average.

In the Astrodome, with its 390-foot power alleys, Niekro could float his 75mph specialty pitch and dare hitters to hit it out. They could drive the pitch 380 feet to a glove held by Cedeno, Terry Puhl or Jose Cruz. Out!

Larry Dierker's Foamer No-hitter

It was a Friday night, July 9, and it was a Foamer Night. In a season with low attendance (less than 900,000), the front office was searching for marketing ideas to draw larger crowds to the Astrodome. The initial plan called for promotional nights with free beer. The beer was free if an Astro hit a home run while a light was lit on the scoreboard. But the Astros hit only 30 home runs at home that season. The plan changed to free beer for the fans if an Astros pitcher struck out a hitter while the light was lit.

Larry Dierker struck out Montreal second baseman Pete Mackanin in the seventh inning, triggering the free beer promotion. Fans lined up at the concession stands for their free beer.

As Dierker later recalled, "Here I am pitching a no-hitter and people aren't watching the game because they're lined up for free beer." Some fans got their beer and proceeded to get in line again, drinking a beer while working their way to the front of the line for their next one.

The small crowd of 12,511 saw at least part of Larry's no-hitter, with his batterymate Ed Herrmann supplying a two-run homer while catching the 6-0 win with eight strikeouts.

1976 MVP

In 1976, James Rodney Richard was honored as the Astros team MVP. Richard joined Larry Dierker as the only pitchers to win 20 games, as he posted a 20-15 record. Richard led the league by allowing only 6.83 hits per nine innings.

While leading the league in bases on balls, Richard also finished second to Tom Seaver with his 214 strikeouts. Richard took over the role as the ace of the Astros pitching staff.

Richard beat the Giants, Dodgers and Padres in his last three starts to arrive at the 20-win mark. Richard established himself quickly as one of the elite and upcoming arms in the National League.

1977

A .500 season at 81-81 in 1977 included a big year by Bob Watson, with 110 RBIs. Watson hit for the cycle against the Giants. He later accomplished the feat for Boston, becoming the first player with cycles in both leagues.

Jose Cruz had a prominent bat as well. Art Howe took over at second base and third baseman Enos Cabell broke out offensively. Joe Niekro established himself in the rotation after deciding to feature the knuckleball as his main pitch.

Niekro remained in the Astros bullpen until being inserted into the rotation in late July of 1977. Niekro pitched a complete game against the Cubs and then followed up with shutouts of the Pirates and Cubs.

But the Astros' choice of Arizona State southpaw Floyd Bannister with the first overall pick in the draft failed to answer their quest for a dominant starter.

Joe Ferguson became the starting catcher after being traded for Larry Dierker. Terry Puhl was promoted from the minors and claimed a starting outfield spot.

Bannister made his debut in the rotation for the Astros and won eight games as a 22-year-old. Andujar proved to be a quality starter, winning 11 games and making the National League All-Star team. Richard became the stalwart of the rotation. winning 18 games.

The pitching staff under the tutelage of pitching coach Mel Wright became one of the best in the league with a 3.54 staff ERA.

1977 MVP

Jose Cruz won his first team MVP award in 1977. Cruz hit a career high 17 homers with a .299 average, while walking more times than he struck out. Cruz didn't homer until mid-May.

Manager Bill Virdon used Cruz mainly in the third spot in the lineup but was willing to move him around as needed.

Cruz's versatility throughout the lineup allowed the Astros to try several of their new pieces throughout the order. Cruz was able to contribute wherever he was placed.

1978

A fall to fifth place was waiting for the Astros in 1978. They plummeted to 74-88. Injuries played a role. Cedeno missed most of the season with a knee injury. The club was in bankruptcy and was unable to acquire difference-making talent on a shoestring budget.

On the positive side, Niekro and Ken Forsch became dependable starters. Cruz had a big year. Denny Walling's bat caused people to take notice.

The Astros continued to add new young players. They were able to sign Vern Ruhle following his release from the Tigers after an injury at age 24 at the end of spring training 1978. The Astros gave Ruhle time to recover and he rewarded them handsomely. He developed into a key cog in the Astros early '80s teams.

By 1978, Mark Lemongello failed to take the next step forward in his third season, despite being just 22 years old. After the season, Lemongello would be the key piece in a trade with the Blue Jays for Alan Ashby.

1978 MVP

Enos Cabell was the first player in franchise history to play in all 162 games in a season. In 1978, Cabell was selected as the team MVP. Cabell was shifted between the second, third and fifth positions in the lineup, and kept his average between .290 and .300 during the second half of the season.

Cabell played most of the season at third base but covered for Bob Watson at first for a week while he was sidelined in August. Cabell also collected 195 hits, the most by a Houston player in franchise history to that point.

1979

By 1979, the transition was completed. The Astros still continued to move for more prospects, but they also traded for shortstop Craig Reynolds and catcher Alan Ashby to give them experience.

The nucleus was in place for their best season yet, finishing second in the West with an 89-73 record.

A quick turnaround rescued the future for the Astros, a 75-1 longshot to win the championship. They traded Floyd Bannister to Seattle for Reynolds.

Ken Forsch pitched a no-hitter April 7 at the Astrodome against Atlanta. Jose Cruz beat Cincinnati 3-0 with a home run at the end of the month, pushing Houston into first place. The team was sold to John McMullen in May.

Bob Watson was traded to Boston in June, allowing Cedeno to move to first base. Cedeno's legs got a much-needed break after his injuries and miles of running for fly balls in the outfield. Terry Puhl moved to center field and Jeff Leonard took over in right. Leonard hit .290 and stole 23 bases.

Manager Bill Virdon put Joaquin Andujar back into the rotation in 1979 and he responded with his second All-Star game selection. Andujar was joined by Joe Niekro and Joe Sambito on the pitching staff for the National League squad.

The Astros stood up to the Reds and opened up a big ten-game lead in July. Tom Seaver of the Reds predicted that the Astros would drop like a lead balloon in the second half. They did, including suffering a seven-game losing streak.

Virdon had little power, but he pushed his club to win with the running game. Four players stole 30 bases or more. Terry Puhl led the club in home runs with just 13. Joe Niekro won 21. J.R. Richard added 18 and broke his own club strikeout record with 313. The Astros pushed the Reds to the finish, losing the division title by 1 ½ games.

They had the foundation for an even bigger year after their 89-73 season, gaining experience in a pennant race.

Rare Protest Win

It is seldom that a team protests a game, and it is even rarer when a team wins the protest. That's exactly what happened for the Astros in August 1979.

While playing the Mets at Shea Stadium, Astros right fielder Jeff Leonard flied out to Lee Mazzilli for the game's final out. However, the umpiring crew called time out before the pitch.

While the umpires conferred, Mets first baseman Ed Kranepool left the field and headed to the clubhouse, not realizing the game was going to continue.

The umpires put Leonard back in the batter's box, but no one noticed that the Mets didn't have a first baseman. Leonard fouled a pitch and then singled and the game continued. Kranepool was busy getting ready to shower after the game in the clubhouse.

195

It wasn't until Kranepool dashed back onto the field to take his position at first base that anyone noticed that the Mets were playing shorthanded.

Mets Manager Joe Torre argued that the hit should be nullified.

After an on-field conference, home plate umpire Frank Pulli nullified the hit. Pulli ruled that the game couldn't continue without the defense having nine players on the field and moved Leonard back into the batter's box.

Astros Manager Bill Virdon came out and protested the game at this point. Leonard flied out to end the game. At least he thought he had.

Since the Astros were in New York, the appeal was heard the following day by National League President Chub Feeney. He ruled in favor of the Astros, and the game was resumed that evening. Leonard was placed on first base and Jose Cruz bounced out to second baseman Doug Flynn.

The Mets starter from the night before, Pete Falcone, had to be replaced and he lost his potential shutout. Kevin Kobel came in and pitched the final third of an inning to complete a 5-0 shutout. Kobel went on to pitch seven innings in the regularly scheduled game. Kobel lost his start to J.R. Richard.

So, while Leonard was credited with a hit, he also flied out twice in one of the most unique at-bats in team history!

1979 MVP

The 1979 Astros MVP was Joe Niekro. Niekro broke the Astros' single season record with 21 victories. Niekro pitched seven innings against the Dodgers on the final day of the season and earned a 3-2 win. The Astros finished only 1 1/2 games behind the Cincinnati Reds. Niekro was joined by his brother Phil of the Braves as 21-game winners. The brothers tied for the league lead. He posted an outstanding month of May, going 6-0 during the month, as he pitched four complete games and two shutouts.

Niekro was also the league leader with six shutouts for the season. Niekro finished second to Cubs' closer Bruce Sutter in the Cy Young Award, while another Astro, J.R. Richard, finished third.

196

1980s: First Playoff Decade

1980

The blockbuster move that pushed Houston to its first playoff appearance was the signing of free agent Nolan Ryan. With John McMullen's decision to make the fireballing righthander from Alvin, Texas the first million-dollar-a-year ballplayer, the Astros gained tons of respect around the baseball world.

Then they added another free agent, Joe Morgan. Morgan left Cincinnati to return to Houston and help lead the Astros to their first title.

J.R. Richard earned his 100th career win early in the season. Heading a rotation with Ryan, Niekro, Forsch and Vern Ruhle, Richard was squarely in his prime. Richard was the first Astro to start the All-Star Game.

But three days later, doctors told him to rest his arm. By the end of July, he suffered a stroke and his season was finished. The Astros fell into third place in August, but they swept a two-game series in early September to tie the Dodgers for the top spot in the NL West. Ruhle took Richard's spot in the rotation and finished 7-2.

The Astros finished their season at home with a three-game lead over the Dodgers and headed for Dodger Stadium needing one win to clinch the division title. They lost three in a row, all close games. The season came down to a one-game playoff.

To cut the tension, Jose Cruz climbed atop a table in the visitor's clubhouse and entertained his teammates with a dance. Joe Niekro was the starter for Game 163. Niekro went the distance in a 7-1 win. Art Howe belted a three-run homer off Dave Goltz after taking a curveball for what could have been strike three. Home plate umpire Doug Harvey said, "Artie, don't take that pitch again."

Catcher Joe Ferguson was hopping mad that the call went against the Dodgers. Goltz came back with the same pitch, and Howe sent it on a long journey. When Howe crossed home plate, he winked at Harvey.

1980 NLCS

The powerful Philadelphia Phillies were waiting for the Astros in the best-of-five NLCS in Philadelphia. As the Astros arrived, Niekro was pushed back in the rotation because he was needed in the one-game playoff against the Dodgers. The tired Astros sent Ken Forsch to the mound for Game 1 against Steve Carlton.

Carlton was the Cy Young Award winner in 1980, and third baseman Mike Schmidt won the Most Valuable Player award. Pete Rose had joined the Phillies as a free agent in 1979. Another of their stars, Greg Luzinski, crushed a two-run homer in the Phillies' 3-1 win.

Game 2 was tied 2-2 going to the eighth. Each team scored once in that inning. The game went to the tenth. Dave Bergman drilled a two-run triple and the Astros claimed the game, 7-4.

The series moved to Houston. Joe Niekro was dazzling for ten scoreless innings, but the Astros couldn't score against Larry Christenson or the bullpen. Denny Walling drove in the only run on a bases-loaded sacrifice fly after Joe Morgan tripled in Houston's 1-0, 11-inning win in Game 3. "In the dugout, you couldn't talk to the player next to you because it was so loud...I never heard the Astrodome like that," said Terry Puhl. One win away from their first World Series, the Astros failed to close their bid. Cesar Cedeno left Game 3 with a gruesome leg injury – a dislocated ankle - and was finished for the series.

Game 4 was a wild one, including a confusing call by the umpiring crew on a controversial play. With Vern Ruhle on the mound and runners at first and second on the move, a Garry Maddox line drive to the mound was gloved by Ruhle and he threw to first for what seemed to be a line drive double play.

However, the umpires could not agree about whether the ball was caught on the fly or on a short hop. The first and third base umps had ruled a line drive catch, but home plate umpire Doug Harvey signaled no catch. After the umpires huddled and conferred with National League President Chub Feeney, they made a compromise decision and called it a double play. At one point they called it a triple play because lead runner Bake McBride was standing on third and first baseman Art Howe ran to second and touched the bag. It was ruled a double play because Harvey felt that his incorrect call was what led to McBride thinking the ball had not been caught. The Phillies did not score in the inning and the Astros maintained their 2-0 lead.

The Sporting News national baseball writer Bill Conlin called it the "Texas Compromise." Conlin said that umpire Doug Harvey "showed more diplomacy than rules-interpreting ability on the non-call".

After the game, Harvey explained his call to pool reporters. "Maddox hits the ball and steps in front of me. There are runners out there wondering if it is a catch or a trap. My first reaction is no catch and I put my hands down to signal the ball is in play. I asked for help and they tell me the pitcher caught the ball and that's good enough for me."

It took the umpiring crew 20 minutes of discussion and arguments before the game could resume. Both teams protested the game, but neither one was upheld by league president Chub Feeney.

The Phillies went on to win an appeal that Gary Woods left third too early on a sacrifice fly by Luis Pujols in the sixth. That run was taken off the board. The Phillies went ahead 3-2 in the eighth but Houston tied it in the ninth. The Phillies won, 5-3 in ten innings, on a double by Greg Luzinski.

Phillies reliever Tug McGraw summed up the game best. "It was like a motorcycle ride through an art museum...You see the pictures but afterward you don't remember what you saw."

Game 5 matched Nolan Ryan with rookie Marty Bystrom. It was 2-2 when the Astros got three runs in the last of the seventh. The roof fell in on Ryan with six outs to go. Some infield scratch hits, including a one-hopper to Ryan by Bob Boone that was deflected off his glove, added up in a five-run inning for a 7-5 Phillies lead. The Astros came back again to tie it in the eighth, but Garry Maddox provided the game-winning RBI in the tenth, 8-7.

Terry Puhl hit .526 in the series and set a playoff record with 10 hits in a five-game NLCS.

.

1980 MVP

Jose Cruz won his second team MVP award in 1980. Cruz moved into the cleanup spot at the start of the summer. He was hitting .329 at the end of May. He was also providing solid contributions, banging out three hits as he knocked in four runs against the Expos early in the month.

Cruz had a dozen three-hit games, including four in the last part of August. Cruz finished the season with a .302 average and 91 RBI and placed third in the MVP voting, finishing behind Mike Schmidt and Gary Carter.

1981

The Astros returned to the playoffs in 1981 because they won a half-title in the NL West. The season was divided into two halves by a players' strike. The players walked out June 12, when the Astros had a 28-29 record. They opened the season by losing 12 of their first 15.

Art Howe put together a club record 23-game hitting streak, but other offensive components were missing. Joe Morgan had moved on to San Francisco. New General Manager Al Rosen traded Enos Cabell to the Giants for pitcher Bob Knepper. Rosen shipped Ken Forsch to the Angels for Dickie Thon.

Dave Bergman went to the Giants for Mike Ivie. Ivie was hospitalized for mental exhaustion and did not deliver one home run for the Astros. The Los Angeles Dodgers won the first half of the season.

After a two-month hiatus, the negotiated settlement provided a fresh start for all teams when they returned August 10. Minor leagues typically divided their season into halves at that time, but it was a different twist for the majors.

It came down to Houston and Cincinnati for the second-half title and a playoff berth. The Astros had a 1 ½-game lead over the Reds when they met the Dodgers in Houston.

Nolan Ryan pitched his fifth career no-hitter that day, breaking a tie with Sandy Koufax in a 5-0 shutout that lowered his league-leading ERA to 1.74. Ryan spent the hiatus during the work stoppage working on his ranch. He battled control issues that day in the NBC telecast, with 32,115 fans in attendance.

He needed 65 pitches to get through the first three innings, including three walks and a wild pitch. Alan Ashby's two-run single in the third provided him with a 2-0 lead.

When Ryan struck out Steve Garvey to open the fourth, pitching coach Mel Wright came to the mound to tell him he was overstriding. Ryan corrected his mechanics and set down the final 19 in order. Terry Puhl made an excellent running catch on a Mike Scioscia deep fly ball to the warning track in right center field in the seventh. Dusty Baker grounded to third on a 2-0 curveball for the final out. "I don't like having my name on the scorecard in a game that made history for Nolan Ryan. But I am happy for him. He is a great pitcher," said Baker. Ryan struck out 11.

His last no-hitter had come in 1975, but he was to get two more on his way to seven no-hitters and 5,714 strikeouts – both all-time records. Ryan called this no-hitter the most important of his five to that point. The Astros held their lead over the Reds and won the second half title with a 33-20 record.

Ryan was on the mound again when the playoffs started, matched with 20-year-old rookie southpaw sensation Fernando Valenzuela of the Dodgers. It was Ryan's next start after his no-hitter. He and Valenzuela left the game at the Astrodome with a 1-1 tie after eight innings. Alan Ashby ended the dramatic game with a walk-off two-run home run with two outs in the ninth off Dave Stewart.

The game wound up a Ryan two-hitter. Ryan was 11-5 during the regular season with a 1.69 ERA – the best in the majors. He retired 16 in a row over one stretch of the first playoff game. Steve Garvey homered in the seventh, tying the game 1-1. Ashby, Manager Bill Virdon and Ryan all made favorable comparisons to the no-hitter when asked about his stuff for the playoff game.

The next night, the Astros again took Astroball to the Dodgers and beat them, 1-0 in 11 innings. Former Astro Jerry Reuss, who in his previous start fractured Astro starter Don Sutton's kneecap with an errant pitch, faced Joe Niekro.

Cesar Cedeno was thrown out at the plate in a collision with catcher Mike Scioscia in the fifth inning. Niekro left after eight and Dave Smith worked two scoreless innings in the ninth and tenth. Reuss was lifted after nine and gave way to Steve Howe. The Astros chose Joe Sambito to work the 11th.

Sambito fanned Reggie Smith and Mike Marshall with two on to keep the Dodgers off the scoreboard. Dave Stewart returned to a pressure situation and allowed singles to Phil Garner and Tony Scott. Tom Lasorda used lefty Terry Forster to retire Jose Cruz with runners at first and third. Then he called on righthander Tom Niedenfuer to intentionally walk Cedeno and strike out Art Howe. Bill Virdon made his move, selecting Denny Walling to pinch hit for Dickie Thon. Lasorda was out of lefthanded relievers.

Walling's lefthanded swing powered a pitch over the head of right fielder Derrel Thomas, who had played shallow since taking over for Rick Monday as a defensive replacement.

The series moved to Los Angeles, where the Astros still could not find their offense. The Dodgers won three straight to capture the best-of-five series. Burt Hooton beat them with a three-hitter. Valenzuela followed with a four-hitter. Reuss finished the series with a five-hitter.

1981 MVP

Nolan Ryan was selected as the Astros MVP in the strike-shortened 1981 season. Ryan was the leader of a pitching staff with five starters with ERAs under 3.00. Ryan tied for the team lead with his 11 wins with another future Hall of Famer, Don Sutton, who had signed with the Astros in the off-season. Ryan benefited from a lighter inning load, and had a 1.37 ERA after the six-week work stoppage. Ryan finished fourth in Cy Young Award voting, losing out to the Dodgers phenom Fernando Valenzuela.

1982

The Astros fell into a four-year downturn starting in 1982. They had a formidable trio of starting pitchers in Don Sutton, Ryan and Niekro, who won his 100th game in 1982. Those three pitchers were all 35 years old or older. Closer Joe Sambito blew out his left elbow. His replacement, Dave Smith, had a bad back. Knepper slipped to 5-15 and Ruhle had a losing record. Phil Garner had a big year at second base, drilling 13 home runs and driving in 83 runs to lead the club in those departments.

Ray Knight arrived to man first base in a trade with Cincinnati for Cesar Cedeno. The Astros stumbled home at 77-85. General Manager Al Rosen fired Bill Virdon, the winningest manager in team history, as the season wound down and replaced him with longtime coach Bob Lillis, the first MVP of the Colt .45s back in 1962.

1982 MVP

Ray Knight led the team in hitting with a .294 average while finishing second on the team with 94 RBIs.

1983

Injuries to Art Howe and Alan Ashby hit the 1983 Astros. Mike Scott came from New York in a trade for Danny Heep, but he did not discover his key to success immediately. Nolan Ryan provided a memorable moment in April at Montreal, striking out future Astros Manager Brad Mills to pass Walter Johnson's all-time record of 3,508.

He later fell behind Steve Carlton in strikeouts that season, but went on to put the record out of reach. Dickie Thon led the club in homers (20) and steals (34). The final record of 85-77 made the year respectable, but a bad April cost the club a chance to be a strong contender.

1983 MVP

Jose Cruz won his third team MVP in 1983. Cruz, at age 35, produced his top season in hitting with a robust .318 batting average and banged out 189 hits. Cruz finished five points behind league leader Bill Madlock of the Pirates. Cruz finished sixth in the MVP voting and was the first Astro player to finish in the top ten in MVP twice in his career. Cruz also collected 92 RBIs, the highest number he had collected so far in his career. Cruz finished seventh in the league in RBIs as well.

1984

The 80-82 Astros of 1984 were short on power. Joe Niekro blossomed with a 16-12 season and a 3.04 ERA. Nolan Ryan had his usual tough-luck year with a 3.04 ERA, but his record was 12-11. Enos Cabell (.310-8-44) had become one of the team leaders, but a young man with awesome Astrodome power came onto the scene – Glenn Davis. The Georgia native was called aside after a game by GM Al Rosen and told to swing the bat, not take pitches. Teammates had told him he should be more selective in his approach, but they couldn't threaten him with demotion to the minors, as Rosen did.

1984 MVP

Jose Cruz was the club leader in many categories: batting average (.312), homers (12), runs (96), hits (187), steals (22) and RBIs (95). He took home another team MVP award.

1985

Dickie Thon was beaned by a Mike Torrez fastball early in the 1985 season, torpedoing a chance for a strong start. The 1984 All-Star was never the same player after that. By the end of April, five other players and broadcaster Gene Elston joined Thon on the disabled list. Elston was struck by a car while jogging in Philadelphia and sustained broken bones. Glenn Davis came up from the minors in September and provided a preview of his Dome-beating power.

Mike Scott (18-8, 3.29) blossomed in 1985 after learning a new pitch from former pitching coach Roger Craig. It was the split-fingered fastball, thrown hard with the index and middle fingers split wide to fit on the sides of the baseball. A large hand was the best tool a pitcher could bring to a bullpen session, coupled with excellent arm strength.

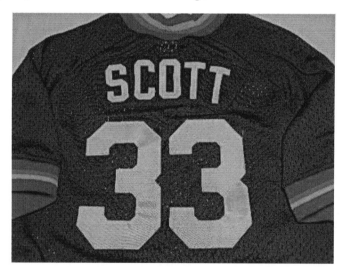

Scott turned it into a dominant combination, as reliever Bruce Sutter of the Chicago Cubs had done earlier. In the 83-79 campaign, the Astros provided hope for better years ahead.

Bob Knepper, Glenn Davis, Kevin Bass and Bill Doran gave Houston fans a preview of exciting times ahead. Jose Cruz collected his 2,000[th] career hit in September.

1985 MVP

Bill Doran was named the Astros MVP for the 1985 season. Doran was inserted into the leadoff spot by Manager Bob Lillis and he flourished. Doran reached base in thirty consecutive games from mid-April until the end of May. During the streak his batting average rose from .237 to .305. His biggest day of the year came when he had a five-hit performance against the Mets in July, knocking in Dickie Thon in the 12th inning to help the Astros inch over the .500 plateau. Doran finished with a .287 average and finished 21st in the National League MVP voting. Despite this, Doran never was able to make an All-Star team.

1986

The 1986 Astros were the most talented team in the club's history to that point. They had great pitching at the beginning of the decade but struggled for offense. It was different in '86.

Glenn Davis and Kevin Bass joined Jose Cruz, Bill Doran and a combination of Denny Walling and Phil Garner (Wal-Gar) at third base to provide multiple offensive threats. Billy Hatcher had been added in center field to provide more speed. New General Manager Dick Wagner and Manager Hal Lanier brought a combination of an experienced front office leader who had success with Cincinnati and a rookie manager who was fiery and aggressive. Lanier decided to open the season with a three-man rotation early in the season because of frequent off days in the schedule.

That gave him more time to develop Jim Deshaies for the fourth starter spot. Lanier's decision paid off in a 15-6 start through May 2. Knepper started 5-0 with a 1.31 ERA. The top three starters each got six starts while Deshaies started twice.

Deshaies proved to be a valuable contributor later. Wagner picked up Aurelio Lopez and Larry Andersen as free agents to bolster the bullpen and traded for Danny Darwin. Andersen was released by the Phillies while they were in Houston. He threw a bullpen, signed with the Astros and switched clubhouses.

The Astros pulled out in front of the pack of the NL West, prompting a comment from Dodger Manager Tommy Lasorda that they were just "renting" first place. Lanier platooned at third base and shortstop (Craig Reynolds and Dickie Thon) and made Alan Ashby his starting catcher.

Ashby, a switch hitter, added to the balance in the lineup. Doran (42), Hatcher (38) and Bass (22) stole bases to force defensive mistakes, and the team was aggressive in baserunning. Lanier was a graduate of "Whiteyball" in St. Louis and believed in pushing the running game. Cardinals manager Whitey Herzog utilized speedsters to great success.

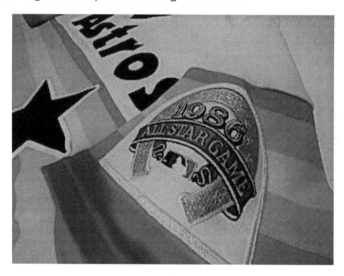

By the time the All-Star Game arrived in Houston, the Astros had slipped into second place after leading the division all season. Roger Clemens led the American League to a 3-2 triumph at the Astrodome. Vice President George H.W. Bush threw out the ceremonial first pitch.

The Astros took three of four from the Mets after the All-Star break and swept Montreal with all three victories in their final at-bat. They pulled ahead in their division and entered September with a seven-game lead.

In the clinching burst, Jim Deshaies struck out the first eight Dodgers for a Major League record in a 4-0 win, twirling a two-hitter. Dodger skipper Tommy Lasorda sent in Larry See to pinch-hit for his pitcher in the third inning, trailing 2-0. See did not see the basepaths, but he broke the strikeout string by hitting a fly ball for an out. Nolan Ryan allowed one hit the next night in a combined two-hitter with Charlie Kerfeld. Then Mike Scott clinched the division title with a no-hitter against the Giants, 2-0. Scott, the first Houston pitcher to win the Cy Young Award, fanned 13 Giants. He finished the season with 306 strikeouts, 18 wins and a 2.22 ERA.

Charlie Kerfeld won 11 games in relief for the 96-66 Astros in their best season in history to that point. Glenn Davis powered 31 home runs and drove in 101 runs. Kevin Bass hit .311 with 20 homers to go with his 22 steals.

In the postseason, the Astros and Mets squared off in one of the most memorable postseason series of that era. It was a best-of-seven series, and the Mets won in six. Afterwards, there was widespread agreement that if it had gone seven, Mike Scott would have won it for the Astros. That's pure speculation, but Scott dominated the Mets and he was in their heads. He fanned 14 in the opener and beat Dwight Gooden on a Glenn Davis home run, 1-0.

Bob Ojeda took Game 2 for the Mets, 5-1. The teams split those games in Houston and headed for Shea Stadium in New York.

Bill Doran belted a Game 3 home run off Ron Darling to put Houston ahead by four, but the Mets countered with Darryl Strawberry's three-run blast off Knepper to tie the game. Houston went ahead in the seventh, but New York thrilled the Mets fans when Lenny Dykstra won the game with a two-run ninth inning walk-off home run off Dave Smith, 6-5.

Scott evened the series by stopping the Mets again, 3-1 in Game 4. Alan Ashby and Dickie Thon drove in all of the Houston runs with home runs.

The Mets benefited from a blown call at first base in Game 5 when Craig Reynolds was called out by umpire Fred Brocklander. Houston lost at least one run on that call. Nolan Ryan and Doc Gooden departed and the game moved to extra innings. Gary Carter won the game on a single in the 12th, 2-1.

Bob Knepper started the epic Game 6 against Bob Ojeda and had a 3-0 lead in the first in Houston. The Astros could have had a fourth run, but Kevin Bass was tagged out at home when a suicide squeeze failed.

Knepper, more animated than ever, proceeded to pitch the game of his life. He dominated for eight innings, allowing two hits, but allowed the Mets to tie it in the ninth. Pinch-hitter Lenny Dykstra ripped a ball over the head of Billy Hatcher, playing shallow in center field, for a triple. Mookie Wilson singled in a run off the tip of Doran's glove. Keith Hernandez doubled in a run. Dave Smith entered to relieve Knepper and walked the first two batters he faced, setting up a sacrifice fly by former Astro Ray Knight. The Astros thought they had Knight on strikes, but Brocklander, umpiring this game at home plate, called a ball on a 1-2 pitch. Brocklander was not on the Astros' Christmas list in 1986.

The game intensified through 16 memorable innings. Roger McDowell was sensational, retiring the minimum of 15 batters in his five innings. Both teams scored in the 14th. Billy Hatcher's home run off Jesse Orosco in the 14th shook the left field foul screen to tie the game as he backpedaled toward first.

Then the fans erupted and filled the Astrodome with sound. The Mets scored three times in the 16th but had to hang on to win, 7-6. The Astros had two men on base when Jesse Orosco struck out Kevin Bass to end it. During the at-bat, Keith Hernandez went to the mound and told Orosco to throw Bass nothing but curveballs. That's what he did. Bass recalled the confrontation many years later and admitted that he tried to win the game himself instead of realizing that the Mets were not going to give him a pitch in the strike zone with lefty-hitting Jose Cruz on deck. Orosco, meanwhile, was pitching on fumes. He faced 14 batters in the game.

Mike Downey of the *Los Angeles Times* wrote, "They [the Astros] made the Mets sweat and suffer, made them charge from behind and gasp to stay in front...They were enervated, drained, battle-fatigued."

With their near misses for World Series berths in 1980 and 1986, the Astros had completed the journey from noncompetitive to elite.

1986 MVP

In 1986, Mike Scott became the first Astro pitcher to win the Cy Young Award. Scott was named the Astros MVP as he joined J.R. Richard as the only pitchers in Houston to strike out 300 batters in a season. Scott won 18 games and had a 2.22 ERA.

 Scott led the National League in ERA, shutouts and strikeouts. He was also the winning pitcher for the Astros in both of their wins in the League Championship Series against the New York Mets.

1987

Nolan Ryan had one of the most unrewarding seasons a pitcher could have in 1987. He was 8-16 despite a league-best 2.76 ERA! Bob Knepper was 8-17, but his ERA was 5.27. Charley Kerfeld had an injured right elbow. The team lost 20 more games than the year before, finishing 76-86.

1987 MVP

Bill Doran put up another stellar season in 1987 and was selected as the team's MVP. Hitting at the top of the lineup, Doran reached base at a .365 clip and led the team with 31 stolen bases. Doran started the year at leadoff and was moved to the two-hole by Manager Hal Lanier in mid-May with the emergence of Billy Hatcher. Lanier moved Doran down to the three-spot when the Astros promoted speedy outfielder Gerald Young. Doran was an on-base machine and hit a career high 16 homers, third on the team behind Glenn Davis and Kevin Bass. His .283 average made it an excellent year.

1988

Jose Cruz and Dickie Thon were released in 1988. Cruz rewrote the Houston record book and still ranks high in many offensive departments after his Astros Hall of Fame career. His friendly smile is still on display at Minute Maid Park and at many charity events. "Cheo" is one of the fans' favorite players for many reasons.

His consistent play and clutch performances helped to establish the team as a factor in many seasons. He was a big part of the renaissance of the organization during his career from 1975 to 1987.

After auditioning several shortstops, the Astros traded for Rafael Ramirez. Gerald Young took over in centerfield. Ken Caminiti claimed third base. Craig Biggio made his major league debut at catcher. Nolan Ryan left after the season and signed as a free agent with the Texas Rangers. McMullen was vilified for allowing Ryan to leave as he was trying to sell the team.

1988 MVP

Glenn Davis was voted the Astros MVP for the 1988 season. Davis joined Jim Wynn as the second Astro to hit 30 homers twice in his Astros career. Davis finished second in the National League in homers and fifth in RBIs. Davis led in homers among right-handed batters. He was an All-Star and finished seventh in league MVP voting.

Davis also was a quality defender, tying the top fielding percentage for an Astro first baseman in their first 22 seasons. A clutch hitter as well, Davis had 14 game-winning RBIs.

Davis told the story of his initial experience as a major leaguer. He was aggressive early in counts when he first arrived, but started taking more pitches on the advice of teammates who cautioned him that pitchers would not continue to throw him as many good pitches to hit in the future. GM Al Rosen called him into a private meeting after a game and threatened him with demotion to the minors if he didn't start swinging at more pitches. Davis complied, and he hit 164 homers from 1985 to 1990.

1989

Hal Lanier was replaced by Art Howe as manager in 1989. A youth movement was coming, but not yet. A patchwork approach brought in veterans such as pitchers Jim Clancy, Mark Portugal, Bob Forsch, Rick Rhoden and Dan Schatzeder. A record of 86-76 was a tribute to Howe, but the team was about to get into a full-fledged rebuilding mode. Mike Scott picked up his 100th win.

22-inning game

The Astros took part in another all-nighter in August 1989. The Dodgers battled the Astros in a 5-4 win that lasted 7 hours, 14 minutes. Not many of the 34,000 fans remained at the Astrodome to watch the end of this game.

Tim Leary matched up against Astros lefty Bob Knepper, but both starters were gone by the sixth inning. Neither team scored after the sixth inning until the 22nd. This, too, was the product of good pitching. Dodger starter Orel Hershiser came out of the bullpen after Tom Lasorda had depleted the six members of their normal bullpen. Hershiser gave up three hits in seven innings and kept the Astros hitters off balance.

Jim Clancy pitched the final five innings for the Astros and picked up the win. Clancy escaped a big jam in the 21st inning. Clancy gave up a walk to Mike Scioscia followed by a single to left by Willie Randolph. The runners moved to second and third on a passed ball by Alex Trevino. Clancy struck out Mike Davis swinging. Hershiser hit for himself and hit a grounder to third. Ken Caminiti threw home for the second out. Eddie Murray lined to shortstop and the Astros had their chance.

With Hershiser's pitch count rising, Lasorda moved his third baseman Jeff Hamilton to the mound for the bottom half of the inning. All-Star pitcher Fernando Valenzuela came in to play first base and Murray was moved across the diamond to third. Hamilton then retired the Astros in order. It was Hamilton's first pitching appearance since his senior year of high school in Flint, Michigan. He was reportedly clocked at 91mph.

Clancy had a clean 22nd inning and the Astros got their second crack at Hamilton. Bill Doran led off with a liner over the second baseman. Shortstop Rafael Ramirez later singled to right and Doran scored the winning run.

The Dodgers used nine pitchers; the Astros seven. The following day, the teams were scheduled to play a matinee and Glenn Davis slept in the training room as opposed to going home. Trevino was used in a double-switch for Craig Biggio and caught 15 innings.

The Home Sports Entertainment broadcast went off, since the game ended at 2:50am. The cable system was sharing channel space with other networks and an automatic timer sent many of the affiliates back to the other channel at 2 a.m.

Astros pitcher Jim Deshaies was used as a pinch-hitter. Deshaies was a career .088 hitter. John Shelby of the Dodgers went 0-for-10.

The next day, Bob Forsch gave up a grand slam to Scioscia in the first inning. He made it through five innings, but Craig Biggio homered with two outs in the bottom of the ninth. This game also went into extra innings, with the Astros prevailing 7-6 in 13 innings.

1989 MVP

In 1989, Mike Scott won his second team MVP award. He won his Opening Day start. Scott won 20 games for the first time and was named National League Pitcher of the Month in June when he went 6-1.

He was 14-5 at the All-Star break and the starting pitcher for the National League. In early June, Scott was called on to pitch two days after a start as the game went into extra innings. Scott pitched the top of the 13th inning and then with one out and the bases loaded, he hit a sacrifice fly to give the Astros the walk-off win. Scott finished second to Padres reliever Mark Davis in the Cy Young voting while leading the league in wins.

ASTROS HALL OF FAME

The Houston Astros initiated their Hall of Fame in 2019. Inductees are honored in a special pregame ceremony before a game in August each season. There are plaques detailing the careers of the players on the concourse in Home Run Alley at Minute Maid Park. Honorees are referred to in this book as Astros Hall of Famers.

Bob Aspromonte, Jeff Bagwell, Lance Berkman, Craig Biggio, Cesar Cedeno, Jose Cruz, Larry Dierker, Joe Morgan, Phil Niekro, Roy Oswalt, Shane Reynolds, J.R. Richard, Nolan Ryan, Mike Scott, Jim Umbricht, Billy Wagner, Bob Watson, Don Wilson and Jimmy Wynn are the players who have been inducted through 2021. Executives, broadcasters and other nonuniformed personnel also are included but are not mentioned in this limited space.

BIGGIO-BAGWELL PLAYOFF ERA

1990

In the final year before clearing the decks for a young club, Bill Doran was traded to Cincinnati. Mike Scott had an off year and Glenn Davis was hit with injuries. Davis was traded to Baltimore after the season for Pete Harnisch, Curt Schilling and Steve Finley. Larry Andersen was traded to Boston for Jeff Bagwell. Bagwell would become the first baseman for the next 15 years. Biggio played some outfield but did not move to second base until 1992.

The 75-87 record signaled to General Manager Bill Wood that he should go all in with a youth movement.

1990 MVP

The 1990 team MVP was Danny Darwin. A pennant drive acquisition in 1986, Darwin started the season as a setup man in the bullpen to closer Dave Smith. Darwin was shifted into the starting rotation and his final 17 appearances came as starts. He was nothing short of spectacular as he won his first eight decisions as a starter that season. He ended the season with 162 2/3 innings pitched, which made him the winner of the league ERA crown at 2.21. Darwin did not give up more than one run in any of his July starts and was named pitcher of the month for the National League.

1991

With 1991 marking a watershed year of moving on from veterans to youth, Mike Scott retired after a shoulder injury sidelined him. Pete Harnisch joined the "old man" of the staff, 31-year-old Jim Deshaies, Mark Portugal, Daryl Kile and Jimmy Jones. Schilling was tried as a closer. But Al Osuna won that job. A new group of position players included shortstop Andujar Cedeno and outfielders Luis Gonzalez and Eric Anthony. Karl Rhodes and Kenny Lofton had their opportunities. It was a dismal 65-97 season.

During September 1991, the Astros went to Cincinnati on their final road trip of the season to meet the Reds. The Astros were in the basement of the National League West while the Reds were struggling to reach .500 themselves.

Astros starter Mark Portugal had been excellent through the first three innings, allowing the Reds only a single walk. The Astros' sticks had given Portugal a two-run lead on a double by Jeff Bagwell.

Mariano Duncan hit the first pitch he saw from Portugal out of the playing field to cut the Astro lead to 2-1. Next up, Reds first baseman Hal Morris blasted a 1-1 pitch out to right center to make it a tie game. Paul O'Neill then connected on a 1-1 pitch for the third solo homer in a row to give the Reds the lead. After each homer at Riverfront Stadium that season by the Reds, a cannon was ignited in the outfield.

Astros pitching coach Bob Cluck went out for a mound visit after those seven pitches. Portugal pushed back to Cluck on why he had come out. Cluck replied that he was coming out to slow him down a bit. "The guy in the outfield needs some time to reload his cannon."

Cluck's stalling tactic worked. These homers were the only hits yielded by Portugal before he was lifted for pinch-hitter Rafael Ramirez with the Astros trailing. The bats came alive later and the Astros came back to win 7-3, but Portugal got a no-decision.

1991 MVP

In 1991, the Astros discovered a hidden gem in newly minted first baseman Jeff Bagwell. Bagwell was shifted to first base in the last week of spring training and went on to become the Rookie of the Year, the first time an Astro had ever won this award. Bagwell received 23 of the 24 first place votes for the award. The 23-year-old Bagwell had a rough first week, collecting only two hits and one RBI. A trip to Atlanta and San Francisco got Bagwell's bat going and it kept going for over a decade.

Bagwell had thirteen three-hit games for the Astros and had his average up to .300 in late September before falling back to finish at .294. Bagwell started in the sixth position in the order but was moved to the three-hole in late June.

1992

In their last season with John McMullen as owner, a revitalized team took the field. They improved to 81-81. That was quite an accomplishment in a year with a history-making 26-game road trip to accommodate the Republican National Convention. The 12-14 record for that road trip spoke to the competitiveness of the new players. Biggio took over at second base on his way to a Hall of Fame avenue for his career.

1992 MVP

The 1992 team MVP was closer Doug Jones, one of a handful of relievers ever to win this award. Doug Jones was also a rather unconventional choice as he saved 36 games for the team, which was then the franchise record. Jones' out pitch was his change-up, which came in under normal hitting speeds. Unlike "Wild Thing," Jones was nicknamed "Mild Thing."

Jones was released by the Indians after posting a 5.54 ERA in 1991. The Astros signed him as a low-budget add to the rebuilding team's bullpen and he became the closer. Jones finished the season with a 1.85 ERA along with 11 wins - all in relief. He was the first reliever to lead Houston in wins in club history.

Owner John McMullen, who made millions in the shipbuilding industry, also had the golden touch when it came to buying and selling sports franchises. He scooped up the Astros out of bankruptcy and sold them for a bundle to Drayton McLane, Jr. late in 1992.

McMullen later did the same thing with the New Jersey Devils of the NHL. McMullen had his battles with adversaries, including General Manager Dick Wagner. Wagner resigned after 1987, replaced by Assistant GM Bill Wood.

218

1993

When 1993 arrived, new owner Drayton McLane made headlines with the free agent signings of native Texans Doug Drabek and Greg Swindell.

In their first season under the McLane ownership, the players wore new blue and gold uniforms with an open star logo. Some fresh paint on the Astrodome covered the revitalized team on the field. Addressing the pitching weakness of his team, McLane sent a message to the fans that he was serious about winning. Mark Portugal surpassed both of those established veterans with a breakout 18-4 season with a 2.08 ERA. Darryl Kile won 15 games and threw a no-hitter against the Mets.

Although the 85-77 record signaled improvement, Bill Wood was fired as GM and replaced by Bob Watson. Howe also was fired and replaced by Pittsburgh coach Terry Collins.

1993 MVP

The 1993 season brought Jeff Bagwell his second team MVP award. Bagwell would go on to win six of them in his tenure with the team. Bagwell hit .320 for the team, when he placed sixth in the league. Bagwell also hit 20 homers, another career high for him. Bagwell reached base in the first 33 games of the season and flirted with the .400 mark in late May. Bagwell was quickly establishing himself as one of the premier players in the major leagues.

1994

With the fiery Terry Collins calling the shots and the young players maturing, 1994 brought a season that might have been memorable if it had not been halted by a player strike in August. The 66-49 record had the Astros in pursuit of a playoff spot when the season ended abruptly.

219

GM Bob Watson provided Collins with a lineup of players entering their prime seasons. Craig Biggio was 28, Jeff Bagwell 26, Luis Gonzalez 26, Scott Servais 27, Steve Finley 29. Andujar Cedeno was 24. The "old man" on the pitching staff was Doug Drabek. He was 31! Greg Swindell (29), Darryl Kile (25), Pete Harnisch (27) and Brian Williams (25) were perfectly positioned at those ages for improvement.

1994 MVP

Jeff Bagwell became the first Astro player to win the National League Most Valuable Player Award and was only the third player in league history to be a unanimous choice for the award. The only other National Leaguers to have been unanimous choices were Orlando Cepeda in 1967 and Mike Schmidt in 1980. Bagwell collected all sorts of hardware, including a Gold Glove and a Silver Slugger Award. Bagwell broke Jim Wynn's long-standing club record with 39 homers and a lofty .368 batting average. Bagwell's season ended in early August when he suffered a broken bone in his hand. He was hit by a pitch by the Padres Andy Benes.

The baseball season ended only a couple of days later with the players' strike and subsequent cancellation of the World Series for the only time in baseball history.

One of the most amazing things about Bagwell's numbers was that he compiled all of these numbers in only 110 games, including 116 RBI!

1995

Drayton McLane was in a payroll crunch for 1995, leading to a massive trade with San Diego. Ken Caminiti, Steve Finley, Andujar Cedeno and three other players headed to the Padres. The Astros received Derek Bell, Phil Plantier, Craig Shipley, Ricky Gutierrez and Doug Brocail. Then Luis Gonzalez and Scott Servais were dealt to Chicago for ineffective catcher Rick Wilkins. Finally, top draft choice Phil Nevin went packing to Detroit for reliever Mike Henneman.

The 76-68 record left the Astros just short of a playoff spot. When they battled the Cubs at Wrigley Field to end the season, both clubs knocked each other out of the picture while the Colorado Rockies slipped past both of them.

1995 MVP

In 1995, second baseman Craig Biggio was named the team's MVP for his outstanding play as the Astros finished only one game out of the new wild card race. Biggio led the league in runs scored at 123, and also led the team in hits. Biggio became the catalyst of the Astros offense as Manager Terry Collins moved him into the second spot in the lineup.

Hitting behind the speedy Brian Hunter, he twice scored five runs in a game. In the last week of the season, Biggio collected four hits and scored five times in a game at Wrigley Field, but the Astros lost a 12-11 decision to the Cubs. Biggio also had a four-stolen-base game at Montreal in September as well. This was also the first season that Biggio led the league in being hit by a pitch with 23.

1996

With Jeff Bagwell healthy after two straight years of broken hand injuries, he put up .315-31-120 numbers in 1996. Derek Bell drove in 113 runs. The "Killer Bees" era of Bagwell-Biggio-Bell and third baseman Sean Berry made the Astros an offensive powerhouse.

Pitcher Mike Hampton mastered his sinker-curveball-changeup mix to give Houston another young factor on the mound to join Kile, Drabek and Shane Reynolds. The 82-80 finish wasn't enough to save Terry Collins' job, but the team was positioned to take off. Billy Wagner had shown after his promotion that he could be a powerful closer.

Andres Reiner

Some of the Astros' success in the late 1990s was due to their aggressive scouting and player development in Venezuela. International amateur scout Andres Reiner was a standout contributor. He helped the Astros open a baseball academy in Venezuela, the first one in the country. The pipeline that was created helped the team to develop several All-Stars and at least six major contributors to the Astros or other clubs.

By the mid-1990s, the Astros' system had produced a couple of impact outfielders, Richard Hidalgo and Bobby Abreu. The Astros only protected one of them, losing Abreu to the Tampa Bay Devil Rays in the expansion draft in 1998.

Two of the prospects, shortstop Carlos Guillen and pitcher Freddy Garcia, were dealt to the Seattle Mariners in the deadline deal for Randy Johnson in 1998. Guillen and Garcia had yet to crack the Astros roster but were major assets for Seattle. Minnesota Twins starter Johan Santana was another of the prizes developed by the team from Venezuela, winning a pair of Cy Young Awards along the way in his 12-year career. He left in the Rule V draft.

Astros field director Carlos Alfonzo said, "Reiner was more than a visionary in the world of baseball. He was a caring human being that made such an impact, not only with the number of players signed and developed by him, but also with the men and women that he touched in all walks of life." Reiner stayed with the organization through the 2005 season before joining his former boss, Gerry Hunsicker, in Tampa Bay.

Once the Astros established their academy in Venezuela, other teams took note of their success. More teams opened academies there. The Astros kept their academy through 2009 when the political situation there caused them to close it. But the pipeline of talent had been opened, and more than half of the major league teams eventually set up shop there. The Marlins found future Triple Crown winner Miguel Cabrera there and the Astros continued to find stars like Jose Altuve there.

"It comes down to believing in him," said former General Manager Bill Wood of Reiner. Reiner was an international businessman and baseball scout who approached Wood in 1984 about opening the academy. Wood, then the Astros farm director, wasn't able to act on it at that time.

A few seasons later, Wood had replaced Dick Wagner as general manager, and soon gave Reiner the approval to implement his plan. Of the first four signees for the Astros, three made it to the majors.

Abreu was joined by shortstop Raul Chavez (turned catcher) and first baseman Roberto Petagine in the first class of signees.

Reiner was born in Hungary but moved to Venezuela as a youngster in 1946 after the end of World War II. After his time in amateur ball, Reiner became ingrained in the game in his country. Reiner became a goldsmith and jeweler in Caracas before devoting his efforts to baseball. He started his career in scouting with the Pirates before joining the Astros.

Reiner knew where to find the talent. In the signing of Santana during the baseball lockout of 1994, the team wasn't funding the signing of any more international players. However, the team did allow Reiner to use his own funds to guarantee a player's signature, and he was able to bring Santana into the Astros fold during the 1994 players strike.

Reiner's contribution to the Astros' success can't be denied, but his impact on baseball was even larger with the number of players who starred in the last couple of decades.

1996 MVP

In 1996, Jeff Bagwell was named the team MVP for the fourth time, tying Jose Cruz. Bagwell's 120 RBIs were the most ever by an Astro player. Opposing pitchers walked Bagwell 135 times during the season. Bagwell finished ninth in National League MVP voting behind former teammate Ken Caminiti of the Padres.

1997

In the cycles of baseball, it's been typical for a team to replace a laid-back manager with a fiery one, reversing the move the next time a change was made. That pattern held true with Houston, with fiery Hal Lanier giving way to patient Art Howe and hard-charging Terry Collins moving out for laid-back first-time skipper Larry Dierker. Dierker had been a top-notch broadcaster for many years. He was insightful. His instincts were to let this good team play. He had few signs. Players often put on their own hit-and-run plays, but Dierker did not want to get in their way by calling pitchouts or running plays.

He was a minimalist who stayed with his starting pitchers as long as possible and limited his pitching changes.

If he had an effective setup man such as Scott Elarton pitching well in the seventh inning, often he did not remove him for the eighth. The 1997 team broke the 11-year playoff drought by holding off Pittsburgh in September and starting a run of four playoff teams in five years.

Dierker was an excellent analyst for radio and television broadcasts. He also wrote an insightful newspaper column for the *Houston Chronicle* for years.

When Drayton McLane was looking for a new manager in the winter of 1996, he challenged his top executives to think outside the box. McLane was unafraid to challenge baseball conventions.

Tal Smith and Gerry Hunsicker were impressed with Dierker's knowledge and his perspective as a successful pitcher for many years. The team needed to improve its pitching to a championship level. Dierker delivered in spades as a manager.

When Darryl Kile was improving as a starting pitcher and on a mission to make a quantum leap in his performance, he searched out Dierker. After his final start of the season, Kile asked Dierker for advice about what he should do in the offseason. Dierker was a broadcaster at the time. He responded, "Play golf." Kile chuckled and added that he was planning on that. Dierker clarified, "Play golf as if every shot is important. Keep your score. Manage your way around the golf course. It's like pitching out of trouble and managing your way through a lineup."

Dierker's Astros opened with a 2-1 victory over Atlanta behind Shane Reynolds and Billy Wagner. The Braves would beat the Astros in the playoffs that year, but they were the gold standard in the National League. Reynolds was 9-10 that year, but Kile stepped up with a 19-7 season. Hampton was 15-10.

The other two spots in the rotation were up for grabs when the season opened. Chris Holt and Ramon Garcia kept things from falling apart, but both had losing records. Luis Gonzalez returned to Houston and put together a 23-game hitting streak to tie the club record.

Jeff Bagwell had another monster year, belting 43 home runs and driving in 135 runs while stealing 31 bases.

Craig Biggio led the league with 146 runs. Some 11 years to the day that Mike Scott clinched the last Houston playoff spot with a no-hitter, Mike Hampton clinched the division title with a four-hitter against the Cubs. The Astros won a mediocre NL Central Division by going 84-78.

The Atlanta Braves rolled over the Astros in the playoffs. The Braves won the opener, 2-1 behind Greg Maddux despite Darryl Kile's strong game.

Tom Glavine enjoyed major run support and beat Mike Hampton 13-3 in Game 2. John Smoltz fired a three-hitter in the 3-1 Braves win in the sweep.

1997 MVP

Craig Biggio played in every game for the second consecutive season in 1997. He became the first player in major league history to play every game and not ground into a double play during the season. Biggio and Jeff Bagwell were both voted as starters for the National League All-Star team as the Astros won their first divisional title since 1986. Biggio scored 146 runs, a franchise record to this point, and was hit by a career high 34 pitches. Biggio finished fourth in the league MVP voting while he became the league's premier leadoff hitter. He also won his third Silver Slugger and Gold Glove awards.

1998

Although Kile became a free agent and signed with Colorado prior to 1998, the Astros were loaded with offense and they powered past teams on their way to a club record 102 wins.

When they acquired Randy Johnson in a deadline trade engineered by General Manager Gerry Hunsicker, the Astros were positioned to make it to the World Series for the first time. It didn't happen.

They ran into a locked-in Kevin Brown at the peak of his career and the best big game Sterling Hitchcock ever pitched, giving the San Diego Padres a 3-1 win in the Division Series.

Outfielder Bob Abreu left Houston as an expansion draft choice by Tampa Bay. Abreu, left unprotected by the Astros in a major mistake, was traded to Philadelphia and turned out to be a tremendous player. The Astros in effect chose Richard Hidalgo over Abreu. Hidalgo was a solid player, but Abreu was better. Actually, the Astros could have kept both of them.

Reliever John Hudek was traded to the New York Mets for outfielder Carl Everett, who had an explosive season in Houston and suppressed criticism of the loss of Abreu. Another insightful trade brought outfielder Moises Alou from Florida for prospects. Alou lit up opposing pitchers for three of the best years of any Astro in history.

Alou belted 38 home runs and drove in 124 runs while hitting .312. He was one of the best clutch hitters in Houston history. His presence in a lineup with Bagwell, Biggio, Everett, Bell and Berry added up to a league-leading 874 runs for the Killer Bees.

Kerry Wood of the Chicago Cubs stopped that club on one scratch hit by Ricky Gutierrez in Chicago May 6 while striking out 20 in one of the greatest pitching performances in recent decades.

The Houston pitching was solid. Shane Reynolds led the staff in wins with 19. Jose Lima chimed in with 16 after escaping the bullpen. Mike Hampton and Sean Bergman were in double figures.

When the Randy Johnson trade hit the media July 31, the Astros had added a dominant lefthander who could stop other lineups cold. Johnson came from Seattle for a large prospect load, including Freddy Garcia and Carlos Guillen.

Both of them went on to All-Star status in their long and productive careers. Gerry Hunsicker said he owed it to the Houston fans to go for a World Series by mortgaging the future for Johnson. Johnson was in the final year of his contract, and he left for Arizona after the season. Before departing, he gave the Astros a dominant two months.

The Big Unit was 10-1 with a 1.26 ERA. He pitched three straight shutouts in the Dome, fanning 16 in the third.

Kevin Brown topped Johnson 2-1 in the NLDS opener, with a save from Trevor Hoffman. Brown struck out a playoff record 16. The Astros evened the series in Houston on a Bill Spiers RBI single in the ninth off Hoffman, 5-4. Billy Wagner blew a 4-2 lead on a Jim Leyritz two-run homer that tied the game, 4-4.

Brown returned to stop the Astros in Game 3, winning 2-1. He pitched two of the first three games since there was a day off after both of the first two games. Leyritz struck a game-winning home run late in the game off Scott Elarton.

Hitchcock and the Padre bullpen held the Killer Bees to three hits and beat Johnson in the finale, 6-1. The Padres won the series, 3-1.

1998 MVP

Craig Biggio repeated as the Astros MVP in 1998. Biggio was again among the elite in the league. He hit a lofty .325 and finished second in the National League with 210 hits. He was the first Astro to collect 200 hits in a season. He also tied for third in the league in runs scored with 123.

He reached base in 41 straight games either by hit, walk or hit by pitch in April until early June. Biggio was named an All-Star for the fifth consecutive season. He was also the first Astro player to break the 50-double mark in a season, leading the NL. He powered 20 homers. Biggio became only the second player in history (Tris Speaker of Boston in 1912 was the first) to combine 50 doubles and 50 steals. He scored 123 and set a club record with 210 hits.

1999

When the 1999 season rolled around, the ceremonial first pitch honor belonged to Neil Armstrong. The first man to set foot on the moon told Drayton McLane on the phone, "I don't do public events" when McLane invited him. When McLane explained the historical significance of the game, Armstrong agreed to do it. After all, Armstrong had been behind the Houston dugout as one of 23 astronauts tossing out first pitches when the Astrodome opened in 1965. This was the final opener in the Astrodome, 35 seasons later. The Astros beat the Cubs 4-2.

They were on their way to another division title. Shane Reynolds, who won the opener, finished third on his team in wins with 16. Mike Hampton had a magical 22-4 season. Jose Lima was 21-10.

By June 13, the '99 Astros were 36-23. They led San Diego 4-1 in the eighth when Manager Larry Dierker suffered a grand mal seizure in the dugout, stopping the game. He missed the next 27 games after brain surgery.

The game was suspended until July 23, the next time San Diego visited Houston. The Astros were 13-14 while bench coach Matt Galante served as interim manager.

Jeff Bagwell smashed Jimmy Wynn's club record for home runs in a career – 224. Bagwell also walked 149 times to edge past Wynn's single season record for walks. Although Moises Alou missed the entire season with a knee injury, Bagwell's 42 home runs and 126 RBIs were supplemented by big seasons by Carl Everett and a combination of other players.

The race for the division crown went to the final day. Houston beat Los Angeles in the Astrodome in the regular season Dome finale, 9-4.

Willie Nelson took the field and sang, "Turn out the lights, the party's over" during the celebration on the field, which included many of the Houston players from the team's history. The team headed for the playoffs for the third straight year after an injury-riddled, 97-65 season.

Unfortunately, the lack of success in the postseason continued when the arch-rival Atlanta Braves knocked off the Astros. The Astros still could not win a postseason series for the first time, although Shane Reynolds beat Greg Maddux in Game 1, 6-1.

Kevin Millwood's one-hitter in Game 2 quickly squared the series.

In Houston for Game 3, the tenth inning featured a highlight-reel play by Atlanta shortstop Walt Weiss. He stopped Tony Eusebio's smash toward left field with a diving effort, springing to an emergency throwing position with his body leaning severely toward third base. Weiss pulled off an Ozzie Smith-type play that was dazzling, throwing out Ken Caminiti at home. Brian Jordan's two-run double in the 12th won it for Atlanta, 5-3.

The Braves took Game 4, 7-5, to close out the series and close the Astrodome for baseball. Since 1999 the Dome has sat in its place on Kirby at Loop 610, gathering dust and waiting for a decision on how it can be used in the future. Its future is being studied.

Its place on the Register of Historic Places prevents it from being demolished. The Astros exited the Dome winless in six playoff series. Six no-hitters were pitched in the Astrodome, all by Houston.

1999 MVP

Jeff Bagwell was selected as the team's MVP for a record fifth time in 1999. Bagwell finished second to the Braves Chipper Jones in league MVP voting. Bagwell was the league leader in runs scored with 143 and in walks with 149. He also hit 42 homers, which was one off of his own franchise best in 1997. Bagwell also broke the career homer mark by passing Jim Wynn's total April 21. His season was also historic. He was the seventh player to hit 40 homers and steal 30 bases in the same season. Bagwell first joined the 40-30 club in 1997. Only he and Barry Bonds had achieved this mark twice in their careers. Bagwell loved the city of Chicago. He had three-homer games at both Comiskey Park and Wrigley Field in the same season. Only Johnny Mize and Ralph Kiner had connected for three-homer games at two different ballparks in the same season. It had been over 50 years since it was done. Bagwell also homered in 17 different ballparks in 1999.

Did you know…

Craig Biggio's first uniform number with the Astros was 4. When veteran Steve Lombardozzi came to Houston in a trade in 1989, he claimed that number. Veterans who have more major league service time typically are granted their requests for uniform numbers. Biggio then took number 7 and made it famous.

Chapter 6

A NEW CENTURY

2000

With a long-anticipated move to new Enron Field in downtown Houston, Drayton McLane had the retractable roof that allowed the fans to enjoy games played on natural grass with the roof open if weather conditions allowed.

The new ballpark brought energy and developments to the east side of downtown Houston. Since the team had made three straight playoff trips, the fans were used to top quality baseball.

Many fans expressed concerns about the parking situation, but they soon discovered that they could get to the stadium from any part of Houston easily and the traffic could empty quicker after games than at the Astrodome. A variety of hotels, restaurants and other establishments developed in the area over the next two decades.

With the new stadium came new branding of the team, with the new uniform featuring brick red and black colors to fit the theme of Union Station, the old train station that was converted into an entrance to the stadium as well as the offices for the team. A locomotive was resting atop railroad tracks above the left field wall to add to the entertainment, blowing its whistle and moving back and forth on the tracks when the Astros created excitement on the field.

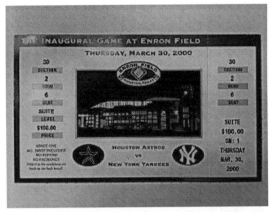

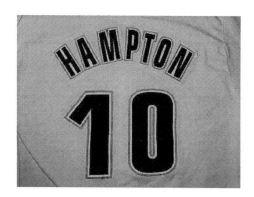

Ace pitcher Mike Hampton and slugging outfielder Carl Everett both made their exit before they could play a game at the new ballpark. Everett was traded to Boston for shortstop Adam Everett and Greg Miller. Hampton announced that he would file for free agency after the 2000 season, prompting a trade to the New York Mets along with Derek Bell for youngsters Octavio Dotel and Roger Cedeno.

Did you know that....

Twice in franchise history have the Astros had two 20- game winners in the same season. Jose Lima and Mike Hampton won at least 20 games in 1999. Justin Verlander and Gerrit Cole matched that achievement in 2019.

Enron Field

Fans flocked to see the new stadium, but the team's performance was disappointing. The style of baseball was totally different from the Astrodome's spacious, pitching-oriented games. With a 315-foot wall down the left field line and balls flying through the air, an offensive explosion accompanied the move to Enron. The Astros slugged their way to a National League record 249 home runs and scored 938 runs. The most runs they scored in a season at the Astrodome was 874. The Astros finished 72-90 in their new uniforms, featuring a red and black color scheme with pinstripes. Jose Lima wound up 7-16 with a 6.65 ERA. Richard Hidalgo, Jeff Bagwell and Moises Alou all put up huge numbers. Lance Berkman and Daryle Ward belted 21 and 20 home runs, respectively. They showed that they would be big factors in future lineups.

Craig Biggio's iron man status at second base was interrupted August 1 at Miami by a knee injury that sidelined him with a torn ACL for the rest of the season. Chris Truby impressed in a trial at third base after being called up from the minors.

During the summer of 2000, Tony Eusebio put together one of the most unique hitting streaks in baseball history. On July 9, Eusebio, the Astros backup catcher, started a hitting streak that lasted nearly two months. Eusebio came in with a batting average of .205 and despite sporadic playing time, raised it to .289 before his 24-game hitting streak was snapped.

Eusebio was not normally assigned to any particular starting pitcher, and had struggled through a 1-for-26 slump before his bat went to work. Eusebio was splitting time with Mitch Meluskey behind the plate. Meluskey hit 14 homers that season. The hitting streak for Eusebio was rather remarkable since it lasted 54 days and was one of the longest for a catcher ever.

Eusebio hit .409 during the streak, but the number sneaked up on people and became the franchise record. Eusebio's mark was eclipsed by speedy Willy Taveras a few seasons later.

"I didn't know the record streak for the Astros was 23 games," Eusebio told reporters after the game. This was not the only unlikely event in the career of Eusebio. In 1997, Eusebio swiped his first career base in the Divisional Series. He had never stolen a base in the majors and was able to swipe only one during the regular season.

Eusebio's season ended a couple of days later when he separated his shoulder falling into the dugout chasing a foul ball. Eusebio spent one more season as the Astros backup catcher before signing with the Expos, but he was released before playing for them.

2000 MVP

Again in 2000, Jeff Bagwell was voted the team's MVP. Bagwell had a career high and franchise record 47 homers. He also led the league by scoring 152 times, the fourth-highest total in National League history. Playing his first season at new Enron Field, Bagwell set the team record for homers at home with 28. Bagwell also became the 87th player in major league history to hit 300 career homers. The club fell back as the pitchers struggled to adapt to the new ballpark, but the hitters loved it.

Bagwell was the first player in National League history to hit 45+ homers, knock in 100 and score 150 runs in a single season.

2001

Despite the disappointment of dropping to a 72-90 record the first year at Enron Field after winning three straight division titles, there was not a major turnover of the roster.

Jose Lima had the Crawford Boxes in his head in 2000 and there was reason to think he might not be able to handle pitching in a home run haven, but he remained on the staff. The biggest offseason move was reacquiring catcher Brad Ausmus from Detroit, along with Doug Brocail and Nelson Cruz. The Astros parted with problematic Mitch Meluskey and mercurial Roger Cedeno in the trade. Meluskey hit better than any Astro catcher ever had, but his game-calling was below average and his ability to work with his teammates was in question after he initiated a fight during batting practice in San Diego with outfielder Matt Mieske.

Craig Biggio opened the season with his first career five-hit game, displaying his return from knee surgery after being knocked onto the disabled list in 2000 by a Preston Wilson slide at second base. Biggio returned to play 155 games and bang out 180 hits.

Moises Alou and Lance Berkman also had big years, both hitting .331 and driving in more than 100 runs. Alou, Berkman and Hidalgo totaled 314 RBIs.

Third baseman Chris Truby could not pull out of a slump, leading General Manager Gerry Hunsicker to outmaneuver the Chicago Cubs for free agent Vinny Castilla after he was released by Tampa Bay.

Castilla rewarded Hunsicker by driving in 82 runs in just 122 games. Jeff Bagwell delivered 130 RBIs with one of his best years, and the offense again thrived.

The pink elephant from 2000 – the pitching staff – underwent some positive change with young hurlers Wade Miller and Roy Oswalt claiming spots in the rotation with strong efforts. Miller worked his turbo sinker to NL Pitcher of the Month honors in April with a 4-1 start. He finished 16-8 with a 3.40 earned run average. Oswalt was promoted in May after a whirlwind ascendancy through the minors, finishing 14-3 with a 2.73 ERA. Tim Redding and Carlos Hernandez also helped as rookies. The huge boost from the rookie corps allowed the club to withstand miserable starts by Jose Lima, Scott Elarton and Kent Bottenfield. All of those three were gone from the rotation by midseason. Billy Wagner tied the club record with 39 saves. He, Berkman and Alou were All-Stars.

The Astros caught the Chicago Cubs in August, but their NL Central pennant race was paused by the attack on America September 11. Baseball was shut down for a week.

With the season pushed back, play resumed October 2 with St. Louis just one game behind Houston. The San Francisco Giants and slugger Barry Bonds were in Houston, with Bonds zeroing in on Mark McGwire's single season home run record.

Houston Manager Larry Dierker was emphasizing that his pitchers not give in to Bonds, but rookie Wilfredo Rodriguez was victimized by Bonds' 70th home run October 4 into the upper deck in right-center field to tie McGwire's record of 70 set three years earlier. Bonds went on to finish with 73. The Giants swept the series and the Astros fell a game behind St. Louis.

The season ended in St. Louis for Houston. Billy Wagner escaped a bases-loaded jam in the last of the ninth with a double play ball in a Houston 2-1 thriller in the series opener. Lance Berkman provided the game-winning home run in the top of the ninth.

The Cardinals won the next game to force a dilemma for Dierker in the regular season finale. The Astros had already secured a playoff spot as the wild card even if they lost the game and finished second to the Redbirds.

Dierker could save his ace, Shane Reynolds, for the playoff opener instead of using him in the final regular season game. Owner Drayton McLane wanted to win the division title. The decision was made to start Reynolds.

The Astros won the finale 9-2 as Reynolds beat former Astro Darryl Kile. They equaled the Cardinals' 93-69 record but held the tie-breaker because of a better record in head-to-head play. Houston moved into the playoffs against archrival Atlanta.

In Game 1, the Houston bullpen failed to protect a 3-2 lead in the eighth inning. Shortstop Julio Lugo booted a double play ball and the Braves went on to score four times in the 7-4 Atlanta win. Wagner surrendered a three-run homer to Chipper Jones.

Tom Glavine was brilliant in a 1-0 Atlanta win in Game 2. In that era, Glavine was able to exploit the wider strike zone of umpires such as Eric Gregg to his advantage. Catcher Javy Lopez routinely planted his right foot outside of the catcher's box and Glavine hit his target with pinpoint accuracy, often several inches outside the edge of home plate. The only run scored when Lugo made another error. Emergency starter Dave Mlicki pitched well for the injured Oswalt.

John Burkett beat Reynolds in Game 3, 6-2. The Braves swept the series from the Astros and beat them in the playoffs for the third time in five years. Dierker resigned, saying he had taken the team as far as he could. Jimy Williams was hired to replace him.

2001 MVP

In 2001, the run of eight consecutive seasons that the team MVP was either future Hall of Famer Craig Biggio or future Hall of Famer Jeff Bagwell ended. There was a new big bat in the lineup, Lance Berkman. Berkman finished fifth in league MVP voting. Berkman led the National League with 55 doubles, and broke Pete Rose's record for the most doubles by a switch-hitter in a season. Berkman had 94 extra-base hits while knocking in 126 runs as a left fielder. He also had an eye-popping 1.051 OPS.

Berkman raised his average above .330 in mid-May and had only one day for the rest of the season below that. He finished the season with a .331 mark, finishing fourth in the league in hitting behind Larry Walker and Todd Helton of the Rockies and teammate Moises Alou. In early April, Berkman homered into the Allegheny River in a game against the Pirates.

Larry Dierker resigned as manager after 2001, saying that he had taken the team as far as he could. He continues to be involved in the Houston community, especially with the Cy-Hope charity.

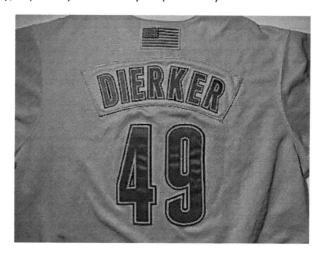

2002

Unfortunately for Dierker's successor Jimy Williams, his career pattern as a manager continued in Houston. An excellent teacher and expert on the fundamentals of baseball, Williams also managed Toronto and Boston in the years prior to their championship seasons. Williams inherited improving young pitchers Oswalt and Miller, but the 3-4-5 starter spots were problematic in 2002. Reynolds was injured, leaving young lefty Carlos Hernandez third on the staff in wins with seven after Oswalt's 19 and Miller's 15. Hernandez could have been another important contributor to the Houston cause for the next few years, but his left shoulder was injured on a baserunning dive into second base, and it derailed his career.

240

Nonetheless, Williams and the Astros fought through early problems and got rolling in the second half. They pulled to within a game of St. Louis August 7 before falling back. They wound up with an 84-78 record, 13 games behind St. Louis.

Despite trades by GM Gerry Hunsicker for infielder Mark Loretta and pitcher Tom Gordon, the Astros could not get a solid team performance, due in part to substandard years from Craig Biggio and Richard Hidalgo, among others. The team needed improvement for 2003.

One of the memorable days of the 2002 season started sadly in St. Louis, although the Astros were in Houston. The Astros were mourning the death of former teammate Darryl Kile. Bagwell, Biggio and Brad Ausmus flew to St. Louis to attend the memorial service and returned to Houston for the game, but all three were on the bench when the game started.

With their emotions raw, all three were pressed into action as the game developed. When extra innings arrived, visiting Seattle played hard for a victory. Bagwell delivered the game-winning hit as a pinch-hitter and was mobbed by his teammates near first base in a tear-filled celebration.

Catcher-first baseman Alan Zinter was promoted from the minors in 2002 to crown a marathon journey to the majors. Zinter, a first round draft choice of the New York Mets in 1989, toiled tirelessly in the minor leagues for many years before finally reaching the big leagues. With an ever-present smile on his face, he told the story of his determination and dedication to continue his quest to reach the highest level of baseball. The El Paso, Texas native was 34 when he played for the Astros, hitting .136 with two home runs during his first season. Zinter served mostly as a pinch-hitter. Two years later he played his second and final season in the majors with Arizona. He later became a major league hitting coach. Zinter played a total of 18 seasons in the minor leagues and one in Japan, hitting 258 homers in almost 1,800 games.

2002 MVP

In 2002, Lance Berkman repeated as team MVP. Berkman got the year off to a fast start by homering in the first three games. Later in April, he connected for two homers in back-to-back games in Cincinnati, including three homers in the April 16 game. He joined Mickey Mantle as the only switch-hitters to slug 10 homers in their team's first 20 games of the year. Berkman led the National League with 128 RBIs after being installed in centerfield. He was named to the All-Star Game and participated in the home run derby. Berkman broke Bob Watson's franchise record by knocking in a run in ten consecutive games. Berkman joined Jeff Bagwell as the only Astros to lead the league in RBIs. Berkman finished third in MVP voting behind Barry Bonds and Albert Pujols.

2003

With the core of the team aging in 2003, Hunsicker reached to acquire an injection of energy. Surprisingly, he signed free agent second baseman Jeff Kent to a three-year contract during the offseason. The signing blindsided Biggio, whose .253-15-58 season in 2002 was below his standards. Nonetheless, he was not expecting to see his position given away.

Without any public comment, he started working on sprinting in preparation for his move to the outfield. At 37, his legs would undergo a major test in a move to center field, with its 436-foot wall at the top of the incline known as Tal's Hill. Drayton McLane embraced different features when his playing field was designed for 2000, but major league centerfielders did not! They were worried about running into the flagpole.

Kent, an NL MVP two years earlier with the San Francisco Giants, hit .334 with 34 home runs that year. Second base was his position and the Astros did not think about moving him. Biggio's athleticism was tested. He coped with a historic turn to his historic career. No everyday player in the modern history of the game had moved from catcher to second base to center field.

Despite his status as an All-Star and Gold Glove winner at second base, he took the challenge and helped to make the Astros a playoff team again by the next year. Lance Berkman moved to left field, with slugger Daryle Ward exiting for Los Angeles in a trade for pitcher Ruddy Lugo.

SHANE REYNOLDS

In a shocking end to spring training, former Opening Day starter Shane Reynolds was released. When Reynolds' career was later judged to be worthy of his status as an Astros Hall of Famer, it must be viewed in a complete context. He won 103 games from 1992 to 2002. He was the Opening Day starter five years in a row, 1996-2000.

Reynolds won 19 games in 1998 and was one of the most consistent pitchers in team history. The durable righthander, a physical conditioning fanatic, made 274 appearances. He walked just 358 in 1622 innings.

Reynolds, who attended the University of Texas, was a third-round draft choice in 1989. He was a marginal prospect as a minor leaguer.

The career turning point for him was similar to Mike Scott's: he learned a new pitch. Minor league pitching coach Brent Strom (later the major league pitching coach) fitted him with a new repertoire.

"For me it was in Venezuela in '91," recalled Reynolds. "I had just finished my second year in AA and Rick Sweet was our manager and he was going to manage our Venezuelan club. Brent Strom was our AAA pitching coach and he was going to be our pitching coach. I think I got lucky as a AA player to be invited and then Strommy just completely changed me. He watched me throw a couple of games and he asked me the question, 'Do you want to spend ten years in the minors or one year in the big leagues?' I said, 'One year in the big leagues.' He said, 'We need to do this. Let's try this.' He completely changed my windup, gave me a sinker, more control over the curveball and taught me the split-finger."

"I have to give him all the credit. I don't think I ever would have made it to the big leagues if that hadn't happened."

Reynolds' spot in the rotation in 2003 went to rookie lefthander Jeriome Robertson, who delivered a strong season. Robertson contributed 15 wins despite a high 5.09 ERA. But the pitching staff was unable to match the offense. Oswalt, Miller, and Tim Redding combined for a 34-32 record.

Redding, who made his debut in 2001, carried the tough-luck label with his 10-14 record despite a good 3.68 ERA. Like Carlos Hernandez, Redding had the potential to form a powerful trio with Oswalt and Miller. His career in Houston (21-28, 4.75 ERA) fell short of his talent.

The offensive boost provided by Kent was part of an improvement from 749 runs scored to 805 by the Astros. Kent delivered what was expected, compiling .297-22-93 numbers. Bagwell (.278-39-100) continued to be one of the top hitters in the sport, unfazed by what others in the lineup did. Berkman (.288-25-93) and Hidalgo (.309-28-88) were excellent bookends in the outfield for Biggio. Newcomers Morgan Ensberg at third base and Adam Everett at shortstop covered the left side of the infield like bluebonnets on a Texas pasture in the spring. Ensberg belted 25 homers with a .291 average. Geoff Blum was an excellent utilityman (.262-10-52).

One of the most significant games of 2003 was a six-pitcher no-hitter at Yankee Stadium in June. Oddly, it was the only win on a six-game road trip which continued in Boston. Even more oddly, Roy Oswalt was their starting pitcher and he failed to complete the second inning. When he left with a leg injury, Jimy Williams turned to the bullpen again and again in the 8-0 win. Peter Munro, Kirk Saarloos, Octavio Dotel, Brad Lidge and Billy Wagner collaborated on the first six-pitcher no-hitter in baseball history. Owner Drayton McLane, Jr. and his family sat near the dugout during the historic game. The no-hitter was so unusual that several of the Astros players did not realize it was a no-hitter when the game ended. The closing trio of Dotel-Lidge-Wagner was perhaps the best end-of-game threesome in the history of the Astros. All of them were closers at some point in their careers.

A 3-6 finish to the season cost the Astros a playoff spot. They were passed by the Chicago Cubs when they faded, finishing 87-75.

2003 MVP

Richard Hidalgo broke the "Killer B's" hold on the team MVP award when he picked up the trophy for his 2003 season.

While not equaling his numbers from 2000, Hidalgo was still at the peak of his career. He slugged 28 homers while knocking in 88. Hidalgo was also a force in right field, throwing out a league-high 22 runners. Hidalgo moved between the fifth and sixth spots in the lineup, often hitting behind Jeff Kent and Jeff Bagwell. Hidalgo knocked in five by hitting three homers in a September game at Coors Field in Denver.

He moved his average over the .300 mark and kept it there for the remainder of the season, finishing at .309.

BILLY WAGNER

As Billy Wagner became an Astros Hall of Famer in 2021, he was celebrated as an unlikely baseball star. Wagner was the victim of a broken home who was raised by different relatives in Virginia, moving from one home to another and finding refuge in sports.

Wagner threw righthanded when he started playing baseball, but at a young age his right arm was broken and he started throwing with his left. As a small kid who was tougher than his teammates, he fell in love with pitching. As he threw baseballs against the side of a barn in his country home, Wagner painted a strike zone on the wall and fired one ball after another at it, in the absence of a playmate.

He rode buses miles over mountain roads to attend school, eventually attracting a scholarship offer from Division III college Ferrum in Virginia despite his lack of velocity and size.

In college, he developed a more muscular body and more force behind his fastball. That turned him into a Houston first-round draft choice in 1993.

Wagner was a starting pitcher in the minors, but when he was promoted to the majors he lacked a curveball and changeup. He found his way to the bullpen and made his future throwing an electric fastball and a snapping slider. Wagner powered through his conversion to closer and became the franchise's all-time saves leader in 2003, just before being traded after the season to Philadelphia. He had been critical of top management during the season for failing to make major trades.

By trading Wagner and moving Brad Lidge to closer, the Astros promoted from within in an obvious succession. Shortly after that, they made two blockbuster free agent signings.

2004

Owner Drayton McLane, Jr. and General Manager Gerry Hunsicker went on a mission to improve the Astros, culminating in the signing of free agent superstar pitchers Andy Pettitte and Roger Clemens, both of whom had lived in the Houston area for most of their lives while pitching for other teams. Clemens and Pettitte had been teammates for the New York Yankees.

Pettitte was a native of Houston suburb Deer Park who left the Yankees after nine straight playoff seasons, with a 149-78 career record in pinstripes and a 1996 World Championship. He had more postseason wins than the Astros had as a team!

A month later, Memorial resident Clemens joined Pettitte as an Astro. Clemens had a Hall of Fame resume, including a 310-160 record with Boston, Toronto and the Yankees.

McLane topped the major splash he created a decade earlier with the signing of Doug Drabek and Greg Swindell. The attention of the baseball world again was directed to Houston.

Clemens brought a brightly-burning fire to the Astros. His intensity on the mound fired up his teammates. He delivered an 18-4 record with a 2.98 ERA in 2004 to bring him his seventh Cy Young Award.

The Rocket was 38-18 with a 2.40 earned run average in his three years with Houston. "The three years that I had here were very special, to have the opportunity to come home and pitch, to work alongside Baggy and Bidge and Andy. For a short period of time, we took football off the map down here."

Pettitte, conversely, was confronted with a left elbow injury while batting in his first game as an Astro, enduring three trips to the disabled list before undergoing surgery for a torn flexor tendon in August of 2004.

Despite all the firepower, the Astros were sluggish early in 2004 and the team was not clicking. Hunsicker was decisive in addressing the major issues. He moved a slump-ridden outfielder Richard Hidalgo to the New York Mets for reliever David Weathers and a minor leaguer. Then he pulled off a three-way deal with Kansas City and Oakland.

Hunsicker sent Octavio Dotel and catcher John Buck into the mix of the three-team deal in order to obtain outfielder Carlos Beltran. Beltran's elite skills allowed Jimy Williams to anchor the outfield by playing him in center field and moving Biggio to left. Brad Lidge took over as the closer. Setup help came from Dan Miceli and David Weathers. Beltran joined the team in late June with the Astros playing below par at 38-34. He caught fire, finishing the season with 38 homers and 42 steals. His elite skillset charged the offense and improved the defense.

But Wade Miller went down with a shoulder injury, joining Pettitte on the shelf, The team reached the All-Star break with a 44-44 record. Minute Maid Park hosted the All-Star Game. Houston Manager Jimy Williams was booed when he was introduced as one of the National League coaches.

Drayton McLane decided at the All-Star break to fire Williams and replace him with Houston resident Phil Garner, a former Astro player and major league manager in Milwaukee and Detroit.

But by August 14 the Astros had sunk even lower, seven games behind the Chicago Cubs for a wild card playoff spot with a 56-60 record.

In Montreal, the Expos were going for a three-game sweep of the Astros behind Livan Hernandez, who took a 4-2 lead to the ninth. The Cuban-born Hernandez led the league in innings pitched and complete games. He needed three outs for his tenth win. He got one. Luis Ayala came in with two on and one out. Jason Lane singled in one run.

Jose Vizcaino tied the game on a ground out. Orlando Palmeiro's two-out pinch single gave the Astros an improbable 5-4 win, snapping the Expos' seven-game winning streak.

Garner had lunch with Hunsicker in Philadelphia amid a sweep of the Phillies. Garner gave Hunsicker every reassurance that the team would fight to the end, but he honestly advised Hunsicker that if it were his team, he'd blow it up. "I'd trade guys and I'd get myself a pile of cash and I'd start all over the next year," Garner told Hunsicker. Hunsicker responded, "I want to give these guys every chance I can."

The Astros dropped two of three to the Cubs in their next series, leaving them 7 ½ games back in the wild card race. Then for the next 16 games, they almost forgot how to lose. From what appeared to be a lost cause, even to their manager, the Astros won 15 of the next 16. They lit up the National League with a 36-10 record from August 15 to the end of the regular season. Only the 1951 Giants had a better finishing kick during that phase of the season. The Astros grabbed a wild card playoff spot by one game over San Francisco.

Berkman was torrid in August and September, hitting .354 with 13 homers and 41 RBIs. "It just seemed that every one of those games coming down the stretch was a playoff game," remembered Berkman. "I think that actually played in our favor, because once we got to the postseason it was really like, 'Well, here we are, it's just another game like we've been playing.' Especially in '04 in this building (Minute Maid Park). No one could beat us." Berkman powered one of the biggest blows of the wild card race in San Francisco, a windblown home run at Pac Bell Park.

The Astros swept their final six-game homestand. The race went to the last day of the regular season. With Roger Clemens scheduled to start against Colorado, he had to be scratched because he was ill the night before. Brandon Backe stepped up with a memorable game on a few hours' notice and beat the Rockies, with Lidge fanning the final four to break the NL strikeout record by a reliever with 157. The Astros won 18 straight at home over the final six weeks of the season. At the end of the 92-70 campaign, the torrid Astros had a strong quest to continue their inspired play in the playoffs.

2004 NLDS

The Astros avenged losses in three earlier playoff series by taking out the Atlanta Braves in the NLDS.

Clemens won the first game, 9-3. Ausmus, Berkman, Beltran and Lane went deep.

The Braves rebounded to claim Game 2 in extra innings. Rafael Furcal gave the Braves a 4-2 triumph in the 11th with a two-run homer off Dan Miceli. Lidge was tagged for a late home run allowing the Braves to tie it, 2-2.

Backe won game 3 with six strong innings, 9-5. Ensberg drove in three runs and Beltran added another homer.

The Braves stormed back in Game 4 to tie the series, 2-2. Biggio ripped an early three-run homer to give Clemens the lead, but the Braves drew even on Adam LaRoche's three-run blast off Chad Qualls. J.D. Drew drove in Furcal in the ninth for a 6-5 Atlanta edge, and John Smoltz closed out the game.

Beltran exploded in Game 5, driving in five in a 12-3 rout in Atlanta. With his two more home runs, Beltran also captured Series MVP honors. He hit .455 with four home runs.

At last, the Astros had won their first postseason series after five failures and 42 seasons of play.

2004 NLCS

Game One of the NLCS was a slugfest. St. Louis captured a 10-7 offensive show despite four Houston home runs.

Albert Pujols and Scott Rolen unloaded back-to-back blasts off Miceli in the eighth to claim Game 2, 6-4.

Clemens and Lidge collaborated on a 5-2 Houston Game 3 win at Minute Maid Park with home runs from Kent, Beltran and Berkman.

Beltran stepped up again with what proved to be the game-winning homer in the seventh inning of Game 4 in a 6-5 Houston decision to tie the series, 2-2. Beltran's home run swing was eye-popping. Oswalt fell behind 3-0 in the first inning with Albert Pujols ripping a two-run homer. Berkman answered with his fourth homer of the series in the sixth. Raul Chavez tied the game, 5-5 in the sixth with a timely single off Kiko Calero.

Woody Williams of St. Louis and Backe dueled to a scoreless tie in Game 5. Jeff Kent teed off with a walk-off three-run homer in the ninth for a 3-0 thriller and a 3-2 Houston series lead.

Phil Garner was strapped for a starting pitcher for Game 6 in St. Louis. He settled on Pete Munro, avoiding using Clemens on short rest. The Cardinals grabbed a thriller, 6-4 in 12 innings, on Jim Edmonds' two-run homer off Dan Miceli.

The series went to Game 7: Clemens vs. Jeff Suppan. The Astros led early, 2-0. They could have broken it open in the second inning when Brad Ausmus crushed a ball into the left center field gap with two men on base. Both would have scored if the ball landed on the outfield grass, but Edmonds dashed over from right center and launched his body into a spectacular diving catch.

"To me, that was the whole series," said Lance Berkman. "Obviously there were other things that happened. But Edmonds almost singlehandedly won those last two games. He hit the walk-off home run in Game 6 and then came back in Game 7."

St. Louis took the game and the series with a 5-2 finale. The Astros went home just as disappointed as in 1980 and 1986, one out or one hit away from a World Series berth but unable to nail it down.

2004 MVP

The local baseball writers selected Lance Berkman the team MVP in 2004. It was his third team MVP award. Berkman became the first Astro outfielder to hit 30 homers in three different seasons. He had a 33-game on base streak through August and September. Berkman took part in the home run derby contest at the All-Star game in Houston and lost in the final round to future teammate Miguel Tejada. Lance grew up learning to switch hit by hitting a tire hanging from a tree limb in New Braunfels, Texas. His righthanded power was tremendous, and he displayed it in the home run derby. But he was more consistent from the left side, where his approach to allow the ball to travel deeper allowed him to capitalize on using the short dimensions to left field and left center at Minute Maid Park. Berkman finished seventh in the league MVP voting behind the Giants' Barry Bonds. Berkman ended the season with 106 RBIs and a .316 average in his third All-Star season. He also was player of the month in the NL in May.

2005

The Astros lost some major talent between 2004 and 2005. Free agent Carlos Beltran turned down the largest contract offer in Astros' history to sign with the New York Mets. Jeff Kent's contract expired and the Astros did not re-sign him. They were about to lose Jeff Bagwell for most of 2005 as well, with his arthritic right shoulder no longer serviceable. Berkman tore up his knee playing flag football and missed the first month of the season, but he was able to take over for Bagwell at first base in early May when the future Hall of Famer underwent shoulder surgery.

The absence of Beltran and Berkman from the outfield forced the Astros to turn to inexperienced players Luke Scott, Willy Taveras, converted infielder Chris Burke and Jason Lane. The return of Andy Pettitte and the surprise contribution of young Wandy Rodriguez bolstered the pitching staff, but the team was offensively challenged.

A horrendous 15-30 start marked by a lack of offense put the Astros in such a bind that the *Houston Chronicle* wrote them off with a story that included a tombstone in the artwork. The players were able to use the premature burial of their playoff chances as a motivating influence.

"We'd walk around the clubhouse and talk to staff and players and kinda look at each other and say, 'Are we this bad?' And I don't think anybody felt that way," said GM Tim Purpura. "I don't think anybody gave up on the talent early. And we certainly didn't either. A lot of people wanted us to tear the club apart, but we stuck to our guns. No. We're gonna go with this group and see what they can accomplish. We just decided to try not to tinker too much and go with what we had."

From June 7 until July 10, they won nine series in a row, improving from 21-34 to 44-43. Coincidentally, they stood 44-44 after 88 games just as the 2004 team had. The hunt for a red and black (team colors) October was alive, especially after witnessing the furious finish the year before. The pattern, in fact, continued.

The Astros captured 15 of 17 games, and by July 30 they had the third-best record in the National League. That's the way they finished, with an 89-73 record, one game better than Philadelphia.

That one-game difference stood out at the end of the regular season. It swung on the September 7 Houston victory over Philadelphia, achieved on Craig Biggio's three-run homer off Billy Wagner in Philadelphia with two outs in the ninth, 8-6.

The Astros' 74-43 record after the 15-30 start was the best in the majors. They joined the 1914 Miracle Boston Braves as the only two teams to reach the postseason after falling 15 games below .500.

Roy Oswalt (20-12, 2.94 ERA), Andy Pettitte (17-9, 2.39) and Roger Clemens (13-8, 1.37) were the key pitching performers. Brandon Backe and Wandy Rodriguez each won ten. Brad Lidge racked up 42 saves.

Morgan Ensberg (.283-36-101) stepped into the cleanup spot and provided important power. Berkman wound up shuffling between first base and left field. Phil Garner deftly mixed in Mike Lamb at first base and Chris Burke in the outfield, with Willy Taveras contributing speed and solid defense in center field. Biggio scored 94 times and hit 26 bombs. Bagwell worked his way back from surgery with the plan to use him as a pinch-hitter in the postseason.

In the final regular season game, Oswalt started against Greg Maddux and the Chicago Cubs. The Astros blew a 3-0 lead, then came from behind as the Phillies score on the scoreboard showed Houston needed to win or head to Philadelphia for a one-game playoff.

The Astros got a pinch-hit RBI from Bagwell to take the lead and went on to win in another final-day epic clincher.

2005 ALDS

Andy Pettitte started Game 1 of the ALDS in Atlanta against Tim Hudson. Morgan Ensberg drove in five runs in a 10-5 Houston victory.

John Smoltz beat Roger Clemens 7-1 in Game 2, with Brian McCann providing a three-run homer.

The series moved to Houston. Roy Oswalt gave the Braves a third straight top-caliber starter to face. Ensberg struck a pair of run-scoring doubles in the 7-3 Houston verdict.

Game 4 was a classic. With a chance to end the series, the Astros took the field without an ill Andy Pettitte. He was sent home by Phil Garner because of his illness, but Pettitte was to return to the stadium later because the game turned into an 18-inning battle royal.

Tim Hudson and the Braves staked their claim to a fifth and deciding game in Atlanta the next day by grabbing a 6-1 lead. A grand slam by Adam LaRoche into the Crawford Boxes and a McCann home run put Atlanta in the driver's seat by five runs in the eighth. Lance Berkman also found the Crawford Boxes with a slam off Kyle Farnsworth in the eighth to cut Atlanta's lead to 6-5 going to the ninth.

With two outs, Brad Ausmus crushed a missile over the 404-foot sign in left center field to bring airport-level noise to Minute Maid Park.

Extra innings wore on. Garner depleted his bullpen. One man was left – Roger Clemens. The 42-year-old volunteered for relief duty, and Garner happily accepted. Little did he know that Clemens had thrown batting practice to his son Koby in the cage inside the clubhouse during the game. Clemens actually entered as a pinch-hitter in the 15th inning, laying down a sacrifice bunt. Then he pitched three scoreless innings.

Chris Burke walloped a game-winning home run in the 18th off Joey Devine, sending the fans into ecstasy at the 7-6 triumph. It came on the 553rd pitch of the game, and it made Burke only the sixth player to end a playoff series with a home run.

"People thought Rocket was going to win the game for us," recalled Burke. "On the 2-0 pitch my eyes had been moved toward the inside corner of the plate. (Joey) Devine runs a 2-0 pitch and...he threw the pitch right where my eyes were. I got the barrel right there, and the rest is history."

2005 NLCS

In the rematch of the 2004 NLCS, St. Louis grabbed the upper hand in Game 1 at St. Louis when Chris Carpenter beat Andy Pettitte, 5-3. Pettitte had been hit with a line drive in pregame warmups and did not have his usual stuff.

Chris Burke was an offensive factor in Game 2 with a triple off Mark Mulder and played a big part in an eighth-inning rally. Roy Oswalt beat the Redbirds, 4-1.

Mike Lamb homered and scored twice to support Clemens in Houston's 4-3 conquest in Game 3 at Houston.

Another one-run win by the Astros in Game 4 finished with a spectacular double play started by second baseman Eric Bruntlett. The Astros won, 2-1.

With the Astros positioned to win the series at home, Albert Pujols drove a dagger into their hearts with a ninth-inning rocket off Brad Lidge for a 5-4 St. Louis thriller. The Astros' charter flight took off for St. Louis for Game 6 with the pilot reading a note sent by Brad Ausmus to the cockpit. The pilot announced over the PA that the object on the left side of the aircraft was Pujols' home run ball. Lidge overcame his initial anger when he realized that Ausmus had orchestrated the joke.

The doomsayers were prominent before Game 6, certain that Pujols' home run was the beginning of the end for Houston. Oswalt was in the clubhouse before the game when Drayton McLane engaged him in conversation. "Drayton's always been upbeat," said Oswalt.

"It doesn't matter what the situation is. It could be one of the worst days in the United States. He's upbeat. I was watching some of the Cardinals on video. The conversation started, 'Are we going to win tonight? Are we going to be a champion tonight?' Then he noticed that I was locked into the video. I was answering him, but I was watching the video too. He had to do something to get my attention. We'd been talking about the bulldozer that he owned, about my buying it from him at the end of the season. Sitting there, he told me that if I won the game that night and got us into the World Series, he would give it to me." Oswalt walked off the field leading after seven innings knowing that his bulldozer would be delivered soon. The Astros won, 5-1. Houston was headed to its first World Series and the first in Texas.

2005 WORLD SERIES

On a cold, damp night on Chicago's South Side, the White Sox played their first World Series game since 1959. Of the 50 players on the two teams' rosters, 41 were appearing in their first World Series. Craig Biggio was about to play in his first after 2,564 games in his career – the all-time record for a player in his first Series. Jeff Bagwell was third on that list with 2,150 games. Because of his right shoulder, Bagwell was the DH and Mike Lamb played first base. Lamb connected for the first Houston World Series home run in his first at-bat in the second inning off Jose Contreras. Houston's Roger Clemens exited with a hamstring injury after two innings and pitched in his final postseason game for Houston, with the 5-3 loss going to Wandy Rodriguez. Lance Berkman tied the game 3-3 in the third with a two-out double.

Game 2 was even colder and more uncomfortable. Morgan Ensberg homered off Mark Buehrle in the second. Berkman drove in three to give the Astros a 4-2 lead through 6 ½. Andy Pettitte left with the lead after throwing 98 pitches. Chad Qualls entered with the bases loaded and Paul Konerko drilled a grand slam for the Sox for a 6-4 lead.

Jose Vizcaino's two-run single off Bobby Jenks tied it in the ninth, 6-6. Scott Podsednik homered off Brad Lidge, his first 2005 home run in more than 500 at-bats, for a 7-6 ChiSox win.

Game 3 brought the state of Texas its first World Series game. Jason Lane struck a home run in the fourth off Jon Garland. Oswalt uncharacteristically lost a 4-0 lead and former Astro Geoff Blum won the game as a pinch-hitter with a home run in the 14th for the Sox off Ezequiel Astacio, 7-5 in a 5:41 marathon. It was the longest by time in World Series history.

Chicago called on former Houston farmhand Freddy Garcia in Game 4 and he stepped up with a 1-0 gem on a Jermaine Dye single off Lidge in the eighth after Backe pitched seven scoreless innings. The Sox had their first World Series title since 1917. The Astros didn't play another World Series game for 12 years. They scored 14 runs in four games against the excellent White Sox pitching staff.

2005 MVP

In his third full season with the Astros, Morgan Ensberg was chosen as the team's MVP. His 36-homer performance was the best by an Astro third baseman, breaking his own record and Doug Rader's total of 25 in a single season. He was also the first Houston third baseman to have a 100 RBI season. Ensberg won his only Silver Slugger award that season and was selected as an injury replacement to the All-Star Game. In mid-May, Ensberg became the eighth Astro to hit three homers in a single game. Ensberg was especially hot leading into the All-Star break. He collected 28 RBIs in the month of June.

Did you know...

Lance Berkman was the top hitter for the Astros in the 2005 World series with five hits and six RBIs. Willy Taveras also had five hits.

Jermaine Dye of the White Sox was the World Series MVP.

257

REBUILDING & RELOADING

2006

Despite a 19-9 start to 2006, the Astros slipped to an 82-80 record by the end of the season despite Roger Clemens' decision to end a brief retirement and join the team in late May.

When St. Louis went into a freefall at the end of the season, Houston cut the margin from 8 ½ games to ½ game thanks to a nine-game winning streak. Nonetheless, trouble was ahead.

Following the Astros' first World Series appearance in 2005, the team was at a crossroads. The Killer B's were getting older and lost Jeff Bagwell to his chronic shoulder injury. Lance Berkman hit 45 homers in 2006. But the rest of the team was aging and struggled to maintain its high level of success.

The Astros fell to second place despite the addition of outfielder Preston Wilson from the Rockies. With Craig Biggio now 40 years old and Brad Ausmus 37, the Astros needed reinforcements quickly.

2006 MVP

Lance Berkman was named the team MVP in 2006 for a fourth time with another stellar performance. Berkman hit a career high 45 homers as he settled into the first base job. He finished fourth in the league with his 45 homers behind Ryan Howard of the Phillies. He also had a career high 136 RBIs, which placed him third in the league behind Howard and Albert Pujols. Berkman led the Astros with a .315 average. Berkman joined Mickey Mantle as the only switch-hitters to have more than one 40-homer season and it was just the 11th time in baseball history that a switch-hitter had reached that mark. He also connected for his 200th career homer and was the fastest Astro to reach that mark.

After the season, General Manager Tim Purpura signed one of the biggest offensive performers on the free agent market, Carlos Lee.

Lee rewarded the Astros with a career high 119 RBIs, but the loss of pitcher Andy Pettitte back to the Yankees hurt. Hunter Pence took over in centerfield for Willy Taveras, who was dealt to the Rockies for pitcher Jason Jennings. That deal did not turn out well, and the Astros were trying to hold on. Purpura was replaced by former Phillies General Manager Ed Wade in September. Wade hoped to rebuild the team around the remainder of the veteran core that still remained.

2007

A fourth-place 73-89 season in 2007 provided further indication that rebuilding the team had moved to the front burner on the stove. The highlight of the season was Craig Biggio's 3,000[th] hit June 28th on a historic five-hit night for the future Hall of Famer. Putting the gemstone on a 20-year career, Biggio got the historic 3,000[th] on a single off Aaron Cook of Colorado and was thrown out at second base trying for a double. His fifth hit of the night started a game-winning rally and led to Carlos Lee's game-winning grand slam in the 11th, 8-5.

ANOTHER MAGICAL NIGHT

J.R. Towles is the owner of the Astros single game record of eight runs batted in, a record he now shares with Yuli Gurriel. Towles' ascent to the top of the franchise RBI list was swift. His stay wasn't very long. He played in less than a season's worth of games scattered across five campaigns, and he never was able to retain the Astros starting catcher job for long.

Towles hit .375 during his September call-up in 2007 including his eight-RBI game. He became the first player to drive in so many runs in a single game so early in a career. Towles had a tremendous month, hitting .375 with three homers. The Astros thought they had their catcher of the future and he was given the starting job in spring training of 2008. Towles was dispatched back to the minors after hitting only .145 in April and May of 2008. He had two other tours of duty with the Astros in 2008 but was not able to find the magic of that night in September at St. Louis.

In only his sixth major league game and his fourth major league start, Towles went 4-for-4 with a homer and a double and plated eight runs. Towles batted in the eighth spot and knocked a two-run double in the second inning off Cardinals starter Braden Looper, driving in Carlos Lee and Cody Ransom. Hitting against Looper in the fourth inning, Towles singled in two more, Mike Lamb and Lee. In the sixth inning, he hit a ground-rule double that scored Ransom again to give him five RBIs.

Towles was hit by a pitch in the seventh, then drew a walk from Brian Falkenborg in the 8th inning with the bases loaded to give him his sixth RBI. With the Cardinals losing 16-1 going into the ninth inning, Cardinals Manager Tony LaRussa decided not to use any more pitchers, calling on former Astros farmhand Aaron Miles to finish the game. Miles entered the game late in left field and then hit the first batter he faced, Ransom. The first pitch he threw to the next hitter, Towles, cleared the wall in left field, and there was a new record setter in the Astros record book.

Towles broke the single game record of seven for the team, twice done by Jeff Bagwell along with Rafael Ramirez and Pete Incaviglia.

2007 MVP

Carlos Lee delivered in the first year of his six-year contract with a .303 average, 32 home runs and 119 RBIs. Houston fans grew lukewarm to Lee over his years with the team, but Lee delivered big numbers consistently at the plate. His outfield play was not noteworthy, but he had never been known as a good defender. Lee played in every game after signing in the off-season from the Texas Rangers and he did not disappoint. He led the team in both hits and doubles, setting career highs in both categories. Lee started fast and was the first player in the league to reach the 100-RBI plateau en route to his third consecutive All-Star nod. Lee tied with Lance Berkman as the leaders in the National League in go-ahead RBIs.

 For his six years, Lee's batting average, homers, and RBIs were: .286-133-533.

2008

Cecil Cooper was hired late in 2007 to replace Phil Garner as manager. GM Ed Wade signed free agent Kaz Matsui to take over for the retired Craig Biggio at second base. Wade also made a couple of big deals, trading for Miguel Tejada from the Orioles and acquiring Jose Valverde from the Diamondbacks.

The Tejada deal sent five prospects to the Orioles, the most prominent being outfielder Luke Scott. The deal for Valverde cost the Astros three young players, including setup man Chad Qualls. Tejada hit well as he had earlier in his career despite hitting into 34 double plays. The team had only two starters, Michael Bourn and Pence, who were under age 30. There was little help in the farm system pipeline and many prospects weren't able to produce.

The 2008 Astros rallied despite losing Lee to a broken finger. From 44-51, they rode the hot bat of Ty Wigginton to a 21-9 August.

Wigginton's 12 long balls that month after he moved to left field to replace Lee ignited the team. The team's 86-75 mark was respectable, with Berkman putting together another solid year. Hurricane Ike threw a monkey wrench into any playoff hopes the Astros had in September. They were displaced by Commissioner Bud Selig's ruling that their home series against the Cubs had to be played in Milwaukee, where they were no-hit by Carlos Zambrano and sent reeling out of contention.

2008 MVP

Lance Berkman was selected as the Astros MVP for the 2008 campaign. The Astros rebounded to a third-place finish behind the Chicago Cubs. Berkman won player of the month honors in May with a lofty .620 average. Berkman tied for the league lead with his 46 doubles and hit .300 for the fourth time in his career. He finished fifth in the league MVP voting behind winner Albert Pujols.

2009

The team won only 74 games in 2009. An aging group plummeted to fifth place as the oldest team in the majors. Manager Cecil Cooper was replaced by Dave Clark late in the season. Personal milestones for Berkman, Lee and future Hall of Famer Pudge Rodriguez converged. All joined the 300-home run club. Lee hit .300 and drove in 102 runs. Rodriguez set a major league record for games caught in a career. Miguel Tejada and Kaz Matsui reached their 2000th hits, Matsui with many of those in Japan before joining Houston.

2009 MVP

Houston native Michael Bourn was voted the team MVP. Bourn had been acquired by the team a few seasons earlier from the Phillies and was inserted into the leadoff spot in centerfield. Bourn was an outstanding defender and won a Gold Glove.

Bourn also stole a league high 61 bases. He joined Craig Biggio as the only Astros to lead the league in stolen bases to that point.

Like Biggio, Bourn was very hard to double-up, as he grounded into a single double play in 606 at-bats. Bourn finished the season with a .285 average and led the team by scoring 97 runs.

2010

The Astros had to add some veterans, since the farm system was not producing for the 2010 season. New Manager Brad Mills led the team into a slight uptick to 76 wins, but the new additions were non-impactful. Starter Brett Myers and third baseman Pedro Feliz signed as free agents. Wade moved Roy Oswalt to the Phillies for J.A. Happ, Jonathan Villar and Anthony Gose at the trade deadline. He also moved Lance Berkman to the Yankees for Mark Melancon and Jimmy Paredes. The rebuild was now fully under way.

2010 MVP

The 2010 Astros MVP was right fielder Hunter Pence. Now in his third full season, Pence hit 25 homers for the third straight campaign. Pence knocked in 91 runs to lead the team. The franchise was quickly coming to a crossroads and this was to be Pence's final full season in Houston.

2011

Catcher Jason Castro was injured in spring training of 2011, and knee surgery caused him to miss the entire season. The bad news just kept coming. Young players Brett Wallace, Chris Johnson and Jordan Lyles failed to find success. Jose Altuve showed promise, but he was one of the few bright lights in a 56-106 disaster.

Wade continued to trade veterans during the 2011 season. The Astros traded Bourn to the Braves and Pence to the Phillies for prospects to replenish the farm system. The sale of the team was approved in November 2011 to Jim Crane. Wade was dismissed as general manager and Jeff Luhnow was brought in from the Cardinals a few days later.

2011 MVP

In 2011, Hunter Pence was once again the team MVP despite being traded to the Phillies at the deadline in late July. The team went on a 3-11 run after the trade, while Pence was removed from his final game in Milwaukee after the deal was completed. Pence finished third in the team in homers and second in RBIs despite playing a third of the season elsewhere. The Texas native slugged 103 homers and drove in 377 runs in his five years in Houston, jump-starting him on a 14-year career in the majors. He was 28 when he was traded for Jarred Cosart, Jon Singleton, Josh Zeid and Domingo Santana.

2012

With new ownership spearheaded by Jim Crane, GM Jeff Luhnow acquired Marwin Gonzalez via trade with Boston after the Rule V draft in December of 2011. There was a new sheriff in town, and he fired off a bang hours after taking over the job. Luhnow knew how to evaluate players. He proceeded to trade closer Mark Melancon to Boston for Jed Lowrie and Kyle Weiland. As the season progressed, the 2012 team did not. Luhnow was undeterred, because his long-range goal did not include winning in 2012. The Astros were 55-107.

2012 MVP

Second-year second baseman Jose Altuve was named the Astros MVP for the 2012 season. Altuve also provided a necessary spark at the top of the lineup with 33 stolen bases while hitting .290. He also led the team in hits, doubles, triples, steals, runs and on-base percentage. Altuve was the second youngest Astro ever to be chosen to an All-Star team. He also stole home and homered in a game at the White Sox, the first time an Astro had turned that trick in nearly 20 years.

2013

The Astros' move to the American League was not successful. The team won only 51 games under new Manager Bo Porter. Jeff Luhnow traded for power-hitting Chris Carter and pitcher Brad Peacock, but other personnel decisions were failures. The team payroll was a scant $13 million.

2013 MVP

In 2013, Jason Castro was honored as the team MVP. Castro broke the franchise record with 18 homers by a catcher and was chosen as a reserve to the American League All-Star team. Castro joined Craig Biggio as the only Astro catchers to be selected to the All-Star team. Castro suffered a knee injury and missed the last games of the season in September.

2014

The Astros put a tourniquet on the 100-loss seasons in 2014, improving to 70 wins. Luhnow traded for veteran Dexter Fowler and promoted George Springer to the majors, starting the improvement toward respectability. Pitching coach Brent Strom and righthander Collin McHugh were a big part of that movement.

2014 MVP

In 2014, Jose Altuve emerged as a budding star. Altuve broke the team record with 225 hits. That topped the majors. Altuve had a franchise best 69 multi-hit games and was a recipient of a Silver Slugger award. Altuve's .341 average also was best in the league and he became the first Astro to win a batting crown. Altuve led the league in average, hits and stolen bases, the first player to lead the AL in these categories since Ichiro Suzuki in 2001. Despite all of the outstanding numbers, Altuve finished 13th in the MVP voting.

The summaries of the 2015-2021 seasons are located on pages 7-52 and 102-137. Here are capsules of the MVPs from the remaining years:

2015 MVP

In 2015, Dallas Keuchel became the first pitcher to be honored as team MVP in over 20 seasons. He was also the first starting pitcher to win the award since Mike Scott in 1988. Keuchel's 20-win season was a catalyst for the team's appearance in the playoffs for the first time in over a decade. Keuchel was the third pitcher in franchise history to win the Cy Young Award. Keuchel and teammate Collin McHugh were the top two winners in the American League. Keuchel led the league in innings pitched with 232.

Keuchel was 11-4 entering the All-Star break after entering the season as the ace of new Manager A.J. Hinch's staff. Keuchel was named pitcher of the month in May and August.

2016 MVP

The 2016 Astros MVP was Jose Altuve. Altuve collected 200 hits for the third consecutive season and led the American League in batting again. He was only the sixth player in baseball history to score 100 runs with 200 hits, along with 95 RBIs, 40 doubles and 20 homers. He also became the first second baseman to win multiple batting titles since Hall of Famer Rod Carew in the 1970s.

Altuve was named an All-Star again and placed third in the American League in MVP voting behind Mike Trout and Mookie Betts. Altuve passed the 1,000-hit barrier faster than any player in franchise history.

2017 MVP

Jose Altuve became the second Astro to win the league's Most Valuable Player award in 2017. Altuve received all but three first place votes, easily outpolling the Yankees Aaron Judge. Altuve collected 200 hits for the fourth consecutive season. He led the Astros to their first World Series championship. Altuve and Houston Texan defensive lineman J.J. Watt were honored by *Sports Illustrated* as their Sportspersons of the Year.

Altuve was awarded the Hank Aaron Award winner, after winning his third batting title with his highest average, .346. He also hit seven postseason homers, including a three-homer game against the Red Sox. During the regular season he clocked 24 home runs and drove in 81 runs.

2018 MVP

In 2018, Alex Bregman hit a career high 31 homers while hitting .286. Bregman finished fifth in voting for the American League MVP award. Bregman was also named to the All-Star team and he was selected as the game's MVP after he and Astros teammate George Springer hit back-to-back homers. He led the majors with 51 doubles, which was the third highest total for an Astro player.

Bregman also knocked in 100 runs for the first time in his career. Bregman was on base in 145 of his 157 games, including a 42-game streak.

2019 MVP

Alex Bregman repeated as the Astros MVP in 2019. After an outstanding season the year before, Bregman produced even bigger numbers as the Astros went back to the World Series. Bregman finished second to Mike Trout in the American League MVP voting. He broke the 40-homer mark and knocked in 112 runs. Bregman was the sixth third baseman to have a 1.000 OPS since 1900. Bregman became the youngest player in franchise history to hit 40 homers.

He was also called on to play 59 games at shortstop while Carlos Correa was injured. Bregman won his first Silver Slugger award.

As the season started early in March, Bregman homered against the Tampa Bay Rays to celebrate his 25th birthday.

2020 MVP

George Springer was selected as the Astros team MVP in the COVID-shortened 2020 season. Springer led the team with his 14 homers as the team's leadoff hitter. He led the team in OPS with an .899 mark.

He added four more in the postseason as the Astros progressed to the League Championship Series against the Tampa Bay Rays.

2021 MVP

Kyle Tucker was named the Astros MVP in the 60th season of the franchise. Tucker normally hit sixth in the lineup but still delivered 30 homers and knocked in 92. There wasn't a hotter hitter in the American League after the start of May. Tucker tied the club record with 30 homers by a right fielder. He came into the season with only 13 homers and exploded with his new career high. Tucker led the team in OPS with a .917 mark.

Willy Taveras 2005 World Series jersey

CRAIG BIGGIO

Houston's first Hall of Famer, Craig Biggio, was a unique player in many ways. He was the first player in the modern history of the sport to start his career as a catcher, then move to second base and be an All-Star at both positions. Adding to his versatility, he moved to center field and left field in his unparallel journey to Cooperstown. His willingness to play different positions stood out as did his willingness to "take one for the team" more times than any player in modern baseball (since 1903). He was uncompromising in his determination to be able to hit the outside pitch, to the extent of sacrificing his body by being close to home plate in his stance. Biggio dared pitchers to hit him, and many took the dare. His tolerance of pain as a way to reach base helped the team and enhanced his opportunities to steal bases and score runs, which he did on a par with the best players. If there were a bone scan of his body, the indentations would look like the hood of a car left out in a hailstorm!

The city of Houston and its fans have enjoyed the benefits of the Biggios as residents of the city where Craig played, contributing to charities such as the Sunshine Kids by being the national spokesman for that organization to assist children with cancer. Craig has enjoyed spending time on his South Texas ranch as well. He and teammate Ken Caminiti bought the ranch. Caminiti is buried there.

This book is filled with statistics. Many of us fans love the numbers of Hall of Fame players. These players are interesting people, too. That's why this page has no statistics about one of the most important sports figures in Houston history.

JEFF BAGWELL

One of the great ironies about Hall of Famer Jeff Bagwell is his loyalty to the Boston Red Sox as a youngster. He and his father Robert watched Red Sox games on television whenever they could. At times their TV reception was not acceptable, so one of them would get on the roof of the house and adjust the old antenna while the other stood in the doorway and shouted up that the antenna needed to be repositioned this way or that way in order to watch the game properly.

When Jeff was drafted by Boston, it was cause for great elation in the Bagwell family. His grandmother was especially thrilled with the news. When he was traded to Houston for Larry Andersen, his grandmother was equally deflated. Quickly Jeff's dad realized that the trade could be good fortune for the third baseman in the family because Boston was overstocked with third basemen. But when Jeff got to spring training with Houston, Ken Caminiti was in front of him and he quickly realized that there was a major roadblock to his major league highway in Houston as well. When Art Howe and Bill Wood gave him a chance to move to first base, he jumped at it just as Craig Biggio had attacked his position changes. He said, "I went to Hartford, not Harvard, but I could figure out that this was the move to make." Bagwell was a first baseman, a Rookie of the Year, and he and Craig started a 15-year career as teammates.

Two players playing and living in the same city year-round for 15 years is a picture just as unusual in the 2000s as those two players winding up in the Hall of Fame. Just as Craig has done, Jeff has settled into the city as a fan favorite well beyond his playing years.

There have been other Hall of Famers who played for the Astros: Joe Morgan, Eddie Mathews, Robin Roberts, Nellie Fox. Only Morgan grew up in the organization. After he was traded his career went into Hall of Fame high gear. In 60 years, only two – Biggio and Bagwell are truly Astros in the National Baseball Hall of Fame and Museum. Many of the fans who traveled to Cooperstown count their inductions among the fondest baseball memories of their lives.

SOLO GAME

It is rare for a major league baseball player to play in only one game in a major league career. Circumstances conspire to limit a player's time, usually caused by an injury of devastating proportions.

The Astros have a handful of single-game players.

In 1963, the Colt .45s were in their second season. To try to create interest for the team, the Colt .45s used all rookies in their starting lineup for a game in late September. Some of the core of the Colt .45s for the remainder of the decade were starters that night like Jimmy Wynn, Joe Morgan, Rusty Staub and Sonny Jackson. The choice for Houston that night on the mound was Jay Dahl, a left-hander who had been signed after pitching at Colton High School in California. Still three months before his eighteenth birthday, Dahl was summoned from the team's Double-A team - San Antonio in the Texas League.

The left-handed pitcher started well against the Mets, but lasted only into the third inning before giving up seven runs on seven hits, although an error allowed for only five runs to be earned. Dahl left the game and was replaced by Danny Coombs and Joe Hoerner, both of whom were also making their Major League debuts for the team. Since the season was ending, Dahl did not pitch again for the Colt .45s.

At spring training in 1964, Dahl did not return to the mound due to a back injury. He was used in a handful of games at Statesville in the Western Carolina League as an outfielder. In the 1965 season, Dahl returned to the mound and started at high A-ball Durham. He made seven starts there, posting one win and a 4.50 ERA. Dahl was reassigned to low A Salisbury. Dahl took off and posted five wins in five starts.

Salisbury moved into first place in mid-June and the team's general manager, G.W. "Bone" Hamilton, hosted a steak dinner for the team. Dahl attended along with right-handed pitcher Gary Marshall and then went to a movie.

As they were driving later that evening, Marshall's Pontiac GTO crashed into a tree, killing Dahl and another person in the car. Marshall never played again.

The Colt .45s had another player who had a remarkable start to his career, but his career was dashed by injuries. The Colt .45s signed John Paciorek following an all-state high school career at Hamtramck, Michigan. Paciorek, only 18 years old, had a remarkable start that September. One day after the all-rookie game, he made his debut in right field for Houston. It was a debut for the ages. Just added from Modesto in the California League, Paciorek drew a walk off Mets starter Larry Bearnarth. Catcher John Bateman tripled Paciorek and Bob Aspromonte home to give Houston a 2-0 lead. In the fourth inning, Paciorek singled home Aspromonte and Rusty Staub to tie the Mets at 4-4. Paciorek was brought home moments later by a sacrifice fly by Pete Runnels. In the next inning, Paciorek singled home Aspromonte and gave the team a 7-4 lead. He walked and singled off Mets reliever Grover Powell in his last two at-bats.

Paciorek was 3-for-3 with four runs scored and three RBIs. He never made it back to the majors. The following spring, Paciorek looked certain to break camp with the Colt .45s but due to a poor camp he was assigned to the minors again. He spent time also at Statesville and Durham during the 1964 season, but back injuries limited him to just 49 games. Back surgery followed and Paciorek was never able to regain his previous success. He was forced to miss the entire 1965 season as well. He was with the Astros system in 1966 and 1967 but never progressed past A-ball again.

He finished his career in the Cleveland organization, making it only to Double A for 29 games in 1969. Paciorek's younger brothers, Jim and Tom also made it to the major leagues.

The next one-game wonder has a unique twist. He also comes from a baseball family, with his brother honored on a plaque at Cooperstown.

The Astros spent their fifth-round draft choice in 1968 on a high school right-hander from California, Larry Yount. Yount made his way up through the Astros system, receiving spring training invites in 1970 and 1971. After spending the entire 1971 season in the rotation at Oklahoma City, Yount was among the call-ups after the end of the minor league season. He was brought in to replace Skip Guinn to start the ninth inning of a game against the Atlanta Braves. With Felix Millan, Ralph Garr and Hank Aaron due up, Yount took his warm-up tosses on the field. His elbow never got loose, and after taking a couple of extra throws he left the game due to injury. So even though Yount never faced a hitter, he was credited with a game pitched. He is the only pitcher in major league history not to face any hitters. Technically, he was in the game. At least he made the Baseball Encyclopedia!

Yount did not return to the mound for the Astros that season but remained among their best prospects for the next couple of seasons. He was dealt to the Milwaukee Brewers at the end of spring training of 1974 along with minor league pitcher Don Stratton for outfielder Wilbur Howard.

Yount did not pitch at all in 1974. He was able to return to action at Double-A for Milwaukee in 1975, but never got a chance to team up with his future Hall of Fame brother, Robin. He went into real estate in Arizona and found his success in that field.

Did you know...Rusty Staub was the first Astro to hit .300 in a full season when he hit .333 in 1967. He led the league in doubles with 44. Both of those numbers stood as the team's best for 27 years.

273

COACHES

The Astros have had more than 80 coaches in franchise history. Many of them have had little major league experience as players, but a handful have had long and prestigious major league careers. A few of them now have plaques in Cooperstown for their careers.

Former White Sox All-Star Nellie Fox came to the Astros at the end of his career. He played for the last Colt .45s team and first Astrodome team in 1964-65. Fox came to the Colt .45s in a trade after the 1963 season to provide veteran leadership. Fox had just become the fortieth player in MLB history to record 2,500 career hits the previous season. The Colt .45s had a young second baseman named Joe Morgan in their farm system, but a 36-year-old Fox played most of the way, batting second behind Al Spangler and hitting .265.

Following the season, the newly renamed Astros made the commitment to Morgan at second base. Fox remained active in spring training and had the game-winning hit in extra innings in the Astros first exhibition game against the Yankees. Fox was activated during the season and joined the team as the infield coach for new Manager Luman Harris. "You've got to realize you are no longer a youngster," said Fox. Fox remained on the staff through the 1967 season.

Yogi Berra, the famed Yankees catcher, became a member of Hal Lanier's coaching staff for the 1986 season. Berra was a neighbor of Astros owner John McMullen in New Jersey. McMullen was able to convince the former Yankees Hall of Famer to come to Houston. Berra stayed on the staff through 1989.

Jeff Bagwell had a brief tenure on the Astros coaching staff following his playing days. Bagwell moved from the front office as a special adviser to become the Astros interim batting coach. Bagwell replaced hitting coach Sean Berry and stayed on Brad Mills' staff for the rest of the season.

274

The record holder in many of the team's offensive categories, Bagwell was elected to the National Baseball Hall of Fame in 2017 as the second Astro to be enshrined.

Larry Dierker lured former Astro Manager Bill Virdon out of retirement in 1997 to become his first bench coach. Virdon was a former National League rookie of the year with the St. Louis Cardinals. He managed the Astros, Pirates, Yankees and Expos before his first retirement from baseball. Virdon was the winningest manager in team history with 544 wins.

Several other prominent former Astro players also spent time on the coaching lines. Dierker made it a priority to get several former players on his staff along with Virdon. Outfielder Jose Cruz served as a coach from 1997-2009. Vern Ruhle spent four seasons as the Astros pitching coach with Dierker, along with former catcher Alan Ashby. Phil Garner coached on Art Howe's staff from 1989 to 1991 before becoming manager of the Milwaukee Brewers, and later leading the Astros to their first World Series appearance in 2005.

Bob Lillis moved to the front office after his playing days with the Colt .45s and was added to the major league staff in 1973. Lillis became the first former Houston player to manage the team when he replaced Virdon during the 1982 season. Howe, Dierker and Garner are the only other former Astro players to manage the franchise.

The first African-American coach for the Astros was Deacon Jones, who was the hitting coach under Bill Virdon. Jones served from 1976-82.

The first Latino coach and first Latino manager for the Astros was Preston Gomez, who was brought in as a coach by Leo Durocher in 1973.

POSITION SWITCHES

The first two Houston Hall of Famers with the Astros both made a position switch that led to a very successful transition. Both Jeff Bagwell and Craig Biggio collected Gold Glove Awards after their positional moves. Others were not quite so lucky.

Biggio was drafted by the Astros in the first round as a catcher from Seton Hall University in 1987. He was rewarded with a recall from Tucson in late June of 1988 and began to share the catching chores with longtime Astro Alan Ashby. Nearly twenty years after he collected his first hit, he collected his 3000th for the team. One of the most dynamic parts of Biggio's game was his speed. Biggio stole bases and presented a threat to run.

The Astros realized that they had a unique player in Biggio and wanted to preserve his speed and save wear and tear on his knees. During the 1989 season, Art Howe tried him in the outfield for a handful of games to keep his legs fresh. Biggio was selected as the Silver Slugger catcher on the National League team. In 1991, he continued to blossom.

Biggio was selected to the National League All-Star team as the backup to the Padres' Benito Santiago. By the end of the 1991 season, the Astros were determined to move him to second base. He began to work daily with longtime coach Matt Galante. By spring training 1992, the Astros were ready to go all in.

They moved their top prospect, Kenny Lofton, to the Indians for catching prospect Ed Taubensee. Taubensee settled in at catcher but was never the equal of Lofton. The move of Biggio to second base turned out to be the great benefit of that deal.

Biggio only appeared in one more game behind the plate, catching the final two innings of his last career game in 2007. He remained in the infield at second base for a decade.

He was a member of five All-Star games during his career and won five Silver Slugger awards, one at catcher and four at second base. The daring move of Biggio from catcher to second base was one of the team's most successful moves.

The Astros also moved their other Hall of Famer from third base to first base. Bagwell was drafted by the Boston Red Sox from the University of Hartford. The Astros traded for Bagwell as a double A prospect at New Britain at the August 31 trading deadline, sending pending free agent Larry Andersen to Boston. Bagwell was stuck behind Hall of Famer Wade Boggs and another prospect, Scott Cooper. The Red Sox made Bagwell available.

Reaching Houston, Bagwell was the third baseman in waiting behind veteran Ken Caminiti. Bagwell had a good spring and showed some pop. The Astros asked him to move to first base just a few days before the end of spring training.

Bagwell made the starting lineup at first base and was there on Opening Day in 1991. Bagwell started at first base for the next 15 opening days, something no other Astro has ever done at the same position. His defense progressed so well that he was awarded a Gold Glove in his 1994 MVP season.

Enos Cabell had played parts of three seasons with the Baltimore Orioles before coming to the Astros in a trade for slugger Lee May in 1974. Cabell had been primarily an outfielder for the Orioles, only appearing in 20 games at third base before the deal. Like most of these position changes, the team was in a state of flux that allowed the Astros to move players around the diamond.

Cabell's first season in Houston was mostly as an outfielder. The Astros had looked at him as a centerfield candidate, but that wasn't going to happen with All-Star Cesar Cedeno patrolling the big ballpark.

He played primarily left field with Cedeno in center and Jose Cruz in right. Cabell's big opportunity came when new General Manager Tal Smith traded third baseman Doug Rader to the Padres. Cabell nailed down third base for the next five seasons and was part of their first playoff team.

Not all of the moves were as successful. The Astros tried moving other players around the field with limited success.

Cliff Johnson came up through the Astros system primarily as a catcher. His bat was his biggest tool and he made steady progress after being drafted out of high school in San Antonio. The Astros also gave Johnson a look at first base and the outfield but thought catcher was his best route to the majors. In his first full season in the majors in 1974, Johnson struggled behind the plate, only throwing out 21% of runners in a league that was now turning to base stealers to create more runs.

The Astros had Lee May at first base and couldn't find another place where Johnson could play. Johnson ended up with 117 career starts for the Astros but was enough of a defensive liability that he was traded to the Yankees in 1977 for prospects.

Hall of Famer Joe Morgan was briefly moved to the outfield during the start of the 1969 season. This experiment didn't last long either. Morgan's time in left field was brief. He was only in left for 12 games before Manager Harry Walker pulled the plug and returned Morgan to second base. Morgan was an All-Star twice for the Astros at second base before being traded to the Reds after the 1971 season. The trade to Cincinnati jump-started the Big Red Machine. And Morgan collected five Gold Gloves at second base.

IMPORTANT TRADES

There have been 940 different players who have worn an Astros uniform for at least one game. These players have been acquired in many different ways. The Astros have signed amateur players and draftees, taken players in the expansion draft, drafted players in the Rule V draft, signed major league and minor league free agents, and of course have traded for many of these players.

The trading for players leads to analysis of the players acquired and the players traded. This has been the source of much discussion over the last sixty seasons. Defining the list of the best and worst trades is not a perfect science, just as making trades is not.

In the category of best trades, the acquisition of future Hall of Famer Jeff Bagwell has to be atop the list. Bagwell was a double A third baseman for the Red Sox when the Astros traded for him. Bagwell was stuck in third place on the Red Sox team depth chart behind Hall of Famer, Wade Boggs, and Scott Cooper.

Bagwell came to the Astros at the end of the 1990 season for veteran reliever Larry Andersen. Andersen had been a solid setup man for the Astros, but pitched only that September for the Red Sox, signing with the Padres after the season at age 37.

Bagwell made the Astros in the spring of 1991 after failing to unseat Ken Caminiti at third base. Bagwell was moved across the diamond in the last week of the spring after no one won the first base job. He did not relinquish the job until 2005, winning a Rookie of the Year and MVP trophy to make this easily the most lopsided deal in franchise history.

Another of the best trades by the team was the mid-summer trade by Gerry Hunsicker for Royals outfielder Carlos Beltran. Beltran played only 90 games for the Astros but hit 23 homers as he led the Astros to brink of their first National League championship. In the postseason, Beltran put on a spectacular show, hitting eight postseason homers and batting over .400 in both the Divisional Series and League Championship Series. The cost for Beltran was high. The Astros sent a key member of their bullpen, Octavio Dotel, to the Royals with catcher John Buck for Beltran.

The Astros made an outstanding move during their rebuilding days in 1993, taking on the contract of veteran outfielder Mike Felder from the Seattle Mariners. In order to shed the contract of Felder, the Mariners had to include young relief pitcher Mike Hampton. The Astros sent Houston native Eric Anthony to the Mariners. Hampton pitched out of the bullpen in 1994 before being inserted into the starting rotation the following season. Anthony had his best years in Houston and was out of baseball by the time Hampton set a team record with 22 wins in 1999. Hampton won 76 games before being dealt to the Mets seven seasons later.

Developing a franchise catcher had been difficult for the Astros, but in 1978 at the winter meetings, General Manager Tal Smith was able to fill a need. Smith dealt three players, including young starter Mark Lemongello to the Toronto Blue Jays for catcher Alan Ashby.

Ashby settled behind the plate for a decade and was one of the cogs in the 1980 and 1986 division-winning teams. Besides Lemongello, the Astros sent outfield prospect J.J. Cannon and shortstop Pedro Hernandez to the Jays. None of these players made a major impact with Toronto.

In the off-season following 1970, GM Spec Richardson dealt shortstop Hector Torres to the Cubs for a promising shortstop prospect, Roger Metzger of Brenham, Texas. Metzger won the starting job at spring training and remained there for several seasons. Torres bounced around with several teams for the remainder of his career. Metzger became a stabilizing force in the Astros infield and spent several quality seasons with the team.

Another of the Astros' finest deadline deals came in 2016. After the trading deadline, the Astros cleared reliever Josh Fields off their major league roster. The NL West division-leading Dodgers traded for Fields to add to their bullpen. General Manager Jeff Luhnow received a newly signed international player from the Dodgers who had never played a game for their minor league system, Yordan Alvarez. Alvarez quickly made his way up the Astros chain and became the third team member to win a rookie of the year award in 2019. That deal continues to pay dividends to the Astros.

Following their World Series team in 1997, the Florida Marlins decided to slash payroll. The Astros went shopping and picked up veteran outfielder Moises Alou. Alou was one of the key players in their division championship teams for the next few seasons. Alou hit 95 homers for the Astros over his three seasons with the team. The Astros sent three minor league pitchers to the Marlins: Oscar Henriquez, Mark Johnson and Manny Barrios. Each pitched briefly in the majors but had only a minor impact in the Marlins' rebuilding effort.

One of the biggest acquisitions for the Astros came as a straight cash purchase. The Astros purchased outfielder Jose Cruz from St. Louis after the World Series in 1974. Richardson made several minor deals with the Cardinals in the previous two seasons, but no one saw the impact that Cruz would have on the franchise. Cruz patrolled the Astros outfield for over a decade and became a fan favorite.

He left the team at the end of his career, but came back to become a coach and then a broadcaster for the franchise.

At the winter meetings in 1975, Smith dealt veteran second baseman Tommy Helms to the Pittsburgh Pirates for a player to be named later. The player to be named later was assigned to the Astros following the Rule V draft. The player was Pirates minor league third baseman Art Howe. Howe was a former college quarterback at Wyoming. The Pirates were in a stretch in the '70s of finishing at the top of their division, and he became expendable to their search for roster depth. Howe became a multi-positional player for the Astros, becoming the Astros starting second baseman in 1977 and 1978. Howe was moved around to first and third base over the next few seasons. Howe played for the Astros for seven seasons, and later came back to manage the team a decade later. He threw out another future Astros manager, Dusty Baker, for the final out in Nolan Ryan's no-hitter in 1981.

Pennant stretch drives have been the place where many lopsided deals are completed. In 2017, just moments before the trade deadline at midnight, Justin Verlander agreed to waive his no-trade contract and come to Houston from Detroit. Verlander was a franchise icon with the then-rebuilding Tigers. The Astros were able to part with prospects from the deep farm system that Luhnow and his scouting team had put together. The Tigers got three prospects: pitcher Franklin Perez, catcher Jake Rogers and outfielder Daz Cameron for Verlander.

The Astros got the final piece the franchise needed to win their world championship. Verlander went on to add another Cy Young Award to his trophy cabinet in 2019 when he led the American League with 21 wins.

Luhnow also made a very successful pickup following the 2017 season in a trade with the Pirates. Gerrit Cole became an Astro and formed a dynamic duo at the top of the Astros rotation in 2018-19. The Astros sent four prospects to the Pirates for Cole. In that package were pitchers Michael Feliz and Joe Musgrove along with third baseman Colin Moran and outfielder Jason Martin. Musgrove and Moran became contributors with the Pirates but haven't reached the success that Cole achieved in his two seasons in Houston.

In 1982 General Manager Al Rosen made one of the top trades in team history with the New York Mets. The Astros sent outfielder Danny Heep to the Mets for Mike Scott, who had struggled to find a role with New York. Scott worked with Astros pitching coaches Les Moss and Roger Craig, and developed a devastating split-fingered fastball to assist him in winning the Cy Young Award in 1986.

Finally, the Astros' trade of slugging first baseman Glenn Davis to the Orioles was one of the best deals in franchise history. The Astros received back pitchers Pete Harnisch and Curt Schilling together with outfielder Steve Finley. All of these players were at the start of their careers. Unfortunately, Schilling did not find a role with the Astros, who tried him primarily as a closer. Since he was out of options, the Astros moved him on to Philadelphia. Harnisch and Finley were parts of the Astros' renaissance in the early 1990s with new Manager Terry Collins.

Not every trade has turned out well, though. The most lopsided trade in franchise history was the 1971 deal with the Cincinnati Reds. Future Hall of Famer Joe Morgan was dealt with outfielder Cesar Geronimo and pitcher Jack Billingham along with two other players to the Reds. The Astros got back slugging first baseman Lee May from the Reds with Tommy Helms and utility man Jimmy Stewart.

May provided the power that could play in the Astrodome, but Morgan's acquisition became the catalyst for the Big Red Machine that took up residence atop the National League West.

Another of the trades that didn't turn out well for the Astros was the December 1994 deal with the Padres. Ken Caminiti was dealt to San Diego. Like Morgan, Caminiti went on to win an MVP award while with his new team. Caminiti had been a prolific player with the Astros and salary considerations had been an issue in this deal. The Astros received back a package that was led by outfielder Derek Bell, and included 11 players changing uniforms, one of the largest in baseball history. However, Caminiti's performance made this deal overwhelming for the Padres.

During the 1991 winter meetings in Miami Beach, the Astros exchanged prospects with the Cleveland Indians with poor results.

The Astros sent outfielder Kenny Lofton and infielder Dave Rohde to the Indians for catcher Ed Taubensee and pitcher Willie Blair. While Taubensee became the Astros starting catcher, he never experienced the All-Star seasons that Lofton did with the Indians. The Astros had Finley patrolling centerfield at the time and Lofton had not looked strong in his initial call up in September. In the spring of 1992, Lofton won the centerfield job and played in six All-Star games and won four Gold Glove awards.

Jeff Luhnow made a trade deadline deal in 2015 with the Milwaukee Brewers to acquire outfielder Carlos Gomez and pitcher Mike Fiers. In return, the Astros sent future closer Josh Hader along with Adrian Houser, Domingo Santana and Brett Phillips to Brewtown. Gomez and Fiers were pieces of the 2015 playoff team and Fiers stayed in the rotation for the next couple of seasons. Hader spent the next several seasons as one of the premier closers in baseball. The other three players all reached the majors.

And finally, the dealing of Schilling to the Phillies at the end of spring training 1992 proved to be disastrous. Schilling was out of options and had to be exposed to waivers if he was to be sent to the minors. The Astros found a trade partner in Philadelphia, receiving back reliever Jason Grimsley in return. Schilling won 212 games after leaving Houston, and is a perennial candidate for Hall of Fame induction who played on three World Series teams.

OWNERS

ROY HOFHEINZ AND R.E. "BOB" SMITH

Roy Hofheinz was the youngest mayor of Houston, Harris County judge and a dynamic orator who rose from a boy who lost his father in a car wreck involving a drunk driver to one of the most powerful men in Texas. His grandiose ideas for baseball turned into a major asset for the city of Houston, including worldwide recognition for the Astrodome.

R.E. "Bob" Smith turned his fortune from the gas and oil business into a partnership with Hofheinz as the major owners of the Houston Baseball Club. Smith had enormous land holdings in the Houston area and the wealth to invest in a sports franchise and its growth.

JOHN McMULLEN

U.S. Navy veteran John McMullen lived in New Jersey and maintained his residence there while owning the Astros from 1979 to 1992. McMullen bought the team from GE Credit and Ford Credit Company for a reported $19 million and sold it after the Astros went to the playoffs in 1980, 1981 and 1986 under his watch.

DRAYTON McLANE, JR.

Drayton McLane, Jr. entered into professional sports ownership when he bought the Astros from McMullen in 1993. McLane had been a partner of Randall Onstead during negotiations with McMullen, but he decided to pursue sole ownership when the Onstead family turned away. He pressed for the move into downtown Houston and encouraged a bond issue election for the financing of Enron Field, a retractable-roofed stadium with the most modern amenities. The Astros reached the playoffs under his ownership in 1997, '98, '99, 2004 and 2005. They played in their first World Series in 2005. McLane signed big-name free agents such as Doug Drabek, Greg Swindell, Roger Clemens, Andy Pettitte and Jeff Kent. He also extended the contracts of Houston's first Hall of Famers, Craig Biggio and Jeff Bagwell.

JIM CRANE

Jim Crane bought the Astros from Drayton McLane, Jr. in 2011 for a reported $680 million. Crane was a record-setting pitcher at Central Missouri State University in Missouri. A native of St. Louis, Crane hired St. Louis Cardinals executive Jeff Luhnow as his first general manager in 2011. Crane promised patience through a rebuilding process while the team could draft wisely and allow the young players to develop until the payroll was expanded to bring free agents into the mix. After suffering through three consecutive 100-loss seasons, Crane hired AJ Hinch to manage the 2015 Astros. Hinch directed the team's improvement into an annual playoff contender, achieving a World Series title in 2017.

Crane's six playoff appearances in seven years has displayed the plan drawn up by Luhnow was a wise one. After firing Hinch and Luhnow, Crane hired Dusty Baker and James Click before the 2020 season. They have collaborated on two playoff teams in two years.

HOUSTON ASTROS TRIVIA QUESTIONS

Who got the first Astrodome exhibition game hit for Houston?

Catcher Ron Brand

Who pitched the first no-hitter for Houston?

Don Nottebart in 1963

Who was Houston's first All-Star?

Dick "Turk" Farrell in 1962

Who managed the most games for the Astros?

Bill Virdon, 1066

Who are the only two pitchers with multiple 20-win seasons?

Joe Niekro and Roy Oswalt

Who had the most stolen bases in one season?

Gerald Young 65 in 1988

Who had the most starts in one season?

Jerry Reuss 40 in 1973

Who had the most complete games in a season?

Larry Dierker 20 in 1969

Who had the most pinch hit at-bats in one season?

Orlando Palmeiro 80 in 2006

Who had the most relief appearances in a season?

Octavio Dotel 83 in 2002

Astros All-Time Batting Leaders

Jose Altuve	.308	2011-2021
Jeff Bagwell	.297	1991-2005
Bob Watson	.297	1966-1979
Lance Berkman	.296	1999-2010
Jose Cruz	.292	1975-1987
Yuli Gurriel	.291	2016-2021
Hunter Pence	.290	2007-2011
Cesar Cedeno	.289	1970-1981
Carlos Lee	.286	2007-2012
Derek Bell	.284	1995-1999
Craig Biggio	.281	1988-2007
Enos Cabell	.281	1975-1980, 1984-1985
Terry Puhl	.281	1977-1989
Richard Hidalgo	.278	1997-2004
Kevin Bass	.278	1982-1989, 1993-1994
Denny Walling	.277	1977-1988, 1992
Carlos Correa	.277	2015-2021
Rusty Staub	.273	1963-1968
George Springer	.270	2014-2020
Bill Doran	.267	1982-1990
Luis Gonzalez	.266	1990-1994, 1997
Ken Caminiti	.264	1987-1994, 1999
Marwin Gonzalez	.262	2012-2018, 2021
Glenn Davis	.262	1984-1990
Joe Morgan	.262	1963-1971, 1980
Phil Garner	.260	1981-1987
Bob Aspromonte	.258	1962-1968
Jimmy Wynn	.255	1963-1973
Craig Reynolds	.252	1978-1989
Alan Ashby	.252	1979-1989

Astros All-Time Home Run Leaders

Jeff Bagwell	449	1991-2005
Lance Berkman	326	1999-2010
Craig Biggio	291	1988-2007
Jimmy Wynn	223	1963-1973
George Springer	174	2014-2020
Glenn Davis	166	1984-1990
Jose Altuve	164	2011-2021
Cesar Cedeno	163	1970-1981
Bob Watson	139	1966-1979
Jose Cruz	138	1975-1987
Richard Hidalgo	134	1997-2004
Carlos Correa	133	2015-202
Carlos Lee	133	2007-2012
Doug Rader	128	1967-1975
Alex Bregman	117	2016-2021
Morgan Ensberg	105	2000, 2002-2007
Hunter Pence	103	2007-2011
Ken Camniti	103	1987-1994, 1999-2000
Evan Garris	96	2015-2018
Moises Alou	96	1998-2001
Chris Carter	90	2013-2015
Kevin Bass	87	1982-1989, 1993-1994
Yuli Gurriel	86	2016-2021
Lee May	81	1972-1974
Marwin Gonzalez	79	2012-2018, 2021
Derek Bell	74	1995-1999
Joe Morgan	72	1963-1971, 1980
Jason Castro	70	2010-2016, 2021
Luis Gonzalez	69	1990-1994, 1997
Alan Ashby	69	1979-1989

Astros All-Time RBI Leaders

Jeff Bagwell	1529	1991-2005
Craig Biggio	1176	1988-2007
Lance Berkman	1080	1999-2010
Jose Cruz	942	1975-1987
Bob Watson	782	1966-1979
Cesar Cedeno	778	1970-1981
Jimmy Wynn	719	1963-1973
Jose Altuve	639	2011-2021
Doug Rader	600	1967-1975
Ken Caminiti	546	1987-1994, 1999-2000
Carlos Lee	533	2007-2012
Glenn Davis	518	1984-1990
Carlos Correa	489	2015-2021
Kevin Bass	468	1982-1989, 1993-1994
Richard Hidalgo	465	1997-2004
George Springer	458	2014-2020
Derek Bell	442	1995-1999
Terry Puhl	432	1977-1989
Enos Cabell	405	1975-1980, 1984-1985
Bill Doran	404	1982-1990
Alex Bregman	397	2016-2021
Alan Ashby	388	1979-1989
Brad Ausmus	386	1997-1998, 2001-2008
Bob Aspromonte	385	1962-1968
Yuli Gurriel	382	2016-2021
Hunter Pence	377	2007-2011
Rusty Staub	370	1963-1968
Luis Gonzalez	366	1990-1994, 1997
Moises Alou	346	1998-2001
Denny Walling	344	1977-1988. 1992

Astros All-Time Win Leaders

Joe Niekro	144	1975-1985
Roy Oswalt	143	2001-2010
Larry Dierker	137	1964-1976
Mike Scott	110	1983-1991
James Rodney Richard	107	1971-1980
Nolan Ryan	106	1980-1988
Don Wilson	104	1966-1974
Shane Reynolds	103	1992-2002
Bob Knepper	93	1981-1989
Wandy Rodriguez	80	2005-2012
Ken Forsch	78	1970-1980
Dallas Keuchel	76	2012-2018
Mike Hampton	76	1991-1997
Darryl Kile	71	1967-1975
Jim Deshaies	61	1985-1991
Wade Miller	58	1999-2004
Collin McHugh	58	2014-2019
Dave Smith	53	1980-1990
Turk Farrell	53	1962-1967
Mark Portugal	52	1989-1993
Danny Darwin	47	1986-1990, 1996
Dave Roberts	47	1972-1975
Dave Giusti	47	1962-1968
Jose Lima	46	1997-2001
Lance McCullers, Jr.	45	2015-2021
Pete Harnisch	45	1991-1994
Tom Griffin	45	1969-1976
Joaquin Andujar	44	1975-1981, 1988
Justin Verlander	43	2017-2020
Bob Bruce	42	1962-1966
Jim Ray	42	1965-1973

Astros All-Time Save Leaders

Billy Wagner	225	1995-2003
Dave Smith	199	1980-1990
Brad Lidge	123	2002-2007
Fred Gladding	76	1968-1973
Joe Sambito	72	1976-1984
Jose Valverde	69	2008-2009
Doug Jones	62	1992-1993
Ken Giles	61	2016-2018
Roberto Osuna	51	2018-2020
Ken Forsch	50	1970-1980
Luke Gregerson	47	2015-2017
Ryan Pressly	43	2018-2021
Frank DiPino	43	1982-1986
Octavio Dotel	42	2000-2004
Todd Jones	39	1993-1996
Hal Woodeshick	36	1962-1965
John Hudek	29	1994-1997
Chad Qualls	29	2004-2007, 2014-2015
Claude Raymond	26	1964-1967
Frank LaCorte	26	1973-1983
Xavier Hernandez	25	1989-1993, 1996
Brandon Lyon	24	2010-2012
Jim Ray	23	1965-1973
Matt Lindstrom	23	2010
Dan Wheeler	23	2004-2007
Bill Dawley	21	1983-1985
Larry Andersen	20	1986-1990
Mark Melancon	20	2010-2011
Jose Veras	20	2013-2014
Will Harris	20	2015-2019

Astros All-Time ERA Leaders

Roger Clemens	2.40	2004-2006
Joe Sambito	2.42	1977-1984
Justin Verlander	2.45	2017-2020
Dave Smith	2.53	1980-1990
Billy Wagner	2.53	1995-2003
Larry Andersen	2.57	1986-1990
Gerrit Cole	2.68	2018-2019
Mike Cuellar	2.74	1965-1968
Nolan Ryan	3.13	1980-1988
Don Wilson	3.15	1966-1974
James Rodney Richard	3.15	1971-1980
Ken Forsch	3.18	1970-1980
Danny Darwin	3.21	1986-1990, 1996
Joe Niekro	3.22	1975-1985
Roy Oswalt	3.24	2001-2010
Octavio Dotel	3.25	2000-2004
Larry Dierker	3.28	1964-1976
Brad Lidge	3.30	2002-2008
Mike Scott	3.30	1983-1991
Mark Portugal	3.34	1989-1993
Vern Ruhle	3.35	1978-1984
Andy Pettitte	3.38	2004-2006
Xavier Hernandez	3.40	1989-1993, 1996
Denny Lemaster	3.40	1968-1971
Pete Harnisch	3.41	1991-1994
Ken Johnson	3.41	1962-1965
Turk Farrell	3.42	1962-1967
Jim Ray	3.53	1965-1973
Lance McCullers, Jr.	3.57	2015-2021
Mike Hampton	3.59	1991-1997, 2009

Astros All-Time Strikeout Leaders

Nolan Ryan	1866	1980-1988
Roy Oswalt	1593	2001-2010
James Rodney Richard	1493	1971-1980
Larry Dierker	1487	1964-1976
Mike Scott	1318	1983-1991
Shane Reynolds	1309	1992-2002
Don Wilson	1283	1966-1974
Joe Niekro	1178	1975-1985
Wandy Rodriguez	1093	2005-2012
Darryl Kile	973	1991-1997
Bob Knepper	946	1981-1989
Dallas Keuchel	945	2012-2018
Ken Forsch	815	1970-1980
Mike Hampton	767	1991-1997, 2009
Lance McCullers, Jr.	750	2015-2021
Collin McHugh	743	2014-2019
Jim Deshaies	731	1985-1991
Turk Farrell	694	1962-1967
Billy Wagner	694	1995-2003
Wade Miller	659	1999-2004
Tom Griffin	652	1969-1976
Bud Norris	643	2009-2013
Justin Verlander	640	2017-2020
Dave Giusti	625	1962-1968
Bob Bruce	609	1962-1966
Gerrit Cole	602	2018-2019
Jose Lima	584	1997-2001
Brad Peacock	583	2013-2020
Pete Harnisch	583	1991-1994
Brad Lidge	561	2002-2007

About the Authors

BILL BROWN

Bill Brown is a native of Sedalia, Missouri. He earned a Bachelor of Journalism degree in the radio-TV sequence at the University of Missouri. Brown was a major league baseball play-by-play television broadcaster for the Cincinnati Reds for seven seasons, 1976-82. He served the Houston Astros for 30 seasons in that capacity, 1987-2016. He was inducted into the Texas Baseball Hall of Fame in 2004 and the Houston Astros Media Wall of Honor. He was voted Texas Sportscaster of the Year in 2013.

MIKE ACOSTA

Mike Acosta is a native Houstonian who spent 22 years working for the Houston Astros. He began his career as a broadcast intern in 1999 before working in ballpark operations and sales. In 2009 he integrated the MLB Authentication program with the Astros and created "Astros Authentics," a brand that makes authenticated game-used memorabilia available to fans. As the longtime Astros team historian, he conceptualized and developed the Astros Hall of Fame, an entity he continues to oversee. Acosta serves on the board of directors of the Astrodome Conservancy, a nonprofit that supports the reuse and redevelopment of the Houston Astrodome. He also serves as the public address announcer at Minute Maid Park when needed.

PHIL BOUDREAUX

Phil Boudreaux is a Houston native and a lifelong follower of the Astros. Boudreaux began attending games with his father and his grandfather in the late 1960s. The first homer he saw was blasted by Jimmy Wynn against the Giants.

While attending the University of St. Thomas, Boudreaux interned in the sports department at KTRH Radio. He began to cover games during the 1981 season and started to do statistics at Home Sports Entertainment during the 1983 season. He has been working the broadcasts ever since and has covered more than 2,500 Astros games.